Producing Success

Producing Success

The Culture of Personal Advancement
in an American High School

PETER DEMERATH

The University of Chicago Press CHICAGO & LONDON

Peter Demerath is associate professor of educational policy and administration at the University of Minnesota. He has published numerous articles and contributed chapters. This is his first book.

The University of Chicago Press, Chicago 60637
The University of Chicago Press, Ltd., London
© 2009 by The University of Chicago
All rights reserved. Published 2009
Printed in the United States of America

18 17 16 15 14 13 12 11 10 09   1 2 3 4 5

ISBN-13: 978-0-226-14239-5 (cloth)
ISBN-13: 978-0-226-14241-8 (paper)
ISBN-10: 0-226-14239-6 (cloth)
ISBN-10: 0-226-14241-8 (paper)

Library of Congress Cataloging-in-Publication Data

Demerath, Peter.
Producing success : the culture of personal advancement in an American high school / Peter Demerath.
p. cm.
Summary: The result of four years at Midwestern "Wilton High," this book seeks to understand the merciless, competitive culture of an upper-middle-class American high school, showing the various things parents, students and community members do to secure different kinds of advantages for themselves and their families.
Includes bibliographical references and index.
ISBN-13: 978-0-226-14239-5 (cloth : alk. paper)
ISBN-13: 978-0-226-14241-8 (pbk. : alk. paper)
ISBN-10: 0-226-14239-6 (cloth : alk. paper)
ISBN-10: 0-226-14241-8 (pbk. : alk. paper)
1. Educational sociology—United States. 2. High schools—United States. 3. Academic achievement—United States. 4. Students—United States—Social conditions. 5. Social stratification—United States. 6. Middle class—United States. I. Title.
LC205.D46 2009
373.1826'22—dc22

2009013806

For Ellen, Olivia, and Sophia

Contents

Acknowledgments

This project would not have been possible without the welcome my research team received from the students, parents, staff, and administrators of Wilton Burnham High School. Harboring an anthropologist for any length of time can be an uncomfortable proposition. Given that data collection for the project lasted four years, I am particularly grateful for the generosity of the WBHS community: the students who shared their high school experiences with us, the parents who invited us into their homes, and the teachers who made us a part of their classrooms. All taught us a great deal about growing up, going to school, and living in Wilton. I would also like to express my gratitude to the Burnham students who permitted their original artwork to appear in chapters 6 and 7. I thank Bob Donmoyer for suggesting Wilton as a site for the study; and Elizabeth Cunningham, principal of WBHS, for seeing the value of longitudinal field research from the outset.

I am also indebted to several anthropologists and educational researchers who have taught me so much about how to study school culture. These include Gretchen Rossman, George Urch, and David Evans at the University of Massachusetts, Amherst; Deborah Gewertz of Amherst College; Fred Erickson at University of California–Los Angeles; Harry Wolcott of the University of Oregon; Erwin Epstein of Loyola University, Chicago; and Patti Lather, Helen Marks, Antoinette Errante, Rick Voithofer, Cynthia Dillard, and Cynthia Tyson at Ohio State University.

The project was supported by an Ohio State University Faculty Seed Grant, as well as research assistance provided through the Ohio State University College of Education Office of Equity and Diversity. I am grateful to Bob Ransom for facilitating that assistance. I discuss the substantial contributions of those research assistants—Mario Davidson, Jill Lynch, Rich Milner, and April Peters—in the next chapter. I also wish to thank the directors of the School of Educational Policy and Leadership at Ohio State for their support of the project while I was a faculty member there from 1997 to 2007: Mary Ann Danowitz Sagaria, Bob Donmoyer, Bob Lawson, and Scott Sweetland.

While the first four years of the project were devoted to data collection, the last five have been dedicated to analysis and writing. My interpretation and presentation of findings from the study have benefitted greatly from the critical feedback of a wide array of anthropologists of education, many of whom I met when I presented initial findings at the Spencer Advanced Institute, "Reconsidering the Interrelationship between Anthropology and Education," in May 2001. I want to thank Bradley Levinson, Kathy Hall, and Amy Stambach for inviting me to be a part of the Institute, as well as Ray McDermott, Dorothy Holland, Ulf Hannerz, Elsie Rockwell, Bryan Brayboy, and Lesley Bartlett. I especially thank Doug Foley, who took a particular interest in the project early on and generously provided extensive and detailed comments on various drafts over the last five years. As I explain in the pages that follow, this book is meant for a broad audience. There are several people who have coached me as to how to go about that, including Jim Peacock, Catherine Lutz, Michele Foster, Peggy Sanday, and especially Debra Jasper.

My wife and I left Ohio in the summer of 2007 so we could be closer to her family in Wisconsin (and reduce the carbon footprint left by our substantial commutes). I also wish to express my appreciation to several of my new colleagues at the University of Minnesota for their support, including Darwin Hendel, Michael Paige, Jennifer York-Barr, Karen Seashore, Rebecca Ropers-Huilman, Fran Vavrus, Joan DeJaeghere, and Dick Nunneley in the Department of Educational Policy and Administration, and Bill Beeman in the Department of Anthropology. I also thank my research assistants Rhiannon Williams and Allison Mattheis, and administrative associates Marcia Finke, Julie Bishop-Hogan, and Sara Beverage.

The comparative perspective that runs throughout the book has been generated largely by my ongoing relationship with the people of Manus Province, Papua New Guinea. I wish to thank the members of the Karol Matawai family for their continued hospitality in Pere village, as well as Birio Frisu and Chokal Pombuai. I also thank the Pere Community Council for the privilege of continuing to work with them on sustainable development efforts, particularly Chokal Manuai, and Piwen Langarap. I remain grateful to the late Barbara and Fred Roll and the Manus Project at the University of Pennsylvania for funding my initial field research in Manus. I also wish to convey my appreciation to Mary Catherine Bateson, an inspiration in her own right, for the way in which she has connected me to the public anthropology done by her mother, Margaret Mead.

I consider myself fortunate to have found an editor and press who saw the potential of this project early on. Sincere thanks to Elizabeth Branch Dyson of the University of Chicago Press for the thoughtful way in which she worked with me to establish a joint vision of what this book could be. I also want to express my appreciation to the press's reviewers for the spirit of collegiality with which they engaged with the manuscript and their valuable suggestions for improvement. Any shortcomings that remain are mine alone. I am also most grateful to Mary Gehl, Anne Summers Goldberg, and Rob Hunt at the University of Chicago Press for seeing the manuscript through the production process.

Lastly, I want to thank my brothers, Loren and Ben; sisters, Janine and Mary; and mother, Judy, educators all, for their support and dialogue over the years that has so enriched my thinking about schooling. I am especially grateful for the advice, guidance, and scholarly example set by my father, Jay Demerath, professor emeritus of sociology at the University of Massachusetts. Finally I thank my wife, a biological anthropologist whose research imagination continues to inspire me, for her help in conceiving the project, and for believing in it from start to finish.

Introduction Producing Success

Julie's jaw was wired shut when she appeared for our interview. She had recently had corrective periodontal surgery, and the liquid-only diet she had been on for the last five and a half weeks had caused her to lose fifteen pounds. She also looked anxious, but that was nothing new—she had told me in past interviews that she was "so busy and tired all the time." Julie Rice was one of the high-achieving students in the study of academic competition and student culture I'd been working on for the past two years, and I knew that she was a very driven young woman. This was her junior year, a crucial year for establishing the academic credentials necessary for admission to a competitive college, and she had been working very hard. A religious young person, she hoped to one day establish a school in a developing country for underprivileged children. "I have it all planned out," she had said. At one point during the previous year her grades had slipped a bit and she had had to reorient her life around her schoolwork. At an interview around that time she had told me, "I am a lot more focused on what I need to be focused on and I need to be focused on that."

As soon as I saw Julie, I asked with concern how she was, motioning toward the brace on her jaw. "Oh, okay, thanks," she said grimly through gritted teeth. But then, as we walked down the hallway toward the quiet corner where we traditionally did our interviews, she began to bitterly recount how the C+ she had just gotten in chemistry would take her grade point average (GPA) from a 3.9 down to a 3.7. At that point, she could not anticipate that the challenges of balancing the demands of school, the college application process, extracurriculars (she was heavily involved in the school's theater program), and her job (she had recently gotten her driver's license and was waitressing at a local restaurant), would seriously affect her health the next year.

Julie's total efforts were typical of the achievement-oriented students at this public suburban high school. These students were so intent on their academic and career goals that their very identities were oriented around competing, maintaining control, and trying to ensure successful futures. The school itself was geared toward scaffolding these efforts. It had a vast array of ways to support and recognize student achievements, and even named all students who graduated with a GPA of above a 4.0 a "valedictorian." (In 2003 there were forty-seven valedictorians—10 percent of the senior class.) The school was located in Wilton,[1] an affluent, though changing, suburb of a large Midwestern U.S. city that often promoted its own distinctiveness and appeal: the Wilton School District motto was "Where excellence is a tradition." Throughout the course of my study, I learned about various things that parents, students, and community members did to secure different kinds of advantages for themselves, their families, and the community. These practices and the ideology that was behind them were almost always referred to as being part of the "Wilton Way."

This book takes a different approach to understanding the role of education in the perpetuation of social inequality in the United States: it focuses on the construction of advantage. It describes the implications of the Wilton Way for how schooling is carried out in this community, particularly in its "Blue Ribbon" high school. Above all, it seeks to explain its cultural basis, meaning the interconnected set of meanings, beliefs, and practices that underlie it. The book argues that the tight—almost seamless—linkages between class ideology, parenting practices, ideal notions of personhood, and accepted school policies and practices make this a cultural system. The result is an integrated network of meanings and practices geared toward: 1) positioning individuals to successfully compete in school and 2) leveraging community resources to support the schools, build up the confidence of individual students, and frame their efforts as successes. In the end, it is this cultural system itself that is these students' primary advantage. The book also discusses some of the negative effects of this unswerving orientation to individual advancement: achievement-oriented students' struggles to habituate to stress and fatigue, the alienation from learning that average and lower-achieving pupils experience; and the marginalization of many African American students, which is attributed in part to how the school handled diversity. The project's overall aim of opening up this cultural system to examination was referred to by an American Indian colleague as "telling secrets."

The compulsion toward self-advancement in Wilton and communities like it certainly has an origin in the great uneasiness felt by many people in this socioeconomic group—a demographic that Robert Reich (1994) labeled several years ago as the "anxious class." Since then, journalists and scholars alike have commented on how many middle-class parents are preoccupied with a "fear of falling" (Ehrenreich 1989, 1), or "falling from grace" (Proweller 1998, 177) for their children. Current neoliberal economic restructuring and the "flattening" of global markets make it likely that today's middle-class children will have a lower standard of living than their parents (Friedman 2005; Lareau 2003; Newman 1993). While young Americans themselves are more ambitious than ever before, they seem to be increasingly aware of their status relative to others and to be preparing themselves at ever earlier ages for the sort of individualistic competition that is ever more central to American life (Elkind 2001; Rosenfeld and Wise 2000; Schneider and Stevenson 1999).

David Labaree pointed out several years ago that such market pressures and social exertions give rise to educational credentialism, at the heart of which is a tension between a view of education as a private good that facilitates individual advancement, and as a public good that provides society with collectively shared benefits. Furthermore, he showed how under credentialism, "teaching takes a back seat to the more socially salient task of sorting, and grading becomes more important for its social consequences than for its pedagogical uses" (1997, 2). Labaree concluded that social mobility goals have promoted the commodification of education in the U.S., which threatens to "transform the public educational system into a mechanism for personal advancement" (p. 12).

During the course of the study, the "academic arms race" around high school students' efforts to gain admission to competitive colleges continued to escalate (D. Callahan 2004, 211). This has become a growth industry, characterized by a proliferation of test preparation services, specialized consultants, and even new "get into college" summer camps. Robbins (2006) recently chronicled the hiring of consultants by well-off parents to coach their children in skills and appropriate behaviors for their preschool and kindergarten admissions interviews. Another journalist recently reported that sixth graders in a suburban community in Virginia believed that colleges would examine their elementary school transcripts (Wilgoren and Steinberg 2000). This is certainly a feature of what David Brooks (2001) refers to as the "big-backpack era." Relatedly, academic cheating has reached an all-time high, and over the last several years there have been a spate of lawsuits over the identification of valedictorians. In addition, the demands of "select" sports teams have continued to intensify, as has the involvement of parents; in July of 2000, a father beat and killed the father of an opposing player at a youth hockey game in Massachusetts (Nack and Munson 2000). There has been a rise in the numbers of adolescents taking growth hormones. These developments are all part and parcel of a society "obsessed with self advancement" (Solomon 2005, 14).

It is no accident that journalists and researchers have registered many ill effects of these young peoples' hyperscheduled lives and competitive routines. One commented on how the pressures for early educational attainment led some first graders to show clear signs of stress (Lareau 2003). Among older students, there have been increases in campus counselor visits by college freshmen. Lastly, among teens, there has been an increase in the numbers who take antidepressants—and attempt to commit suicide. One writer aptly termed this demographic group "generation stress" (Sontag 2002, 58). Finally, various writers have commented on how the culture of competitive individualism has led to a narcissistic preoccupation with the self, disconnection with others, and a decline in civility (Lasch 1991; Putnam 2001). A clear concern is the extent to which young people in the United States are learning the basic habits of democratic citizenship.

In addition to presenting an anthropological explanation of the local logic, or culture of schooling in this community, this book deepens our understanding of persisting educational inequities in the United States. Certainly the low academic performance of students from disadvantaged communities is a primary reason for the persistence of achievement "gaps," though Gloria Ladson-Billings (2006) recently argued that such gaps are actually products of the "education debt" in the United States. Research has shown how resources, parent education, socioeconomic status (SES), and schools themselves may disadvantage certain groups of students (Anyon 2005; Education Trust 2001; Kozol 2006; National Center for Education Statistics 2003; Rusk 1999); how curricular differentiation or tracking can reproduce existing social divisions (Oakes 2005; Page 1991); and how, through their "cultural productions," some students may inadvertently disadvantage themselves (Fine 1991; Foley 1990; Fordham 1996; Fordham and Ogbu 1986; Levinson, Foley, and Holland 1996; P. E. Willis 1977). In this regard, scholars interested in educational inequities have begun to link research into the reproduction of disadvantage with the production of advantage, and have called for more study of how the social position of the middle classes is constructed through schooling (Apple 1996, 1997; Ball 2003; McCarthy 1998; Reay 2004; Varenne and McDermott 1998).

The book builds on and seeks to contribute to a long sociological and anthropological tradition of research into the role of schooling in ongoing class stratification in the United States, including "culture and personality" studies on student identity and educational experience, critical ethnographies of schooling, and more recent understandings of the social dynamics and dictates of neoliberalism. Almost eighty years ago, the Lynds (1929) described how social and economic changes in Middletown at the turn of the twentieth century resulted in a tendency for the city's residents to "subsume more and more of its living under pecuniary considerations" (p. 501). Relatedly, they asserted that schooling began to take over more and more of children's waking hours. In 1949, Hollingshead argued that the social system of Elmtown "organizes and controls the behavior of the high-school aged adolescents who are reared in it" (1949, v). Most importantly, he advanced the notion of "class culture" to capture learned differences in behavior, lifestyle, and aspirations across the socioeconomic status groups of the community.

Margaret Mead turned her anthropological gaze on America throughout her career, and in 1942 wrote explicitly about the American emphasis on individual success:

> It is possible to describe the American system without mentioning class, to talk instead of the premium on success, and to go directly to the dynamics of character formation which lie back of the American will to succeed. (1942/1965, 66)

Mead argued that Americans must succeed in order to be regarded as "good," and that therefore young Americans start their lives "with a tremendous impetus towards success" (91). Riesman asserted more particularly that a new social character type emerged in twentieth-century American society that emphasized achievement. He wrote that a hallmark of this "other-direction" was competency in "manipulating others and being oneself manipulated" (1950, 45). He maintained that this was becoming the typical character of the "new" middle class.

Shortly thereafter, Jules Henry published his sweeping critique of American culture, socialization, and schooling. He referred to the "ideal" American as an "inexhaustible reservoir of drive and personality resources; one who, while not using up what he has, yet exploits his personality to the best advantage" (1963, 16). More specifically, Henry described the "pecuniary logic" underlying the system of American consumerism that trains American children to "*insatiable* consumption of *impulsive* choice and *infinite* variety" (70; original emphasis).

Similarly, Hervé Varenne provided deep insight into the role of education in American society in his portrayal of the contradictory traditions of individuation, sociality, and exclusion that shape life in Appleton, a Midwestern town. He argued that the structure of American culture: "consists mainly of a refusal to set boundaries on individual action" (1977, 187), and showed how this was apparent in Appleton residents' instrumental view of education—as a means to self-reliance, as well as community involvement.

Laura Nader first called for anthropologists to "study up" over thirty years ago in order to understand the processes "whereby power and responsibility are exercised" (1969, 284). Since then, however, anthropologists have consistently complained that the privileged communities in the United States. that are commonly the sites of such success are "overanalyzed and underethnographized" (Ortner 1993, 412). Indeed, many of the ways in which school policies, social networks, cultural capital, and student identities and practices themselves enable these groups of pupils to continue to pull farther ahead remain unclear. Accordingly, an assumption of this study is that social stratification and ongoing social inequality is the result of intentional activity and "informed agency" (Brantlinger 2003) rather than static structures. Hence, as Asa Hilliard (2002) recently put the matter, "we need to decode success, rather than continue the autopsy of failure."

My primary aim in the book, then, is to carry out this decoding: to make explicit the hidden assumptions, beliefs, and concerns that made up the Wilton Way and to show how it had such a powerful influence over the everyday lives of the people of this community. I use the tools of anthropology to bring these class cultural practices to light: long-term fieldwork along with particular understandings of culture and schooling. This book offers detailed descriptions of the lives of students, parents, teachers, and administrators in the community, drawn from a four-year anthropological study carried out in Wilton from 1999 to 2003. It also includes the voices and experiences of people in the community and school who were critical of the community's and school's emphasis on individual advancement, and in various ways, strove to defy it.

Furthermore, the book adopts a cross-cultural view of specific aspects of life in Wilton by making occasional comparisons with another community where I have lived and done research: the coastal village of Pere, in Manus Province, Papua New Guinea. On the face of it, it would be hard to imagine two societies that have less in common: the inhabitants of Pere are relatively poor subsistence fisherpeople who are struggling to achieve a measure of economic development with little outside support. However, one of the guiding principles of anthropology is that we know best about something when we can see it in comparative perspective:

comparisons throw the cultural basis of specific beliefs or actions into sharp relief, thereby enabling us to locate ourselves relative to other groups, and ultimately identify potential prospects for change (Peshkin 2000; Sanday 1998). It is in this way that anthropologists frequently use comparison to "make the familiar strange and interesting again" (Erickson 1986, 121).

For example, one early afternoon in May of 1995, I was sitting in the shade of a dilapidated classroom building in Lorengau, the provincial capital of Manus, with a sixteen-year-old boy whom I had been interviewing about his high school experiences and aspirations. It was very hot (Manus is three degrees south of the equator) and we both wore shorts, half-unbuttoned shirts, and flip-flops. He had just told me that it was "hard" to be a good student in his school, because given the rising unemployment and ever larger numbers of high school graduates across the nation, he and his peers had doubts about whether or not they would be able to get a good enough score on the national tenth-grade proficiency exam to get a scholarship for further education, or even a job. Most likely, he said, he would end up going back to his home village, becoming a subsistence fisherman, and trying to "come up good" so that he could pay back the hard work that his parents had put into raising him. I had heard other students say similar things, and I sympathized and said I understood. Then, surprisingly, he looked at me and said, "Peter, what do you want to do with your life when you go back to America?" During the ten months I had been there, none of the students had asked me that. "Well," I said, "I think I want to teach, and try to get a job at a university, and maybe write a book someday." "Ah," he said nodding, "So you want to be *somebody*." At first I wasn't sure what he meant. But then, after reflecting for a few moments, I said, "Yes, I think I do."

Being somebody, or trying to be somebody, is in many ways what the United States is all about. Our society was founded on laws intended to give individuals certain rights and opportunities to better their lot. We generally value individual growth and self-improvement. These core beliefs are reflected in such American values as "individualism," "self-betterment," "competitive individualism," and "upward mobility."

But it is different in Papua New Guinea, or at least, it has been. For thousands of years most traditional societies in this part of the western Pacific adapted primarily collectivist practices—fishing, hunting, and agriculture—that have served them well over time. There has generally a premium on reciprocal sharing of resources and labor. Relatedly, while there have been status difference between women and men, and men and "big men" (political leaders), most of these societies have historically been more or less egalitarian. There are regular exchange rituals at certain life stages where wealth is redistributed throughout communities. Also, people tend to think of themselves very relationally, as much as members of families, clans, and villages, as individuals. And this can be apparent in many ways, from a compulsion to share to a reticence to state an individual opinion. While much of this is changing under pressure of neoliberal globalization, there is much less of an emphasis on being an individual there; in fact, acting out of self-interest can be sanctioned in different ways. I had learned a bit about this from these students. They told me that students who tried hard in school, wore fancy Western clothes, and spoke a lot of English—or, in other words, tried to elevate themselves above other students—were ridiculed, ostracized, and labeled as "acting extra"—a comment on these egalitarian norms, and young people's efforts to preserve them.

Where I grew up, in a college town in Massachusetts, acting "extra" was what was expected. It was central to the personal goals that differentiated young people with aspirations of joining the upper middle and professional classes. My classmates and I were encouraged to do well in school and in our extracurricular activities. We were taught to feature our achievements prominently in our applications to college, and to write essays that called attention to our unique qualities.

Being Born Three Times: Generating an Anthropological Perspective on the United States

After spending that year in Manus, I returned to the United States, wrote up my research study, got my degree, and was fortunate enough to get a job in my field of educational anthropology. My new colleagues soon began asking what I was going to do for my next research project. One of my interests was in understanding how schools were involved in processes of cultural reproduction, or how it was that students from certain social classes went to certain kinds of schools, and ended up getting certain kinds of jobs that landed them in more or less the same social class. I had benefited from these processes myself. My parents were both educators, and I grew up in a middle class home, went to public schools that were well-supported by the community, and had certain privileges and opportunities that enabled me to go to graduate school and pursue a university teaching career. I thought, then, that I would like to focus on a suburban public high school, somewhat like the one I had attended. Rather than being an outsider, like I was in Manus, I would be something of an insider, and that could bring with it certain advantages. Also, I knew that there was comparatively little research on suburban schools, though they are by far the most common type of public high school in the United States (National Center for Education Statistics 2005).

I was also curious as to whether or not there was any truth in a saying I had read about years before in graduate school, that some anthropologists are "born" three times. The first is their natural birth, the second is when they achieve a deep understanding of the cultural patterns of another group, and the third is when they are able to turn their gaze back on their own society and understand it in new ways. I admired the work of anthropologists and researchers who had been able to do this, people like Sherry Ortner, Lisa Delpit, Peggy Sanday, Harry Wolcott, Doug Foley, Gloria Ladson-Billings, and, of course, Margaret Mead.

My wife and I already had a distant connection to Mead. Pere, the village in Manus where we did our fieldwork, is the same village where Mead did a much of her research on childhood, socialization, and social change, between 1928 and 1974. This posed certain challenges while we were there, particularly people comparing our research approach to hers and questioning why we didn't ask them about the same things that "Magrit" did. We tried to explain, sometimes to no avail, that we were doing applied projects in health and education. Nevertheless, today my wife and I have an ongoing relationship with the people of Pere, and we are honored that they refer to us as "lain bilong Magrit Mid" (Margaret Mead's lineage).

The book's viewpoint is partly inspired by Mead. This requires a bit of explanation, because her reputation has been tarnished in recent years by Derek Freeman's criticisms of her first field project in Samoa (which she carried out when she was twenty-five years old). While the critique was, in some ways, valid, it has unfortunately distracted attention from the rest of her vast body of work, which has withstood critical scrutiny over time.[2]

This book is intended for educators, students, and parents, as well as for anthropologists, sociologists, and other social scientists. As such, some of the anthropological assumptions that underlie the work deserve some explanation. Very briefly, anthropologists assume that culture, or cultural assumptions, consists of learned patterns of behavior that make up a kind of "blueprint" for perceiving the world and acting in it, and that these blueprints consist of systems of meanings, ways of being, even ways of feeling and moving one's body. It is important to keep in mind that these blueprints are only just that, and that there is always room for the personalities and idiosyncrasies of individuals to shape their experiences. However, these blueprints can make things appear to members of social groups as "normal" or "natural" when they are actually the products of culture and, furthermore, may be based on internal inequalities within a group that are hidden from view. This state of affairs can make it very difficult to "see" or account for one's own cultural assumptions or background.

Anthropologists often try to understand these cultural assumptions through notions of holism and relativity. What this means is that anthropology uses a very broad canvas and constantly strives to understand linkages among behaviors, values, and environmental forces. These underlying principles were best expressed by Margaret Mead some fifty years ago:

> Cultural relativity demands that every item of cultural behavior be seen as relative to the culture of which it is a part, and in that systematic setting every item has positive or negative meaning and value. (1964, 93–94)

Through this chain of reasoning, anthropologists generally try to get at the *emic,* or insider point of view, constantly asking themselves: how could it make sense, from the perspective of these people and how they apprehend the world, to believe this, say this, feel this, or do this? This process is frequently referred to as "problematizing" local practices and behaviors.

Overall, then, anthropology might be understood as a "way of seeing" that seeks to uncover the taken-for-granted assumptions and hidden rules of logic that underlie the way that people go about their everyday lives (Wolcott 2008). It is this unique perspective that enables anthropologists to make connections that are not made elsewhere (Nader 2001). In general, in pointing out the role of culture in our everyday lives as well as our everyday abilities to change and adapt, anthropology teaches us that our cultural assumptions are not static, but rather, they can be opened up to discussion and modification. This is why Mary Catherine Bateson said at the centennial of Mead's birth that her mother believed above all that anthropology was a "liberating way of thinking and seeing" (2001).

Class Culture and Schooling

Since this book is devoted to understanding cultural processes that underlie individual advancement and social inequality, it injects this cultural view with the analytical lens of class. This leads to the key concept of *class culture* that refers to class-based practical logics that guide everyday ways of life. Willis (1977) was the first ethnographer to mobilize the notion of class culture in educational research, showing how the class relations of the larger society were reproduced in school through communicative labor. Several years later, Foley wrote, "The class culture concept is a way of focusing class analysis on the cultural politics of how economic classes are culturally reproduced and resisted" (1990, 170).[3] Foley himself showed how socially prominent youth in a Texas border town and high school learned a communicative style that enabled them to manage their impressions and manipulate adult authorities. Teachers unconsciously rewarded these communicative styles as the cultural ideal, thus alienating immigrant minority students and reinscribing the school as a site of popular cultural practices that "stage or reproduce social inequality" (p. 1). Foley's "impression management" self construct extended existing understandings concerning how the demands of American society shape the identities and expressive practices of its youth.

Certainly several concepts developed by Bourdieu are useful in understanding the strategies people use to maintain or improve their socioeconomic standing (1998; Ladwig 1996). First is the view of environments of socialization and education as *social fields,* where students' possible futures are negotiated and constructed within structural constraints. Second is the notion of *habitus,* referring to the more or less durable, class-based dispositions that people are socialized into that serve as unconscious guides for personal action. Third is *capital,* which refers to those acquired attributes that actually have exchange value. Fourth and final is the concept of *agency,* which refers to the ability of people to act in the world.

While, as mentioned above, most studies concerned with the reproduction of inequality through education have focused on students from disadvantaged backgrounds, an emerging international literature is using the concept of class culture to understand how middle-class families negotiate the contemporary education market (see, e.g. Connell et al. 1982; Cookson 1985; Power et al. 2003). Steven Ball (2003), working in the United Kingdom, argued that the market works as a "class strategy" by operating as a mechanism that the middle classes can exploit in their quest for social advancement and mobility. He observed that these strategies of social advancement have become more important in the last ten to fifteen years, and that this has had the effect of making the education market one of the most important sites of class struggle.

Annette Lareau (2003) recently offered a detailed description of how both black and white parents in a large metropolitan area in the northeastern United States sought to actively "develop" their children by engaging in a process of "concerted cultivation." Lareau argued that these families align themselves with the standards of gatekeeping institutions responsible for "social selection," and that this sort of explicit training in the "rules of the game," conferred important advantages on these children.

Finally, Ellen Brantlinger's recent book showed how members of the professional class use their agency "in crafty ways to secure the best of what schools have to offer" for their children (2003, xi). Her study described the ways in which educated middle-class people went about securing school distinctions for their children. She also described how middle-class and high-income students incited accommodations from their teachers, particularly through specific communication styles and "manipulating behavior." Eckert has argued that such students' sophisticated "adult handling skills" (1989, 116) derive from the very American middle-class family ideology described above by Lareau: a stress on participation of the child in decision making, as well as parent-child negotiation, which accords the child a certain level of adult status and gives them experience in dealing with adults on a more equal footing (p. 116). In sum, Diane Reay commented that many middle class families are engaged in

> individual competitive practices to gain advantage for their own children. Such practices are routinely considered to be normative middle-class behavior—part of a moral agenda of putting one's child first. Any notion of common good is subsidiary to getting the best for one's own child. (2004, 556)

Two recent books have also illuminated how schooling for well-off youth sustains a culture of privilege. Alan Peshkin's study (2000) highlighted the institutional advantaging inherent in a privileged education and probed how students made sense of such resulting inequities. More importantly, it illuminated how an elite private high school "stamps" its students with particular attributes and skills, which, along with the school's exclusivity, ultimately convince them of their own superiority. Adam Howard's more recent study (2008) showed how several schools for advantaged youth inadvertently instill in them specific lessons about privilege, such as a narrow view of what makes for valuable knowledge, that success comes from being "superior to others," to do "whatever it takes" to win, that fulfillment comes from accumulating, and that "Others are too different from us to relate" (p. 217). Howard argues that these hidden lessons are normalized through the everyday routines of these schools, and are central processes in the cultural production of privilege.

All of these writers point out that education can only promote social mobility to the extent that it keeps most students from reaching the top of the education hierarchy (see Varenne and McDermott 1998). This historical contingency of success on failure led Jules Henry to remark over forty years ago, "to many cultures such success would seem cruel beyond belief"

(1963, 296). Indeed, from this point of view it begins to make sense why so many students in Manus, as well as their peers in places like Washington D.C. might ostracize and degrade their high-achieving peers.

Entry and Methods

In the spring of 1997, a colleague told me about a suburban high school near the university where I worked that had just received a Blue Ribbon designation from the U.S. Department of Education. The principal actually had a degree in anthropology. When we met, I shared a research proposal with her, saying that I would like to study a diverse group of students to understand how they experienced the school. I planned to interview them, their classmates, teachers, and parents along the way; observe regularly throughout the school and community; and at some point administer a questionnaire to students based on emerging findings. The principal enthusiastically welcomed my plans for the study, saying, "I'm so glad you want to do long-term research, and not just come in, do a single survey, and leave." She actually encouraged me to expand data collection to four years—to identify a group of freshmen and follow them all the way through high school.

I took her up on her invitation. After securing permission from the school district and parents of students, we started the project in the fall of 1999. The research team was initially made up of myself, Jill Lynch, and Rich Milner—two doctoral students at my university. I was aware of recent scholarship that said that in qualitative research like this, the research findings can be strongly shaped by the perspective and background of the researchers. As a white male, I wanted to have co-researchers who could enrich project findings with their own diverse points of view. I hoped that Jill, who is white, and Rich, who is black, could help with that. In subsequent years, two other black doctoral students joined the project—April Peters and Mario Davidson. Jill and Rich worked on the project for the first year, April for the second, and Mario worked on the questionnaire data analysis after the data collection was completed. All made significant contributions to the project. Most valuable, probably, were the regular meetings we had after observing the same classroom or event. We carefully noted the differences between what each of us had noticed—I still marvel at how large some of those differences were.

We spent one to two days a week at the school during the first two years of the study. For the third and fourth years, I did the data collection on my own, and was unable to be at the school as frequently due to increasing responsibilities at the university. We observed regular classes as well as "enriched" and advanced placement (AP) classes. We spent time in the cafeteria, in hallways, and outside of school. We attended school events such as concerts, games, staff meetings, in-services, and award celebrations. From the beginning of the study, we chatted informally with dozens of students and teachers. We recorded our observations in hundreds of pages of field notes. In December 1999, we selected a diverse group of eight high- and under-achieving students to be focal participants in the study. These students were identified primarily through consultation with teachers concerning their academic engagement, classroom performance, and scores on standardized tests. While diverse in terms of gender and ethnicity, these students shared an ability to teach us about their experiences—what it was like to be a son or daughter, a young person in the community, and a student in the school. We interviewed these students for each of the next four years (except for one, who moved out of state after his freshman year); their parents during the first year of the study; and many other students, teachers, and administrators throughout the study. Though I draw primarily on the experiences of the high-achieving focal students for the first several chapters of the book, the under-achieving students' experiences are a critical part of the cultural scene as well and are examined in detail in chapter 7. All told, we conducted over sixty tape-recorded interviews for the study. In March 2002, we administered a grounded survey to 605 students that was based in part on the observational and interview data that had been collected and analyzed up to that point. Findings from the survey are presented throughout the book, and the survey itself is included in an appendix on page 185.[4]

From the beginning, the intent of the project was to achieve an in-depth understanding of the class cultural processes in the community and school that seemed to confer advantages on students. Though the project had a longitudinal design, it did not explicitly set out to track changes in the students, the school, or the community over time—that would be a distinctly different study purpose (see Donmoyer 2001). We did, however, notice certain developments that were relevant to the processes of advantaging that concerned us, and these are noted throughout the book.

Because the book draws heavily on the experiences of the focal students, I include brief snapshots of them below. First, however, I should mention that Cindi Criswell lived with her mother during ninth grade, her father during tenth grade, and then with friends. She dropped out of school in the middle of eleventh grade but remained a participant in the study. Nuako Konadu moved to Toledo, Ohio, in the middle of his

Key study participants

			Occupation		
Focal student	Race/ ethnicity	Residing caregiver	Father	Mother	Achievement level
Sharon Sosa	African American	Father and mother	Sales representative	Commission clerk	High
Nuako Konadu	African/ European American	Father and mother	Auditor	Teacher	High
Julie Rice	European American	Father and mother	Architect	Health care professional	High
David Sterling	European American	Father and mother	Corporate executive	Health care professional	High
Sofia Rhoades	African American	Father and mother	Engineer	Social worker	Under
Bryan Bowen	African American	Mother	Deceased	Management professional	Under
Cindi Criswell	European American	One	Unemployed	Artist	Under
Kevin Madsen	European American	Father and mother	Engineer	Corporate executive	Under

eleventh-grade year. I interviewed him there in the spring of his senior year. Bryan Bowen moved out of state following his ninth-grade year, and I was unable to maintain contact with him.

Sharon Sosa's mother was from the Bahamas, and her father, from the United States. A basketball player, sprinter, and baritone horn player, Sharon also became one of the school's best ceramic artists. She had a winning smile, engaging personality, and spoke very *very* fast. During Sharon's freshman year, a senior member of the Social Studies Department predicted that she would be the first female president of the United States.

Nuako Konadu's father was from Ghana, and his mother, from the United States. When his father first came to America, he worked as a janitor to put himself through college and accounting school. Nuako had

Other study participants

Other participants	Race/ethnicity	Subject or position
Students		
Dianne Heinlen	European American	
Yuki Kato	Asian	
Jeff Kalmakoff	European American	
Anna Norquist*	European American	
Parents		
Barbara Gelb	European American	
Pat Webb	European American	
Teachers		
Gene Foster	European American	Math
Sarah Fusako	Asian American	Science
Jim Greylock	European American	Social studies
Gary Linwood	African American	Music
Neal Richards	European American	Social studies
Monica Stabler	European American	Art
Brian Stanton	European American	Social studies
Ann Vidich	European American	Special education
Administrators		
Elizabeth Cunningham	European American	Principal (1999–2000)
Bobbi Taylor	European American	Athletics director
Laura Trent	European American	Principal (2000–2003)
James Welkes	African American	Assistant principal
Research assistants		
Jill Lynch	European American	
Rich Milner	African American	
April Peters	African American	
Mario Davidson	African American	

*Alumnus of WBHS.

a very quick wit and was always ready with a pithy remark to liven up conversations in class. He was a gifted athlete who played football and basketball and ran track. He favored baggy cargo pants—the baggier the better—and liked to collect "throwback" video games and athletic jerseys.

Julie Rice's family was devoutly Methodist, and Julie herself was active in her church. Julie ran track early in high school but became more and more involved with theater and choral music as she moved through Burnham. She referred to the group of other white girls she hung out with through high school as the GRT—"Girls at the Round Table" (referring to the shape of the table at which they usually sat at lunch). Though an intense conversationalist, Julie tended to avert her eyes while speaking.

David Sterling's father was a top executive at one of the largest corporations in central Ohio. His older brother had been a valedictorian at Burnham and had gone on to Notre Dame. David loved baseball, though he didn't play for Burnham. He was slender, wore glasses, and had a fine high tenor voice. By David's junior year, he had been to Europe three times with his family. Dinnertime conversations in the Sterling home were usually animated and involved discussion of politics. David himself was an articulate speaker who knew how to make an argument.

Sofia Rhoades's father worked at a large corporation in the area and her mother was a social worker for the state. Her family were Jehovah's Witnesses. Sofia's older sister went to Duke, and she prided herself on being a good big sister to her two much younger brothers. She became the goalie on the school's field hockey team and loved football, especially the Ohio State Buckeyes. Sofia was a self-proclaimed "daddy's girl" and considered herself a "good person to get along with." She said, "I don't have problems talking to anybody."

Bryan Bowen was originally from Michigan, where he had twenty-one half brothers and sisters—one in prison serving the end of a term for murder. Bryan's approach to fitting into Burnham was to "establish" himself—which frequently got him sent to the dean's office for conflicts with other students. Short yet solidly built, Bryan was devoted to his mother, and said that she gave him the sort of social support that many other students most likely didn't have. Bryan was the student we got to know least well through the study; he left Wilton and moved back to Michigan after his freshman year.

Cindi Criswell was one of the school's goths. She always dressed in black, adorned herself with chains and studded bracelets, and wore very dark eye shadow, sometimes with designs drawn on her face. Cindi acknowledged that she had a "violent side" and was kicked out of her mother's house during her junior year for threatening her sister with a knife. She was a talented artist who aspired to design her own line of clothing. She also loved horses.

Kevin Madsen's mother held three different executive positions with three different companies in three different states during his time in high school. His father, however, never went to college. After 9/11, his father went to New York with his construction crew to assist in the search for survivors. Kevin got noticeably taller and heftier during his high school career, the new bulk in part due to the soccer team's off-season strengthening program. While in his freshman year, Kevin told us he was in the "Abercrombie" group; as he moved through Burnham, he was generally in the most popular group of students, consisting largely of male and female athletes and several girls that he said were "really hated" because their families were "rich." He generally wore his pants low with the top of his underwear showing.

Over the course of the study, we got to know this group of students very well. They shared their hopes and worries, triumphs and disappointments. They went through a lot during those four years, some more than others. One dropped out of school and two dealt with serious health problems. All faced the sometimes-bewildering predicaments of today's adolescence with a fluctuating combination of angst, excitement, despair, and anticipation. We also became a part of the school community. During the study, I was invited into several classrooms to give talks on human difference, culture, Papua New Guinea, and the work of anthropologists. Rich Milner conducted a dissertation on teacher planning in the school. I assisted the school with a survey and staff meeting on bullying and harassment, and I served on the school's regional accreditation team. A report of findings from the study was presented to the school and used as the basis of a staff development session where staff, teachers, and administrators could discuss the research in light of their own concerns about the school. Finally, when I mounted a drive in 2003 to collect books for school libraries in Manus, the school district generously donated approximately four hundred titles. I have become friends with many of the staff there.

Meanwhile, as the project ran its course, I became a parent. My wife and I had two daughters and began to face some of the same challenges as the parents I had interviewed for the study: we struggled to balance work and family life, worried about what was best for our children in terms of their education, and did our best to deal with stress and fatigue. As I began to share with my wife what I had been learning about what it took to compete in today's high schools, we began to wonder aloud about the environments in which our daughters were going to grow up.

Plan of the Book

Figure 1 provides a display of the elements of this middle-class logic of personal advancement through education and also serves as a guide to the first five chapters of the book. The display illustrates the interaction of the five central elements of this cultural system: 1) the guiding ideology of the Wilton Way; 2) parental support, leverage, and policy manipulations; 3) the institutional advantaging and hypercredentialing of the school; 4) student identities for control and success; and 5) student instrumental strategies for achievement and advancement. Key linkages and feedback mechanisms that bind the system together are described throughout.

Chapter 1 introduces the community and the Wilton Way. It details the more-or-less shared beliefs that comprise this ideology, including the distinctiveness of the community, community members' awareness of competition, expectations for individual success, and paramount beliefs in the importance of self-worth. The chapter then shows how these class cultural beliefs underlie the local philosophy of schooling, and discusses how this fluid linkage between the community and its schools was a key point of articulation in this cultural system. Finally, the chapter illustrates how the school's efforts to meet the needs of minority students were subordinate to its broader goals of remaining competitive. The Wilton Way is described here, at the outset of the book, because it provided the ideological basis for how its residents lived their everyday lives, including the parenting practices, school policies, student identities, and academic strategies that are discussed in the chapters that follow.

Chapter 2 explores the role of parents in supporting their children's academic achievement. It discusses the distinctive combination of affective support, high expectations, and pressure or "pushing" that were typical of the parenting styles in the community. It also describes the ways in which they routinely intervened with individual teachers when they judged that their child's work had been evaluated unfairly. Finally, it examines the ways in which some parents used their class cultural know-how and social and professional networks to appropriate special education policy for the benefit of their children. (Between 1996 and 2002 there was a three-fold

FIGURE 1   A local logic of middle-class personal advancement.

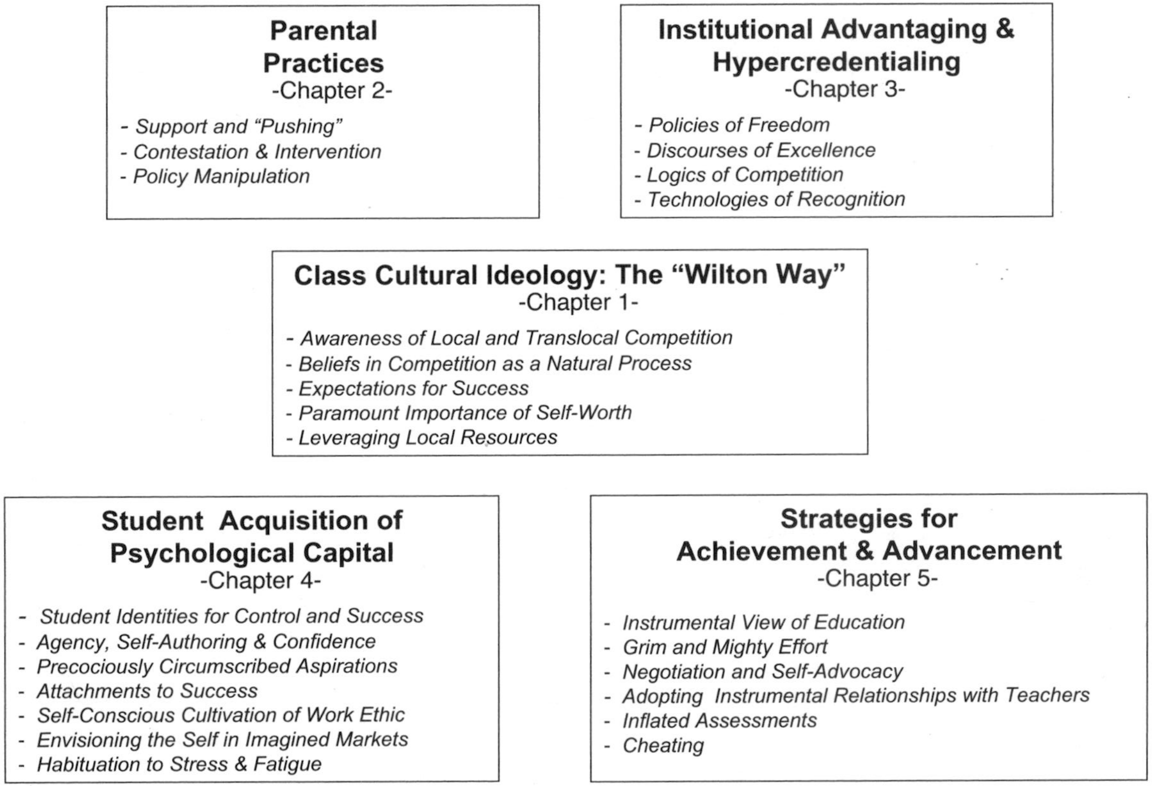

Parental Practices
-Chapter 2-

- Support and "Pushing"
- Contestation & Intervention
- Policy Manipulation

Institutional Advantaging & Hypercredentialing
-Chapter 3-

- Policies of Freedom
- Discourses of Excellence
- Logics of Competition
- Technologies of Recognition

Class Cultural Ideology: The "Wilton Way"
-Chapter 1-

- Awareness of Local and Translocal Competition
- Beliefs in Competition as a Natural Process
- Expectations for Success
- Paramount Importance of Self-Worth
- Leveraging Local Resources

Strategies for Achievement & Advancement
-Chapter 5-

- Instrumental View of Education
- Grim and Mighty Effort
- Negotiation and Self-Advocacy
- Adopting Instrumental Relationships with Teachers
- Inflated Assessments
- Cheating

Student Acquisition of Psychological Capital
-Chapter 4-

- Student Identities for Control and Success
- Agency, Self-Authoring & Confidence
- Precociously Circumscribed Aspirations
- Attachments to Success
- Self-Conscious Cultivation of Work Ethic
- Envisioning the Self in Imagined Markets
- Habituation to Stress & Fatigue

increase in the number of students classified as other health impaired [OHI] in Wilton. By 2002, there were more OHI-classified students in Wilton than in Cleveland, Cincinnati, or Columbus, Ohio.)

Chapter 3 brings readers inside Wilton Burnham High School itself: a Blue Ribbon high school with a rich curriculum and extracurriculum and dedicated teaching staff. It explains that a corollary of the local cultural emphasis on the maintenance of self-worth and the pursuit of individual success was a belief that ceding control to young people and accommodating their preferences would help them to be successful. Accordingly, the chapter shows how the school was organized around policies that gave students great latitude and input. It also provides examples of the variety of ways in which the school sponsored students and socialized them for individualistic competition, from its continuous emphasis on "excellence" and "success" to the many ways in which it formally recognized students' achievements.

Chapter 4 describes the identities of the high-achieving students in the school. It inventories the suite of identity characteristics in these students that were oriented toward controlling their school experiences, in part to allay their anxieties over uncertain futures. These student characteristics included strong beliefs in their abilities to shape their own futures, predispositions to self-advocate, precociously circumscribed aspirations, deeply held attachments to individual success, consciously cultivated work ethics, and a keen awareness of what knowledge, skills, and demeanors might benefit them on education and employment markets. The chapter interprets these identity characteristics as components of psychological capital oriented to maximize students' abilities to compete.

The fifth chapter examines the implications of achievement-oriented students' fixation on "getting good grades" for classroom learning. It describes how these students perceived the purposes of school, and the specific practices they developed to maximize their academic achievement ("get the good grade with the least amount of work") and future prospects. These included constantly judging the utility of their classes and the effectiveness of their teachers; negotiating for extra points, easier assignments, or extra credit; personalizing their relationships with teachers; and cheating. The chapter also explores how many teachers "padded" or "built up" grades, and how these, along with the school recognition programs mentioned in chapter 2, make up a process of "hypercredentialing." The chapter shows how such an emphasis creates disjunctions between processes of credentialing and learning.

Chapter 6 describes how these students went through their daily lives with more or less ever-present high levels of stress and fatigue, and it relates important gender differences in this area. The chapter gives readers a glimpse inside these students' stress-filled days and illuminates their successful and unsuccessful attempts to cope. Over 70 percent of students reported being stressed out "frequently" or "all the time," and while female students had significantly higher cumulative GPAs than male students, they also reported higher levels of stress than male students and were much more likely to identify their schoolwork as the most important source of stress. The voices and experiences of these students demonstrate that the most successful are those that are able to habituate to more or less ever-present levels of stress and fatigue.

The final data chapter tells the story of students who seemed to suffer within this school climate, which was oriented so strongly around individual competition: average- and low-achieving students, as well as many African American students. The chapter explains how it was that many under-achieving students seemed to connect their academic disengagement to the competitive emphases of the school, feeling "defeated" or "alienated" from the school and ultimately deciding not to "play the game." The chapter attributes the rising rates of student harassment and vandalism in the school in part to the frustration many average and below-average students had with the school's rigid hierarchical ranking system and its emphasis on competitive success. It draws on multiple examples and perspectives in an effort to understand why an AP social studies teacher said, "civility is dead here." The chapter also shows how African American students were marginalized within the school. They were consistently underrepresented in higher-level classes during the study and did not seem to adopt many of the same instrumental strategies oriented toward academic success as their white peers.

The conclusion discusses what these findings mean for our understanding of what it takes to succeed in the current educational system, as well as of the role of education in the production of inequality. The chapter calls attention to these suburban students' and parents' keen awareness of the competitive education and employment markets as well as what was needed to compete in them. It recounts key components of the high-achieving students' psychological capital and how they articulated with a school system that leverages community resources and frames students' efforts as successes. Above all, I argue in the conclusion that Wilton students' primary advantage is this integrated cultural system itself. It is a robust and self-reinforcing system that extends across multiple domains of community and school and is continually remade through its members' very identities and practices. I suggest that the existence of such entrenched cultures of personal advancement raise new equity questions regarding the American public education system's reliance on local control.

Part One
Community, Home, and School Settings

Chapter One The Wilton Way:
Middle-Class Culture and Practice

Locating Wilton

Wilton is a middle- to upper-middle-class "historic" suburb of Columbus, Ohio, that has long been a favored residential spot for the area's professional class. Located less than ten miles from the city center, it has a quaint downtown where the Wilton Inn and various shops and restaurants border the village green. It also has well-maintained parks and libraries, two country clubs, and an expansive public recreation center. At the time of the study, nearly 60 percent of adult residents had a bachelor's degree or higher (the U.S. average was 24.4 percent), and over 60 percent of households reported gross income of $50,000–$199,999. The median home value in 2000 was $163,000 (the U.S. average was $111,800) (U.S. Census Bureau 2000).

Of its population of approximately fifty thousand, nearly half of employed adults in Wilton at the time of the study were in managerial and professional occupations, and over a third were in technical, sales, and administrative support. The largest employers in the area were in the government, education, insurance, banking, and technology sectors, and included the State of Ohio, Ohio State University, JPMorgan Chase, Nationwide, Ohio Health, Limited Brands, Honda of America, and the Batelle Institute.

This chapter describes the community of Wilton as well as the class cultural ideology known locally as the "Wilton Way." It discusses local views regarding the distinctiveness of Wilton, community members' awareness of competition, associated beliefs concerning competition as a natural social process, and expectations for individual success. Then it describes local beliefs regarding the importance of the maintenance of individual self-worth. Finally, it shows how these class cultural beliefs underlay key tenets of the local educational philosophy. This philosophy functioned as a key linkage in Wilton that authorized the extraction of private goods from public schools. Other key linkages that bind together this cultural system oriented toward self-advancement are discussed in subsequent chapters.

Wilton's ethnic makeup has remained relatively constant over the last two decades: over 90 percent white; less than 3 percent Asian American; less than 2 percent African American; approximately 1 percent Latino; and less than 1 percent Native American (U.S. Census Bureau 2000). However, socioeconomic diversity has increased—more low-income people have moved there largely to take advantage of employment and educational opportunities not found in the larger city. Throughout the study, parents, students, and teachers commented on the fact that there were poor people who lived in Wilton; some expressed concern that there had been an increase in rental properties in the community (in 2000, of the 5,845 homes in Wilton, 904 were renter-occupied). During the 1999–2000 school year, 4.7 percent of students in the Wilton district qualified for free and reduced-price lunches (U.S. Census Bureau 2000). Cindi Criswell was evicted with her father from their home during her junior year because he could not pay the bills on time.

Nevertheless, virtually all of the parents interviewed for the study who were not originally from Wilton said they had moved there for a combination of economic and educational reasons. Parents generally mentioned the quality of life and the reputation of the schools. David Sterling's father said, "It was supposed to be great schools and just a great community." A school librarian mentioned that she had moved to Wilton because the district would pay for her master's degree.

Most Wilton parents were well-off, and many were able to provide a variety of enriching opportunities for their children, such as private music lessons, trips to England with the select soccer team, and family vacations to far-flung locations. Students and parents showed various degrees of awareness of the privileged lives led by residents in the community. One white parent said:

> Um, we kind of refer to it as pretty much a bubble, because it's not like living in a—city. I mean it's not like living—even in Pittsburgh, or Cleveland, or even Cincinnati where my daughter lives. I mean you—you don't see anyone that is a different ethnic background! [Chuckles.] It's very . . . isolated from the real world." (Interview 7/21/03)[1]

Data from the study suggested that this isolation from other kinds of people seemed to foster a naturalized view of privilege and the social order. One white parent said, "To live in Wilton, you have to be doing a certain amount of good stuff." Parents and students often expressed meritocratic beliefs, ascribing success or failure more or less entirely to individual talent or effort. This theme is discussed in more detail later in this chapter, as well as in chapter 4. Typically, Wilton students had little interaction with people from more disadvantaged backgrounds. When taken on a field trip to visit a homeless shelter, two white male students commented repeatedly on how "weird" it was, how it "totally sucked," and how one shelter resident had tried to take one of the boy's money (which turned out not to be true).

Other students, however, demonstrated an awareness of their good fortune to live in such an area and undertook activities to help others who were less fortunate. When one of the researchers commended two freshman girls for the amount of money they raised for the school's "Adopt a Child" program, one of the girls, of Southeast Asian descent, said, "I think it's definitely important to help people . . . . You're still a very lucky person to be living in this area."

Finally, Wilton had a reputation for an outstanding school system. One of the local metropolitan magazines consistently ranked it as one of the top three suburban districts in the area. The average standardized test scores for students in grades three, five, seven, and ten were between the eightieth and eighty-fifth percentiles nationally. The 2002 Wilton District Profile noted:

> Results on state proficiency tests generally are among the top 10 percent in the state. Average scores on the ACT and SAT college-entrance exams are well above state and national averages. Results in 2000–01 were the highest in many years. The district met all 27 state standards on this year's District Report Card, placing Wilton in the top 5 percent of Ohio's 612 school districts. Wilton is the largest district in the state to achieve this status and a rating of "Excellent." (Wilton School District 2002a)

The district also had a strong resource base and had expanded over the years. Wilton's original high school was founded as Wilton Academy in 1808—at the time it was the first secondary school in central Ohio. In 1951 this was expanded to Wilton High School, which served the needs of the community for the next forty years. In 1973 the district opened the Douglas Alternative Program for high school students, which offered a greater degree of curricular choice and emphasized experiential education. Due to rapid population growth through the 1980s the community approved funds to build Wilton Burnham High School (referred to hereafter as WBHS, Wilton Burnham, or simply Burnham), which opened in 1991. The school was named for one of the "pioneering businessmen" who originally established the town in 1803. (Wilton High School was renamed Robert Wilton High School after another of the community's original founders).

At the time of the study, there were 11 elementary schools, 5 middle schools and 3 high schools in the Wilton District, staffed by approximately 620 teachers. In December, 1999 the district bought a 60,000-square-foot glass-and-steel office building for $5.4 million to house its central administration (an additional $2.2 million was spent on renovations and moving costs). The architectural firm that completed the renovations on the building donated a $27,000 conference table for the center's new boardroom.

The Wilton School District's accomplishments and resources should be considered in the context of persistent public education funding inequities across the state. The state supreme court had ruled the state school funding system unconstitutional three times since 1991. However, the state legislature had persistently failed to address the issue and the situation remained unchanged up until the time of the study, when the state had some of the largest disparities in per-pupil funding in the United States. The Wilton School District was at the upper end of this spectrum: in 2001–2002 it had a per-pupil expenditure of $8,681. These funding disparities underscore the fact that at the time of the study, education in Wilton was conducted in a state funding environment rife with inequities.

The Wilton Way

The study generated a great deal of data concerning local beliefs, practices, and appropriate dispositions related to individual success. I have come to understand them in the context of a local saying or trope known as the Wilton Way. The Wilton Way consisted of more-or-less shared beliefs concerning the distinctiveness of the community, the importance of individual self-worth, and competitive strategies for individual and community advancement. It also comprised the local achievement ideology (or "status ideology") through which parents and community members "constructed a symbolic boundary" around their school community (Holme 2002, 194). In this sense, the Wilton Way is a local instance of upper middle class or professional class beliefs and practices. Jim Greylock, a white WBHS AP history teacher in his thirties, described the Wilton Way as follows:

> So the Wilton Way is the Upper Alexandria Way, is the Townsend Way [other nearby upper-middle-class suburbs], is the upper-middle-class way.

It has nothing to do with what is intrinsic to you, but with what is outside of you. Your consumption. Your capacity to consume. How your capacity for consumption determines your worth. (Interview 4/17/00)

When asked what the Wilton Way was, Gary Linwood, the veteran African American WBHS choir director exclaimed, "Oh my gosh! If I knew that, we'd have it in a bottle."

A central contention of the book is that the Wilton Way provided an ideological basis for the class-cultural beliefs, identities, and practices that characterized its residents' everyday lives.

The Distinctiveness of the Community

While a fairly typical suburb in most respects, Wilton lays claim to a "New England heritage" through the fact that it was originally established over two hundred years ago by settlers from the northeastern United States. The distinctiveness that Wilton attributes to itself and its citizens is apparent in many ways, including the glossy publications and events that were produced to mark its bicentennial in 2003. The motto on the bicentennial brochure was "Wilton—1803–2003—Building the Future with Pioneering Spirit." It announced:

> The Wilton community is commemorating our Bicentennial through
> a series of extraordinary Signature Events. The major events showcase
> Wilton's pioneering spirit and create a legacy for future generations.
> (Wilton Historical Society 2003)

Held between October 2002 and October 2003, the events included a costume ball, a commissioned play, a lecture series, a recreated historic wagon train, a homecoming for former residents, and a memory project to archive historical resources. According to John Dorst (1989), "elite suburbs" that devote this much energy to maintaining such a historical identity are motivated in part by an awareness of the commoditized value of their promotional efforts.

Wilton's sense of exceptionality was also present in its schools. The Wilton School District motto was, "Where Excellence is a Tradition," and permanent signs affixed near the main entrance of each school building noted that they were in one of the state's "Best Communities." In 1998, WBHS was recognized by the United States Department of Education as a "Blue Ribbon High School," which some faculty referred to as the school's "crown jewel."

Some residents were critical of this aspect of Wilton. A math teacher identified a central component of the Wilton Way as "Wilton coming up with ways to distinguish itself." An alumnus of Wilton High School referred to the Wilton Way as "the kind of plastic facade that Wilton carries around, and the kids at Burnham carry around." When asked on the survey whether they were familiar with the Wilton Way, twice as many eleventh graders (21.5 percent) as ninth graders (9.6 percent) answered affirmatively. This suggests a growing awareness of this trope as students get older. The open-ended responses to the question asking what the Wilton Way meant to students were generally split between earnest and cynical replies[2]:

Doing things with pride, excellence and doing them well. (ninth-grade European American female)

The Wilton Way is the way people in Wilton live their lives. It has to do with a certain pride and work ethic for doing well. (eleventh-grade European American male)

The "Wilton Way" is a path of excellence in academics, and a little in sports. We're forced to do more work, harder classes, and less vacation. We [Wilton] want our kids to go to really good colleges so it looks good on the community. (eleventh-grade European American male)

I think it means a snobby, stuck-up way of doing things. Doing things to look good / advance in society. (eleventh-grade American Indian male)

The "Wilton Way" unfortunately implies, to me, a stuck-up, preppy, elitist way of doing things. Image is everything and success is expected. (eleventh-grade American Indian female)

Rich boy snob gets what he wants way. (ninth-grade European American male)

They push us harder, make us work longer, and try and make us learn faster to keep us this "Tradition of Excellence." How stuck up can you get? (eleventh-grade European American male)

No, most likely it means something like people in Wilton are stuck up and are a bunch of posers [sic] but hey—I'd agree with that. (ninth-grade European American female)

Local Responses to Translocal Competition:
Status Anxiety and Expectations for Success

At the core of the Wilton Way are preoccupations with socioeconomic status and class mobility and associated beliefs concerning the naturalness and ubiquity of competition. These may be seen anthropologically as adaptive responses to extremely competitive environments and uncertain fates. At the time of the study, residents of Wilton shared an uneasiness about the future with other members of what the economist Robert Reich (1994) several years ago labeled the "anxious class."

Researchers have commented on how many middle-class parents are preoccupied with the possibilities of "declining fortunes" for their children (Newman 1993; Lareau 2003). Consequently, as Varenne and McDermott noted in their comparative study of suburban schools (1998), students and parents in Wilton were generally keenly aware of being in competition with others.

For example, when we asked students in an AP U.S. history class, "What drives you—to work so hard?" A sophomore Asian American student responded, "It's harder for our generation to live the same lifestyle as our parents do." Julie Rice's mother spoke of "wanting her to stay with the flow, caught up with the pack, even with all those other kids." The father of Sofia Rhoades, who was a chemist at a local pharmaceutical corporation, had an especially sobering view of the local culture of competition. He said that he had always taught his daughter to "play the challenge game":

> I mean, you're always going to be challenged to do better, or outperform . . . because before you show your potential, or what you can do, you're always going to be a negative. And so it's never a level playing surface per se—you're always at an incline, you're always walking uphill. (Interview 12/6/00)

In Wilton there were pervasive and pronounced community expectations for success. A special education supervisor at WBHS said, "Here in Wilton, it's like you *will* go to high school, you *will* go to college. You *will* go to a good college. And nobody wants to go to some teeny, tiny college somewhere." David Sterling said in his first interview in ninth grade, "It's just, Wilton, everyone has to do well in Wilton. It's like, you can't *fail* if you live in Wilton. And that's what you see." A special education teacher said the local expectation was simply, "the best of the best at all times. Every one gives two hundred percent."

When asked in an interview about the Wilton Way, Anna Norquist, a WBHS alumnus laughed, then said:

I don't know. I think—I think ideally I mean it's probably a good—it's probably a healthy ideal, you know? In a sense. I mean that, just to accept, I think to excel, to, you know, to excel, to achieve, um, you know, accomplish your goals—I mean it's all these lofty ideals. And, but I mean, unfortunately it becomes a little bit muddled, I think when they're actually there [in school]. It becomes much more like, you know, get the grades, get the recognition in sports or activities, you know, get recognized somehow. Because you're just lost in a sea of seventeen hundred students . . . . But I think overall, I think that's what they want. I think that's what teachers and administrators think that Wilton's about. In producing, you know, kids that are definitely going to go to college.

Later in the interview she elaborated on the source of the expectations— and their implications:

It seemed like expectations came with the wealth and money, and you know, just—and conformity. And you automatically *assume* all these things about kids, and as a kid, you're supposed to *do* all these things, and *be* all these things. And . . . but now I realize that there *are* good—there *are* good aspects to living in a wealthy community and attending a really great school district, and there are pressures, and um . . . it's just—it's—it's a *battle*. (Interview 8/27/02)

This quotation from Anna Norquist illustrates her own developing awareness of the broad national competitive environment and the degree to which a Wilton education positioned her to succeed in it (she later was admitted to medical school). Furthermore, her description of the struggle to succeed in Wilton as a "battle" is telling: As I detail in chapter 5, many students used language drawn from the military, security, and business worlds throughout the study to describe their academic triumphs and challenges.

The district had high expectations for success at every grade level, including kindergarten. After formal data collection for the study was concluded, two parents shared their experience of attending a kindergarten screening meeting at the elementary school to which they were planning to send their five-year-old boy.

Before the meeting began, the children were taken to a different room, which the parents had not been told about beforehand. Then the principal began by saying, "OK, I want everyone to try and remember what you can about when you were in kindergarten." And then the parents all shared warm and fuzzy memories, like playing with their friends, sitting in the teachers lap and reading, and various special things their teachers did for them because they cared about them so much. Then the principal said, "OK, well it's not like that anymore. Now, children really need to learn to read this year. And they have to be independent. The state standards and testing have pushed things down, so kindergarten is now the new first grade." She then told the parents that if they thought their child might not be ready, that they might want to think about holding them back a year, adding that many parents were doing that in light of the standards. The mother who related this story said she left the meeting feeling "shaky." (Field notes 2/22/07)

The district's lofty expectations became clear to Pat Webb, a white parent, when she moved to Wilton from a community that placed less emphasis on competition and testing. She said she and her husband began to feel pressure even when their children were in kindergarten, as preparations began for testing into the Extended Projects Program in elementary school—the entry point for the district's elaborate and well-funded gifted and talented program.

PAT WEBB: The pressure was just so minimal compared to what these kids get just from the, you now, day one. Like, you know, you're being tested constantly . . . . And every single year, you know, there's something, there's something, there's something, can we do extra reading, can we— you know, help these kids at home, prepare for the proficiency tests, you know. Are we—spending extra time with our flash cards.

PETER DEMERATH: And so—

PW: It's totally different.

PD: And so—are you saying that you and your husband began to feel that pressure even when she was in kindergarten?

PW: Oh yeah. Oh, you feel that right away, because—you know, there's just some kind of, immediately, there's some sort of testing. Okay, well we're going to do the—pre-reading groups. You know, these kids are in this group, you can be in the A group, the B group, the . . . [chuckles slightly.]

PD: Yeah.

PW: I mean, there's, even if it's not, just it's like a typed list that gets handed out, I mean, there's just definitely a division. You know, well, these are the advanced kids, and these are the kids that aren't advanced. I mean they can call it umpteen different things, but—you know.

PD: Sure.

PW: We offer this—advanced program, you know, or you can stay an extra hour, or you can come a little early, or you can . . . [laughs softly.]

PD: Yeah.

PW: You know? There's always this distinction of—of well, you know, so
and so is already reading, and so, in our free reading time, you know,
you can choose your book from this tub over here, or you can choose
your book [from this other tub]. You know, you're in the red tub, or
you're in the blue tub.

PD: I understand.

PW: You know? There's a distinction just immediately. (Interview 7/23/03)

Pat Webb summarized her impressions by saying, "When you dig a little
deeper you find out this is just a real competitive school district" and that
"there are an awful lot of kids who test high by those standards." Of the
district itself, she said, "It just sorts you out right from the word 'go.'"

Such expectations for personal success were ubiquitous throughout the
community. Not surprisingly, parental bragging about children's accomplishments was commonplace, as was posting AP test results on refrigerators and discussing colleges to which children were applying and gaining
admission. Gaps between parental expectations and student capabilities
are explored in more detail in the next chapter.

Community expectations for success certainly extended to the school's
extracurriculum. Bobbi Taylor, the Burnham athletics director, was acutely
aware of what parents expected from the school's teams.

PD: What does that sound like, that high level of expectation? What do
parents say to coaches, or to you?

BT: For most parents [knocking on table for emphasis], they would sit here
and say it's not about the winning. But to them that's the first obvious
sign of a successful program. And I know that I have had several parents talk to me about, "I don't know that our coach can take us to the
next level." And for them it might only be a five hundred season [.500
winning percentage]. They want to be able to find that magic formula
because of the hard work and because our parents are involved. I mean
they send their kids to camps. They want to know what it will take
to make their kid a better player in that particular sport. So they've
invested the time. So the tradeoff is, hey [knocking on desk again for
emphasis], you'd better have a coach in there that can get the *most*
and the *best* from our kids. And, they won't accept too much of
anything else.

PD: So winning is important to parents—

BT:—It's important to some, it's just teaching your kids, or letting them feel
what it's like to win . . . . Once you have that sense that, "Hey we can
win," and you have that little natural arrogance which comes with it, I
think you, I mean, kids can really do some incredible things when they

have the confidence and the sauce, and the trust in their teammates to be able to win. (Interview 5/29/02)

Ms. Taylor here goes beyond parents' desires to have their children play on winning athletic teams. She suggests that experiencing winning is an intrinsic part of a person's "natural" sense of self-confidence. Indeed, the data in this section illustrate how competition was regarded as akin to a natural process in this community. The ensuring chapters illustrate how competition and the drive for individual success imbued virtually all domains of practice in the high school itself.

"This Is Wilton—*Everyone* Is a Special Person!"
The Paramount Importance of Self-Worth

Another tenet of the Wilton Way that was closely related to these community expectations for individual success was the paramount importance of maintaining self-worth. This tenet infused a wide array of community practices, in and out of school, and seemed to have its basis in unspoken beliefs about the role of positive self-regard in competitive success.

These beliefs about the importance of self-worth were readily apparent one day when we were shadowing Cindi (accompanying her through an entire school day). At the beginning of her history class, Cindi commented to her teacher that she was a "special person" that day because she was being shadowed by a researcher. The teacher smiled broadly and responded, "This is Wilton—*everyone* is a special person!" This belief in the "specialness" of Wilton residents seemed to be based on the widely held views about the distinctiveness of the community, the socioeconomic and professional status of its residents, and the arc of success that defined their lives.

When I asked David Sterling's parents what the Wilton Way meant to them, they initially laughed. Then they said the following:

SUSAN STERLING: Some people take it, the Wilton Way, is to make sure every child feels good about themselves regardless of if they're learning anything or succeeding. And with the Wilton Way self-esteem will be at an all-time high.

MICHAEL STERLING: Like Lake Wobegon [the fictitious town described in the radio program *A Prairie Home Companion*], we're all above average.

SS: Exactly, exactly, and so I think there's some of that too.

PD: Okay, because the second part of this I've heard was that in Wilton every person is a special person.

SS: [Laughs.]

MS: [Laughs.]

SS: Well, you don't know this, James [David's brother, a senior] came home today. He's home, he said at the thing today [WBHS's Celebration of Excellence, which also doubles as the graduation rehearsal], he got his cord from National Honor Society. And he said, "You see what this is?" And I said, "What?" "This is what everybody gets to wear because some parent complained a few years ago that her kid didn't have anything to wear and felt bad. So now we all wear these."

MS: [Laughing.]

PD: Which one, the cord?

SS: No, the long one with the badge.

PD: Oh, the medal [The school's new "Celebration of Excellence" medal]?

SS: "Yeah," he said. Now *that* would be the Wilton Way. Okay?

PD: So it has to do with recognition?

SS: Every child will feel good about him or herself. (Interview 6/1/00)

That year the school had decided to give every student a "Celebration of Excellence" medal and ribbon which would be hung around their neck at graduation; each graduate also received a wallet sized card with the school's crest and the rights and responsibilities to which they were entitled embossed on it. The Sterlings' sentiments regarding the importance of the maintenance of self-worth in Wilton were echoed by a white eleventh-grade female student in part of her response to the survey question regarding the Wilton Way: "Money buys agreements, everyone must feel good and fuzzy." Data from the study suggest that one effect of such a focus on maintaining individual self-worth was that a great many youth had an air of entitlement about them. This is certainly consistent with what Lareau found to be a product of the middle-class parenting strategy of "concerted cultivation" (2003). This facet of these students' identities is explored in more detail in chapter 4.

Local beliefs regarding self-worth were also grounded in assumptions about the average intelligence of community residents. The district special education supervisor mentioned above said that a guiding assumption for parents in the community was that, "There are no average kids in Wilton. You are either gifted or special ed. And that's taken from the mindset that the average IQ is 115." She pointed out that, as a consequence, special education services were perceived as "a good thing" in Wilton. Parents' assiduous efforts to get such students special education services are discussed in the next chapter.

Community Influences on Local Educational Philosophy

The "State of the Schools"

The final section of this chapter examines what these local expectations for success and conceptions of personhood meant for the relationship between the community and its schools. As in many communities, the quality of the schools meant a great deal to its identity and economic health (see Bartlett et al. 2002). The primary way in which school quality was judged in Wilton was by performance on state-mandated proficiency tests. Real estate agencies routinely used school report cards in their sales efforts, noting the specific school feeder patterns and which schools had passed all parts of the proficiency tests.

A particularly poignant instance of the importance of proficiency test scores occurred at a Wilton elementary school in June 2003. The school had posted uneven test scores for the previous five years, and when it was revealed that the school had only passed two of the ten state standards for the 2002–2003 academic year, there was an uprising among the school's parents. Saying they were "tired" of the low scores relative to Wilton's other elementary schools, the parents demanded that the principal be replaced. Some even said a "population gap" was responsible for a large number of "slow students" slowing down the "fast students" (while the school had a proportionate number of ESL [English as a second language] students compared to other Wilton elementary schools, it had a larger number of African American students). The principal resigned two weeks after the scores were made public (P. Willis 2003).

The importance of academic success to the overall well-being of the community was demonstrated at the first annual "State of the Schools" presentation on the evening of January 31, 2002. Held at the Wilton Mall and hosted by the superintendent and school board, the event provided insight into key components of the cultural logic that underlay educational practice in Wilton. Approximately three hundred parents and community members were in attendance, and each school had a table with staff members present and various materials on display (including thick "Crisis Management Plan" binders—a reflection of the post-Columbine, post-9/11 environment). Other education-related programs and organizations also had tables, including:

Wilton Education Foundation—a "community-wide, tax-exempt organization that funds projects that enrich the learning experiences for the students of Wilton Public Schools." (Wilton Educational Foundation 2001)

Leadership Wilton—whose stated mission was to "enhance the under-standing of leadership qualities and to develop individual and group leadership potential in order to create a better Wilton area community." (Leadership Wilton 2001)

Partners for Citizenship and Character—a "grassroots, community-wide organization dedicated to raising awareness of character issues in the schools, neighborhoods, and businesses of the greater Wilton commu-nity" (there were "Seeking Success with Character" bumper stickers on their table). (Partners for Citizenship and Character)

Wilton Libraries "Homework Now"— a program that offered live online homework assistance that enabled students to "chat" and "co-browse electronic resources" with librarians twenty-four hours a day, seven days a week.

Wilton After-School Program—which included a variety of offerings for elementary students, including a Science Enrichment Club, a Creative Thinking with Computers class, a Chess Club, and classes in karate and tae kwon do.

These organizations and programs exemplify the rich educational re-sources available to Wilton students and parents. Attendees who had each table stamp their program were eligible to win one of the fourteen door prizes donated by the merchants in the mall.

The superintendent, a white male in his late fifties, began his address by saying, "We are extremely pleased to be able to partner with the mall in bringing you this evening's program. It is just one example of the strong relationship that exists between the schools and the business community of this school district." He then noted how integral the schools were to the local community: "They help create an identity for an area that defines the level of quality an area expects, and over time, maintains." After thank-ing the many people involved in the success of the Wilton schools, the superintendent moved into the centerpiece of the address—assessment. The superintendent first lamented the fact that assessments had become comparison tools among districts and schools. Then he said, "All argu-ments aside, if it's the playing field we're on, then we're going to continu-ously work hard to be the best of the class." He then said that one of the most important things that he could say to the audience that night was that Wilton's students were "exceeding the collective expectations held for their performance." Citing the importance of this observation, he then repeated it. The superintendent spent the next twenty minutes going through twenty-five PowerPoint slides that demonstrated the

Wilton School District's relative academic success, concluding with the state proficiency test results, which indicated that the district had an "excellent" (highest possible) rating. Furthermore, he noted comparative data, which suggested that, "Once again on this year's report card the Wilton Schools can proudly boast that there is no district in the state with more students who as a school district performed as well as we did on the state report card." He then moved into a discussion of district resources, noting that Wilton's total expenditure per student was $8,681, compared to the comparison group district's expenditure of $7,626. He mentioned various successful district educational programs, and then concluded with the following statements:

> The people of this school district can continue to take great pride in its schools because no matter how good the results, we will always have room for improvement, and we will continue to be relentless in seeking that improvement. . . . We will not and cannot rest on any past accomplishments or laurels. A person or entity is constantly in a process of either getting better or getting worse. We never stay the same because staying the same has a connotation of maintenance or inactivity. . . . As a school district, meaning we who work in it and those of you who reside in it, we are about shaping the future through the young people we serve. Our hearts, our minds, and our actions must be riveted to that end. (Wilton School District 2002b)[3]

The president of the school board then thanked the superintendent and said, "As you can see, the Wilton schools are living up to their slogan, 'Where Excellence is a Tradition'" (Field notes 1/31/02).

A primary purpose of the State of the Schools presentation seemed to be to assure parents and community members that the district was competing well. As such, it conveyed important assumptions about the centrality of improvement, growth, and achievement in this community. The "level of quality an area expects" seemed to be an oblique reference to local expectations for standard of living and perhaps class status. Above all, the address revealed the grim determination with which, as Alexis de Tocqueville noted nearly two hundred years ago, Americans seem to go about "acquiring the good things of life" (1838; see also Henry 1963).

The Material Challenges of Remaining a "Destination District"
While, as mentioned above, the Wilton School District was generally well-resourced, it faced many of the same funding issues as its neighboring suburban districts. This was a relatively recent phenomenon: regular new housing construction had historically enabled the district to pass fairly

modest levies at fairly wide intervals and still build very high-quality educational programs. During the time of the study, however, Wilton's residents voted on school funding issues three times. This was due to the district's slumping investments at the time, a lack of new homes being built, and declining enrollments (Wilton School District 2003). The last two factors were related to Wilton's geographical status as a "landlocked" district, meaning that because of a lack of land for new construction there was little prospect of population growth over time. The dialogues and events surrounding these votes illustrate another facet of the Wilton Way: rationales and strategies to leverage local resources for the support of its schools.

For example, during the spring of 2003, the district was faced with having to cut $12 million from its budget by 2006 in order to accommodate state reductions in education spending. A levy failure would mean position cuts, increases in class size, and eliminations of specific programs. Indeed, when the possibility was raised of eliminating the Extended Projects Program in the elementary schools, there was a huge uproar among parents. Many came to a board meeting and complained that their children would not be adequately served if the program was discontinued.

Parents and staff were similarly worried about possible cuts in extra-curricular activities. As mentioned above, many Wilton residents took considerable pride in their winning athletic programs. When Burnham was built in the early 1990s, Bobbi Taylor said that at the time there was concern among parents as to whether the community's two schools "would have the same success" as the original school. At a community meeting before the levy vote in the spring of 2003, the Burnham head football coach commented that a proposed elimination of middle school football would have "a big effect" on the high school, in that the football team would then only be coming together for the first time in ninth grade and would have a difficult time competing with teams from other districts that had been together for two to three years. He emphasized that Wilton needed to remain a "destination district."

The coach here makes a clear connection between the competitive success of the high school's athletic teams and the appeal of the school district as a whole for potential residents. This shows how the emphasis on competitive success pervades the local logic of this community.

Preparation for Individualistic Competition: The Logics of Authority and Recognition

Certainly the local expectations for success mean a high degree of community ownership of and involvement in the schools. The planning process for Wilton Burnham High School offers deeper insight into how community members, teachers, and administrators conceived of the purpose of education as well as how it ought to be conducted. When Wilton Burnham was being conceived, a Climate Committee was formed of parents, teachers, and students to decide on various school policies and structures. The committee's work was certainly driven by the widely shared community expectations of its schools detailed above. More specifically, the committee's recommendations were shaped by unspoken yet widely accepted class cultural beliefs that positive self-regard is required for developing the confidence needed to successfully compete. Over time the community had developed two primary means of developing the self-regard of its youth: granting them authority and recognizing them. The attribution of authority to children and young people was certainly consistent with key aspects of the middle-class parenting style identified by Lareau. She observed that in general children of middle-class parents "have a sense that they are special, that their opinions matter, and that adults should, as a matter of routine, adjust situations to meet children's wishes" (2003).[4] Throughout, the study uncovered broad local beliefs in and beyond Wilton homes regarding how the attribution of authority to young people could aid them in their pursuit of success. Elsewhere, I have written about how this aspect of the local achievement ideology led many of these youth to develop a deeply-felt sense of authority that led them to think they knew what is best for them, and to constantly try to exert influence over their lives in and out of school (Demerath 2007). I return to this theme in chapter 4.

Accordingly, one of the founding principles of Wilton Burnham was to grant students significant authority. A WBHS science teacher who was a member of the Planning Committee said of their deliberations, "We wanted to work with kids on managing their time, so it is more like when they go away to college." So the school adopted a "blended schedule" with some blocks and some regular class periods. In addition, juniors and seniors whose GPAs met a standard were afforded "options" wherein they could leave the campus during their free periods.

The Planning Committee's first goal for the school emphasized success: "opportunities for students and staff to experience success and to reach their fullest potential." Strategies for reaching this goal included "hav[ing] every student involved in one or more activities" and "creat[ing] a mechanism for student recognition." (Wilton Burnham High School 1990). Hence, the planning committee held that "the achievement of each student is important and should be recognized." In this way, the school developed a guiding logic of using external recognition to support self-worth and enhance prospects for competitive success. They decided, for example, that varsity letters should be awarded to band members and artists as well as athletes. Other examples are given in chapter 2. Accordingly, freedom and recognition became central pillars of Wilton Burnham's philosophy and, as the next chapter shows, its policies and practices.

Institutional Bulking Up: Infusing and Extracting Private Goods
Study data illuminated a variety of ways that parents supported the Wilton schools' academic and extracurricular activities, in part to ensure that their children's futures would not be held hostage to the uncertainties of public school funding. One of the most important means of doing so at WBHS was through elaborate and well-endowed booster organizations. The largest and most visible was Bears Inc., a registered 501(c)3 nonprofit organization devoted to supporting the school's athletic teams. Between 1997 and 2000, Bears Inc. successfully raised several million dollars for the construction of a four thousand square-foot "strength and power room" adjacent to the school's gymnasium—the largest privately funded project in the history of the Wilton schools (one visitor compared the weight training room to a health club). It would not be too much of a stretch to say that such infusions of private funds over time have allowed the school itself to "bulk up," compared to other public high schools.

In the first months of fieldwork in the school, I learned of the extensive involvement of the Academic Boosters group—who were not a part of Bears Inc. A letter sent to parents at the beginning of the 1999 school year identified the group's mission as follows:

> We are a broad-based association of people from the community foster-
> ing the academic achievement of *all* students, recognizing faculty com-
> mitment, educating parents, and facilitating enrichment opportunities
> for students. Our goal is not only to applaud high-achievers, but also to
> encourage effort, improvement, and the academic accomplishment of *all*
> Wilton Burnham High School students.

Since their founding in 1987, the Academic Boosters have organized annual appreciation functions for school staff, funded a speaker series for note-worthy visitors to address the school community, and given annual gifts to the school, such as large maps, science posters, art prints for hallways, and library books. The Academic Boosters have also instituted and supported an extensive array of recognition programs for students such as Academic Honors Night, Academic Signings Day, the Student of the Month program, the Socratic Society, and the Junior Book Awards. They also provided permanent award plaques and displays for national award winners and for the Wilton Burnham High School Hall of Fame inductees. In May 2000, I phoned the chairperson and expressed an interest in learning more about the organization. She invited me to their next meeting.

The meeting was held in a conference room at the school on a weekday evening and there were eight white women and one white man in attendance, all in their forties or fifties. Fruit and yogurt were set out on a side table as snacks. The chairperson explained that this would not be a typical meeting, because they were not having an outside speaker.

After introductions and the approval of the minutes from the last month's meeting, a discussion ensued as to whether the Academic Boosters should become their own 501(c)3 or whether they should move under the larger umbrella of Bears Inc. One member explained that the vocal and instrumental music booster organizations had been able to become part of Bears Inc. because they gave varsity letters. The group then discussed whether or not they should give out "academic letters." They asked me if I knew whether schools in other countries, such as Papua New Guinea, did this, and I said there were no letters given at all there, and because of funding shortfalls most schools didn't even have athletic teams.

The next point of discussion concerned what gift the boosters ought to give to the school. One woman said, "Well, when my son was inducted into the Spanish National Honors Society the candle wax dripped all over his hands . . . so we could get candle holders." After more discussion, the group eventually decided on another display case for awards and plaques.

Then came a longer discussion concerning standardized test score indications that Wilton middle school students were weak on grammar. A woman across the table from me shook her head and commented, "It doesn't match with the aptitude." When another member suggested they ask the new superintendent, who had just been hired, to look into the issue, the woman across the table responded, "I'd like to hear what the superintendent has to say before I charge him with any new duties." The chairperson then said, "We should have a whole lot more National Merit Scholars than we do. And our downfall is the verbal [on the PSAT]." The woman across the table looked at me and added, "We want lots of plaques. Lots of National Merit Finalists." The chairperson nodded, and sighed, "Yeah . . . only three this year."

Toward the end of the meeting the group asked me to tell them a bit about the study and what I had learned so far. I began by explaining we had set out to understand school culture and student culture most broadly, and that now we were focusing on a diverse group of eight ninth graders whom we planned on following all the way through high school. At the mention of the group of focal students, two women immediately said, "Really?" The women across the table quickly said, "I have a ninth-grade student. How were these students selected?" (Field notes 5/10/00)

Several aspects of the Wilton Way are apparent in this vignette. The first part of the meeting took up whether or not the group should develop another school-sponsored form of recognition for students—academic letters. The rationale was that such awards would not only allow the Academic Boosters to join Bears Inc., but an unstated assumption was presumably that they would also confer advantages on the recipients. Next, in making her suggestion for a school gift, one of the members called attention to the achievements of her own child. The discussion regarding National Merit Finalists illustrated: 1) community expectations for success (and the boosters' function to make such success visible in the school); and 2) the boosters' proprietary relationship with the new superintendent. Finally, the intense interest regarding how focal students for the study were selected suggests a vigilant awareness of opportunities through which the booster's children could receive recognition.

Conclusion

Wilton is similar to other middle- to upper-middle-class suburbs in the United States. Though its residents belong primarily to the professional and managerial classes, the last two decades have seen an increase in socioeconomic diversity. Moreover, like many other communities, it proudly features its distinctive historical identity—in part out of a compulsion to maintain and enhance its appeal and value. Indeed, the predominating worldview in Wilton of extremely competitive environments and uncertain futures is certainly shared by other members of the "anxious class."

The Wilton Way, as a set of class-based beliefs and strategies adapted to these environments, is also by no means unique to Wilton. Rather, it is a broad-based, middle-class ideology oriented toward self and community advancement. At its core are views of a meritocratic social order, competition as a natural process, pronounced local expectations for individual success, and a strong emphasis on self-worth. While the central tenets of the Wilton Way may be found in other similar communities, they likely take on different forms and are apparent in different ways.

One of the book's central points is that social stratification is the result of cultural activity and "informed agency" (see Brantlinger 2003). From this perspective, this chapter demonstrates how the community funnels additional private resources to the schools to assure their continuing quality and, in turn, promotes their accomplishments—thus adding public value to the community. More importantly, it illustrates how the almost seamless linkages between Wilton's class ideology, use of community resources, conceptions of personhood, and purposes of schooling make this part of a cultural system: an integrated network of meanings and practices oriented toward advancing individuals and the community. One of the most important linkages in this cultural system is between personal and community worth, both of which are primarily assessed through academic and professional success. This synergy leads to a philosophy of schooling oriented toward advancing the material interests of individuals as well as the community as a whole.

This chapter has described several of the means the community developed over time to accomplish this highly directed socialization of its youth: preparing them for competitive academic success as early as kindergarten, granting them great authority and control, and bestowing on them a wide array of forms of recognition. In this way, one can see how the local philosophy of schooling authorizes community members to extract private goods from the school, from the Academic Boosters' efforts to develop school-based forms of recognition that would aid in the process of credentialing to relying on the school to provide their children with the vital experience of winning (see Lipsitz 2005). The resulting cultural assemblage positions individuals to successfully compete in school and leverage community resources to support the schools, build up the confidence of individual students, and frame their efforts as successes.

Certainly these community members' views of the importance of effort and merit in competitive success recall Bourdieu and Passeron's well-known arguments about the role of schools in the social order (1977). As seemingly neutral institutions, they convert cultural capital, which is inherited, into academic capital, which can then be exchanged into economic capital. Sociologists of education refer to this process as a kind of meritocratic whitewashing of more structural socioeconomic inequities: that hard work or a strong work ethic underlies success and that it overrides structural factors such as inherited class status. This is commonly understood as a central way in which economic inequality is reproduced through schooling (P. E. Willis 1982; Foley 1990; Levinson, Foley, and Holland 1996). The next chapter examines the role of parents in the education of young people in Wilton.

Chapter Two Parental Support, Intervention, and Policy Manipulation

While Wilton's class cultural expectations for individual success influenced its educational philosophy and school policies, they also shaped parenting styles and practices. As mentioned in the previous chapter, the local educational philosophy in Wilton provided a warrant for parents to extract private goods from their public schools (see Lipsitz 2005). Accordingly, many parents, especially the parents of high-achieving students, had a proprietary stance toward the schools and the people who worked in them. This chapter examines the distinctive combination of affective support, pressure, and "pushing" that characterized parenting styles in the community. Then it describes specific parents' skillful abilities to intervene with individual teachers and to draw on their class cultural knowledge and professional networks to appropriate special education resources for the benefit of their children. These practices devoted to negotiating special circumstances for parents' own offspring are certainly a central component of the Wilton Way: they make up another key linkage that binds together this suburban cultural system oriented to personal advancement.

As mentioned in the introduction, much of the most compelling recent research on how the "class practices" of middle-class parents influence educational experience has been done by Annette Lareau. In *Home Advantage* (2000), she examined how parents draw on their class-based resources and skills to improve their child's performance in school and ultimately reap "educational profits." More recently, in focusing on both black and white families in a large metropolitan area in the northeastern United States, she observed that middle-class parents sought to actively "develop" their children by engaging in a process of "concerted cultivation" (2003). This process, practiced by both white and black parents, included actively fostering and assessing children's talents, opinions, and skills; reasoning and negotiating with children; intervening in institutions on behalf of the child, and training children to advocate for themselves. Lareau observed that a sense of entitlement emerges in the child as a consequence of these practices. Most importantly, Lareau argued that these families align themselves with the standards of gatekeeping institutions responsible for "social selection," and that this sort of explicit training in the "rules of the game," conferred important advantages on these children. Lareau's work is central to this book, because it raises important questions regarding how these middle class child rearing techniques shape young peoples' identities, their experiences in school, and their futures.

Families in Wilton

There were many family arrangements and parenting styles in Wilton at the time of the study. Survey data indicated that 71.2 percent of students lived with both parents, 20.3 percent lived with one parent, and 7.2 percent had some other sort of living arrangement (several students lived on their own). In addition, while some families were dispersed during the school week and rarely spent time together, others consciously scheduled family time every day.

This was certainly a challenge in David Sterling's family. His father was the comptroller of a large corporation, and his mother was a health care professional. However, the family had always prioritized having meals together. During busy stretches of the school year, the Sterling family found that breakfast was the one meal they could all eat together. David himself was aware of research from the National Longitudinal Study of Adolescent Health, which indicated a significant relationship between frequency of dinner with family and psychosocial well-being among American high school students (Resnick 2000). During his junior year, David said, "I just know from things I've read that—numerous studies have shown that when kids eat dinner with their parents, when they have an active relationship with their parents, they're more successful."

In contrast, Kevin Madsen, one of the under-achieving white focal students in the study had a family that was, in the words of his mother, "scattered." While his father worked in the metropolitan area as an industrial construction contractor, his mother held several different executive jobs in different states during his high school career. She commuted to a job in Boston, Georgia, then moved to a job in Ohio an hour and a half away; then, before his senior year, his mother took a position as a vice president for customer relations at a company based in Charlotte, North Carolina.

During that year she commuted to North Carolina during the week and flew back to Wilton on weekends. Kevin said:

> She stays for the weekend, and then heads out again. It's kind of rough on the family, but at the same time, it's—what she needs to do to keep her business going kind of thing. Where she's vice president of customer service, you know, it's a big thing. . . . It's like a real big company. So she's got a lot to do. I mean, she comes home, you can tell—she's just real stressed out kind of thing. So we kind of like—let her to herself I guess. (Interview 5/14/03)

By Kevin's senior year the family had realized that not keeping the house in order was adding to his mother's stress. Kevin's father then began to pay his own mother to come to the house and clean it before the weekend.

The family was hoping Kevin would go to college in North Carolina; once he did, his mother would move there more permanently, while the father stayed in Wilton with the younger brother so he could continue to go to Wilton schools, which, the parents thought, were superior to those in Charlotte. Kevin's mother said that it was a challenge to have time together as a family:

> Making time together is incredibly important. Having the TV off, going out on the porch, having dinner together. . . . And the kids will actually joke about that: "Here comes our mandatory family time," you know, that sort of thing. (Interview 6/7/01)

Other students in Wilton, such as Cindi Criswell, had more tumultuous family lives. During the four years of the study, her parents divorced, and her father, unable to maintain consistent employment, was evicted from his apartment and could not afford to have her live with him. During her junior year her mother kicked her out of her house for threatening her sister. She then dropped out of school and moved in with friends. Overall, Cindi moved three times from 1999 to 2003. Throughout high school, Cindi certainly dealt with what Clark (2004) recently asserted is the defining issue for contemporary adolescents in the United States: abandonment. The academic struggles of under-achieving students like Kevin and Cindi were likely attributable in part to their turbulent family lives. Their school experiences are taken up in detail in chapter 7.

Parental Support and Resources

The survey revealed three distinct, significant associations between parental background and student academic achievement. First, there was a significant difference in the mean GPA of students living with both parents (2.62) and students living with one parent (2.26).[1] Second, students from more affluent socioeconomic backgrounds had higher GPAs.[2] Third, students whose mothers had high educational attainment had higher GPAs.[3]

While the quality of parental support varied as much as student GPAs, several high-achieving students commented on the importance of their parents' support in their school success. David Sterling's father proofread his English papers before he handed them in. David described his parents' support as "incredible" and said that in general, he had his parents help him "whenever they can." David said that he was able to focus better on his schoolwork at home when he thought his parents were in the house—even if they weren't. As a senior, David attributed 95 percent of his success at Burnham to the support of his family.

Students also occasionally drew on their parents' professional resources to enhance their schoolwork. One day in the spring of 2000, I was observing a group of boys conversing about their plans for a group project in their ninth-grade science class. They animatedly exchanged several ideas, then an Asian American student raised his voice above the din and said excitedly, "Whoa, guys, we can use my dad's Lucent account at Kinko's and do this whole thing in color!"

Other parents used their resources to incentivize their children's academic achievement. We learned of several parents and grandparents who paid money for certain grades, including Kevin's father. Kevin's father also promised to pay him in cash half of whatever amount he received in tuition assistance for college. Kevin said:

He's got good deals, too, though. Like if—if I go to the—any school, they'll say I get ten thousand dollars off, he'll give me five thousand dollars a year. He'll give me half of whatever I get off. So if I got free tuition out of a forty thousand–dollar school, he'd give me twenty thousand dollars a year. (Interview 6/5/02)

Parental Pressure and "Pushing"

Another form of parental support took the form of yearbook vanity ads. These were advertisements of various sizes in the school yearbook that parents could purchase; they typically included a picture of the student as a baby. This was a discourse that was simultaneously encouraging, congratulatory, and pressure-inducing:

Laura, we are so proud of you! Keep swinging your way to success.
Love, Mom, Dad, and Katy (2002–2003; the published picture was one of an infant Laura in a swing)

Son, the sky's not the limit nor are the stars. Live long and prosper. Congrats.
Love, Mom & Dad (1999–2000)

You can and do anything you set your mind to, Theresa. Keep on dreaming big and achieving your goals. We are so very proud of you.
Love, Mom, Dad (Kim, Chris, Michael, and Amanda, too) (1999–2000)

Congratulations Sean on your success at WBHS! Remember, supersuccess is not a matter of talent, it's character. It's what kind of person you are. You have to choose a winning attitude, and in order to succeed you must first affirm and then believe . . . May all your dreams come true. You just have to T-R-Y. Trust and Respect Yourself.
We love you, Dad and Mom, Jennie, Hallie, Dan, and Rosie (1997–1998)

School staff members expressed concern about the last sort of advertisement above. The intervention assistance team coordinator referred to it as parental "pushing," which she described as parents attempting to get their children to "achieve beyond what their kids are capable of achieving"—a practice that certainly was related to the community's high expectations for individual success. She said, "There's a lot of parental support, there's a lot of parental pushing. Sometimes there's more pushing than support." She went on to explain, "Sometimes in meetings I will get these parents who have got this little freshman, they're going, 'But he needs to know what he's going to do with his life!' And you want to say to them, 'at fourteen, did you know?'" An English teacher commented on how such pushing could confuse students:

> And then sometimes I think they feel like they're getting mixed messages. From their parents too, you know, where their parents are saying, "Well hey, now you need to back off and handle . . . this particular situation, or maybe the grade's not everything, you know, try to learn something," and the kid sees the real mixed message there. That you know, you want me to learn something, but at the same time, if I don't come home with an A, then there—there had better be a good reason why not. (Interview 6/6/01)

Intervention and Contestation

As mentioned above, many parents had a proprietary view toward the school, and the administration's consistent accommodation of parental concerns certainly reinforced this stance. Several parents identified this "responsiveness" as a significant positive and exploited it in their efforts to help their children get good grades. One parent of a high-achieving student remarked, "A strength of the administration is that when you have a concern, they listen to you. They're very willing to sit down with you and ask, 'What is your concern?'"

Teachers experienced the school's stance toward parents somewhat differently. In interviews, teachers identified a range of ways in which parents intervened in the school. First, parents often complied with their child's request to excuse them from school on test days, especially in difficult subjects like science (thus netting their child extra time to study for a makeup exam or to possibly learn about test content). The chair of the Science Department reported that more students were noticing when their peers were absent on the day of a test. "They point it out in class," he said; "they didn't use to do that." In addition, parents helped their children get extensions for projects or permitted them to call in sick on days when papers were due . Second, parents influenced student placement. A math teacher said, "You can make a recommendation for a kid to go into a certain class, but if a parent says they want them in another, they're going to go into it. I just don't feel like my opinion was being heard." Third, parents who perceived that their child's work had been evaluated unfairly brought pressure to bear on teachers and administrators. Several teachers described how parents tended to "walk up the ladder of authority" in their efforts to get grades changed—they ask the teacher to change a grade or threaten to go to the principal. Two teachers reported that they had changed grades under the direction of administrators, one because the original grade would have jeopardized the student's athletic eligibility. This teacher said after the event, "I feel like I have no authority." Similarly, one of the school deans said it was not unusual for parents to tell him, "You'll meet me with my attorney and my tape recorder." He said, "A good part of what we do is struggle with parents." Another teacher noted that the parents who were more likely to exert the most pressure on the school tended to come from Wilton Estates—one of the community's most affluent areas. One parent who also worked at the school defined these sorts of parental interventions as part of the Wilton Way. Gary Linwood, the

African American choir director, who regularly had parents call him about choir placements, summarized this view succinctly: "If parents push hard enough, it's going to happen."

A closer look at Julie Rice's mother's involvement with her daughter's academics is telling. At the beginning of our interview, she expressed concerns about where Julie stood in the landscape of academic competition.

> PD: What kinds of concerns do you and your husband have about the future? Concerns, anxieties, can you talk about that?
>
> MARTHA RICE: Um, one that just came up recently. Ron [her husband] was reading an article in the paper that said that you've got schools now that have, I mean, Burnham is going to have thirty valedictorians this year. And a lot of schools are saying you've got to be in the top, colleges are saying we want top 10 percent or better. And I can have Julie with a 4.0, who might not be in the top 10 percent of her class. And so, we're three years away from college with her. And so, I don't think it will be an issue for her; she's a bright enough kid, she's going to have enough on her resume, and that's another thing that just irks me. I mean, these kids have to produce basically a resume to get into college, you know. I did Key Club for four years, I ran track for four years. And colleges want it loaded. (Interview 6/2/00)

Throughout Julie's educational career, her mother demonstrated a keen awareness of very specific aspects of her schooling and a tendency to intervene with teachers. From the time Julie entered Burnham as a freshman her mother began to communicate her concerns to teachers—usually about assessment. One note she wrote to her English teacher in January 2000 read:

> Mrs. Kohl—
> I have a couple of questions about Julie's West Side Story quiz. I believe that question #4 is correct the way Julie responded. I'm also not sure what else was needed for her essay. She gave several examples that did support her thesis statement. I'd appreciate it if you could clarify this for me.
> Thank you—
> Martha Rice

During the weekend before our interview, Martha Rice put fifteen hours into Julie's group science project. She explained in the interview that she knew that one of the students in the group "didn't pull her weight," saying, "I was talking to another mother the other day and I said if they don't get an A on this project, I'm on the phone so fast to that teacher. And she said, 'So am I.'"

As in similar settings there was a heavily gendered dimension to these sorts of parental interventions in school. Other researchers have observed that mothers are usually the key educational decision-makers in middle-class households, as they, much more than fathers, tend to be "hooked into the life of the school" (Graue 1993, 474). The intense oversight and unpaid labor of these middle-class mothers seems to contribute significantly to their children's academic success (see Smith 2000). The remainder of this chapter is given over to describing the most questionable parental interventions that we came across in the study: stringent efforts to obtain special education resources for children with vague or undiagnosed disabilities.

Policy Manipulation: Parental Attempts to Ensure "Optimal Performance"

I first learned about parents' attempts to appropriate special education resources after I shared preliminary findings with the Burnham teaching staff in the spring of 2002. After the talk, several special education teachers approached me and said I really ought to talk with their whole department; they invited me to their next meeting. At that meeting, eight special education teachers and supervisors shared concerns about how the community's and school's emphasis on individual success was affecting the distribution of special education resources. They began by explaining that many parents had high expectations for their children that were probably "unrealistic." One teacher elaborated:

> What you're talking about is the competitive environment—not in the school, but just in the community—parent expectations for their children, you know, in the community. And one of the things that has happened through special education is that we do provide modifications and accommodations for students that have disabilities, to equalize their access—that is the principle behind it. But a parent will hear that so-and-so's son has unlimited time on the ACT test. [And they will say] "Well, how do I get that?" . . . I have had parents refer and call a meeting to start that process, on juniors or seniors who were 4.0 students. It's happened twice. (Interview 5/28/02)

The special education staff went on to say that the end point of the process was the student obtaining an IEP (individualized education plan), some sort of tutorial assistance during the school day, and certain testing accommodations—usually untimed tests in school and extra time on standardized tests such as the ACT and SAT. One of the teachers said of parents, "They're looking for a better grade, so the kid can get into a better college." When I asked if this was part of the Wilton Way, there were smiles and chuckles throughout the room. One teacher said, "The best of the best at all times. Everyone gives two hundred percent." Then a newer staff member named Ann Vidich explained that after her hiring in the district two years ago, she had begun to collect quotes from various people regarding special education and schooling in Wilton. She said, "The classic one was, there are no average kids in Wilton. You are either gifted or special ed. And special ed. is a good thing here." She explained that this was "taken from the mindset that in Wilton the average IQ is 115," so if students were functioning at 97 or 100, they were seen as impaired, because they could not compete. She added, "And the perception is that we want optimum performance. We want all the help, so that they can compete with students that are gifted."

Ann Vidich said she had ethical concerns about the ways in which the district was identifying special needs students. I asked if she would talk with me further, and she agreed, but insisted that we meet outside of district boundaries. On a June afternoon in 2002, in a coffee shop in a strip mall about three miles from the school, she painted a more complete picture of her ethical concerns regarding this trend. She began by saying, "This district is identifying students a lot more readily than other districts—their numbers are way out of control." She showed me documentation of a three-fold increase in the number of students classified as OHI in Wilton between 1996 and 2002 (see the table below). By 2002, there were more OHI-classified students in Wilton than in Cleveland, Cincinnati, or Columbus, Ohio. This, despite the fact that Wilton's student enrollment was a fraction of these larger districts, and less than a third of Cincinnati—the smallest of the three (Wilton School District 2002).

Ann Vidich was involved in the evaluation processes of potential special education students and indicated that she had dissented on three cases in the past year. She referred to classroom observations where she had recorded "high percentages on task" and one child's parents had expressed concern that the child was playing with their shoelace. She said, "Sometimes I don't consider off-task behaviors what somebody else would, in Wilton." She went on to say that some parents were incredulous when confronted with her dissents. The last case Ann Vidich mentioned as of two parents of a kindergartener who were, in her words, "looking for a label" to explain the child's poor performance in school. She explained that

Wilton School District other health impaired (OHI) identification, 1996–2002

Year	OHI identification
1996	39
1997	53
1998	63
1999	76
2000	90
2001	101
2002	122

Note: OHI is defined as "having limited strength, vitality, or alertness, due to chronic or acute health problems such as a heart condition, tuberculosis, rheumatic fever, nephritis, asthma, sickle cell anemia, hemophilia, epilepsy, lead poisoning, leukemia, or diabetes that adversely affects a child's educational performance" (Ohio Department of Education 1995, 18).

the evaluation team's discussion had focused on how "performance anxiety" and "internal emotional anxiety" interfered with the student's learning, and had ultimately linked the anxiety to ADHD (attention deficit/hyperactivity disorder). Ms. Vidich said that it came to light through interviews that the parents drilled the child in the car on the way to school, and that he only had approximately one or two hours of "down time" per day. She concluded that the parents were "stressing their own kid" and that the child actually had an anxiety disorder, which would not make him eligible for special education services under OHI. Overall, Ann Vidich said the pattern among the better off parents in Wilton was to pay for whatever special services their children required: "The special economics are such that they try to fix whatever's wrong by paying for it. . . . You know, fix the kid. If they need medication, fix the kid."

Indeed, subsequent interviews with other special education staff members, the Burnham school psychologist teachers, and parents of special education students revealed a pattern of special education resources being appropriated by mostly middle-class parents seeking to enhance their children's abilities to compete—a phenomenon that has recently received national media attention (see Cowan 2005). The school psychologist referred to "parents. . . . looking to get any edge they can." A special education teacher observed that "The IEP has become a vehicle. . . . so the kid can get into a better college." A math teacher in the school referred to these practices as parents' "tricks."

Knowledge, Networks, and "Tricks":
How Middle-Class Parents "Battle" in School

Parents were clearly the main impetus behind the rising number of OHI students in Wilton. What follows is a closer look at how one mother used her class cultural know-how and social network to secure and maintain special education services for her daughter at Burnham.

Barbara and Thomas Gelb, both white, met at the University of Michigan in the 1970s. After graduating, they lived in Saginaw for five years, then Thomas, a sales executive, was transferred first to Cincinnati, then Cleveland, then to Columbus. Barbara Gelb worked as a teacher for five years after graduating, and then after the birth of their two daughters became a full-time "domestic engineer." When they moved to Columbus, they chose Wilton both for the school district and for the neighborhood of Wilton Estates, which Barbara Gelb described as a "real close community around a country club." The Gelb's older daughter went through the Wilton schools and then went to Bucknell. Their younger daughter, Katherine, attended Wilton Elementary School from kindergarten through fourth grade; Covington, a private school in Columbus, for fifth through eighth grade; and then Burnham, from which she graduated in 1998. Barbara Gelb said that their concerns with Katherine began with reading in elementary school.

> PD: Well, let's go ahead and talk more specifically about Katherine, and her experience. What is the nature of . . . Katherine's special needs or disability?
>
> BG: That's a good question. I don't know if we've ever put a real name on it. Um [sighs], she just, she struggled on a lot of things. I think she—you know, like I said, I struggle to put a name on it. I'm sure it's some form of dyslexia, but it's mild enough that she did very well. I mean she, she needed the help when she got it, and we had to really battle to keep, keep her getting that help, especially at Burnham. What she did was, around fourth grade, she . . . just kind of, kind of started to give up a little bit, which is why we switched her to another school. She would sit in the class, and I think she behaved herself, and she was quiet. She didn't have any hyperactivity or anything like that, so she was just getting kind of left behind. (Interview 7/21/03)

Barbara Gelb went on to explain that Katherine had difficulties sounding out and spelling words. At this point they switched her to Covington and began to work with a school psychologist in the area, Kay Easton, who administered various tests to Katherine. The tests did not yield a specific diagnosis, but were low enough to qualify Katherine for certain special services at Covington (which, located in a neighboring suburb, had a lower threshold for qualification than Wilton). However, at the end of eighth grade, administrators at Covington told the Gelbs that they did not think Katherine could do the work at the high school level—they predicted that she would earn C's and D's. Barbara Gelb said, "And we really were kind of like, 'Oh!' Like they acted like they didn't want her, and we said, okay, you don't want her [laughing angrily], we don't want *you!*" So they went to Burnham, accompanied by Kay Easton, to ensure that "she would continue to have some help there." The meeting went well, and even though Katherine's testing numbers "didn't go with what Wilton required," the school assured them that they would keep her IEP and provide her with special education services.

When I asked Barbara Gelb about her motivations in making sure that Katherine kept her IEP, she said, "We just didn't want her to get up there and kind of get lost again. . . . I also knew the value of an IEP, as far as testing, you know, for college. . . . I knew from what Kay Easton had said, well from all of her test scores, she's going to need help. And she's going to need to take her ACT and SAT, or one or the other, untimed."

When Katherine began attending Burnham, she met every morning with a tutor in a small group of three to five other students. They would go over all of the work in their classes, tests they got back, and various assignments. Katherine began to think of the tutor as "one of her best friends." In addition, Katherine was able to take untimed tests in all of her classes and get special help with homework assignments and projects. Barbara Gelb said that Katherine was a "very good advocate for herself. She would tell these teachers, 'Hey, I can't do this, I need more time.'" However, by the end of Katherine's sophomore year, Burnham's enrollment had significantly increased, and there were many more students that qualified for special education services. The school attempted to take away Katherine's IEP and tutor. Barbara Gelb conferred with other parents, and especially Kay Easton, who advised her, "Don't let them get rid of her IEP, whatever you do." She explained that there was also concern about college, "because if you have an IEP in high school, then you go to certain colleges, they have to provide help also."

Looking back, Barbara Gelb said that she and her husband "fought and fought" and "really battled" to keep the IEP. There were two separate meetings with teachers, a vice principal, and a Burnham school counselor, Connie Thompson, whom Barbara Gelb described as "our advocate." Connie Thompson advised the Gelbs to exercise their option of not allowing the school to see certain tests scores that had been administered privately.

BG: So we did that. . . . Anyway, Susan just advised us. She said, then you can look at the results, and then you can decide whether you want her tested by the school. You can decide whether you want the school to know the results or not.

PD: I see.

BG: Um, it sounds kind of tricky.

PD: No, I understand that. And so also if the results were—

BG:—And, you know, you want to get the best results for your child.

In the end, Katherine was able to keep her IEP and her tutoring services. She went on to score a 19 on the ACT and graduated from the University of Dayton four years later. When I asked Barbara Gelb if the special services at Covington and Burnham had made a difference in Katherine's experience at school, she said, "Oh, I'm really sure it did. It would have been a lot different story without that. . . . I'm just not sure she would have done as well." At the time of the interview Katherine was working as a graphic designer in Cincinnati. Overall, Barbara Gelb said that she had learned that in order to secure these services for her daughter she had to be "real persistent." She concluded by saying that since Katherine's graduation from Burnham she has advised friends with the same kinds of "difficulties."

The experiences and strategies of the Gelb family are certainly a part of the Wilton Way. The family's history followed an upwardly rising trajectory, culminating in their settling in one of the most affluent areas of Wilton. The parents' awareness of academic competition in Wilton was evident in how they assessed Katherine's academic experience (being "left behind") relative to other students. Though their daughter was never diagnosed with a specific learning disability and did not obtain the test results to merit an IEP, the parents used their networks to gain knowledge of special education policy in the district and drew on their sense of proprietary ownership of the schools to mobilize resources in the service of their child. The way in which Katherine referred to her tutor as a "really good friend" shows how this sort of support became naturalized through her school career. Most notably, though Barbara Gelb recognized that some of these practices were questionable, this did not dissuade her from adopting them. Indeed, she disclosed that she herself had become a part of an advising network for other parents seeking such services for their children. At the end of data collection in 2003, the district was getting queries from the Ohio Coalition for Students with Disabilities concerning the identification of students.

Conclusion

Wilton parents' involvement with Burnham was strongly shaped by concerns about their children's academic competitiveness and future status. Though parenting styles and patterns of involvement with the school varied, robust themes emerged from the data concerning the centrality of parental affective support, high expectations, and pressure. Teachers commonly referred to certain students being "pushed" by parents.

Parents' proprietary stance toward the school seemed to afford them a license to intervene with teachers and to appropriate resources for their children. The survey finding regarding the association between student SES and GPA suggests that a set of cultural competencies originating in the home may play a role in the school success of some students—and that more research is needed in this area. Many parents maintained keen vigilance over what was going on in their children's classes and frequently intervened with teachers or administrators if they believed that assessments had been made unfairly. A smaller group of parents drew on their networks and knowledge of policy to appropriate special education resources for the benefit of their own children—including some who were carrying 4.0 GPAs.

The stringent efforts of Wilton parents to exert control over their children's educational experiences and futures contrast sharply with the stance of parents in Manus. Historically, parents in Manus had prized education for how it led to jobs in the cash sector and ultimately to cash remittances back to the village (Carrier and Carrier 1989). However, as mentioned above, at the time of my study there in 1995, due to rising unemployment and educational credentialism, it was very difficult for young people to get a cash-paying job. More and more high school graduates were returning to their villages, unable to find work. Meanwhile, the subsistence base of most villages was intact, and most people continued to survive on fishing, gardening, gathering, and bartering (Demerath 1999).

When we surveyed parents in Manus in 1995, we asked them, "If you had your choice, what do you want your children to do? Go to town and work? Or stay in the village?" Parents consistently answered in effect, "If he/she can finish school and get work, okay, that is good. If they can't, then they can come back here and help us. There is plenty of work here." This response demonstrated a somewhat conditional, fatalistic cultural orientation, wherein parents seemingly recognized and accepted matters which they could not expect to influence. In this sense, the question itself might have seemed a little absurd to Manus parents, as was another question that I posed earlier in the study about fishing. As an older fisherman was about to head out of the lagoon on his outrigger canoe, I asked him what kind of fish he was going to catch. He looked at me quizzically for a moment, and then replied, "That depends on the kind of fish that decides to bite my hook."

But in Wilton, most parents sought to assuage their anxieties about their children's futures by tirelessly exerting control over their schooling. Most broadly, such efforts at control are an essential part of the "life planning" that, according to Anthony Giddens, characterizes peoples' efforts to pursue their best interests under conditions of Western modernity (1991, 125). More locally, in the American suburban context, they are clearly central to the Wilton Way. Parents' support of their children's academic work, interventions with teachers, and manipulations of policy, all to varying degrees, drew on their middle-class cultural know-how and social and professional networks. Overall, the depth and scope of parental intervention in Wilton Burnham suggests that this is another key linkage that binds together this class cultural system oriented toward personal advancement. These sorts of parental expectations and practices continually reify the school's emphasis on credentialing and reauthorize the extraction of private goods from a public institution. Ball points out that parenting activities such as "the development and maintenance of social networks, engagement with and involvement with schooling, and the elicitation of information about and application of pressure on the school," all need to be considered as everyday practices that contribute to social reproduction (2003, 177).

Chapter 4 considers the identities of high-achieving Burnham students and examines the extent to which they themselves had internalized the central modern precept of control. The next chapter, however, moves inside Wilton Burnham High School itself.

Chapter Three The Role of the School: Institutional Advantaging

Inside Wilton Burnham

Wilton Burnham High School is a modern sprawling brick structure set on several acres about four miles northwest of downtown Wilton. There are athletic fields arrayed around it and a small wooded area along the eastern side with a creek that runs underneath the school and through a central courtyard. Upon entering the building, visitors pass the attendance office, a well-resourced library, and the state-of-the-art auditorium, and then enter into the capacious two-story central area known as the "Commons." This large space has a wall of windows looking out to the small woods to the east, national flags arrayed along the north wall (with the school's Blue Ribbon flag displayed above them), and an open corridor along the second floor of the west wall leading to other hallways and classrooms.

All classrooms were equipped with a new centralized video information and cable system which allowed for school-wide viewing of videos as well as the weekly WBHS News—a "student bureau" for CNN. The second floor housed several labs with late-model computers that had comprehensive software packages. Centrally located in the middle of the second floor was the "teacher resource area" where all teachers had a cubicle with desk and storage space. In the center of this area was a room with computer terminals and copiers: unlike other public schools in the metropolitan area, at Burnham there was no limit on the number of copies teachers could make.

Along the first floor of the west wall of the Commons were the counseling center and the administrative and cocurricular offices, and then further to the north, a hallway leading to the arts and home economics classrooms, the gymnasium, and the field house with indoor track and tennis courts and the adjacent strength and power room. The Commons itself functioned as dining hall, study hall, and meeting place. Beyond the north wall was the cafeteria which featured numerous hot and cold choices for lunch and a cappuccino machine by the cashier. Until the winter of 2003, students could take the cookies they purchased in the cafeteria to a designated counter to have them warmed up.

This chapter moves inside Wilton Burnham itself and describes its curriculum, extracurriculum, teaching staff, and policies. Above all, it shows how the local emphasis on competitive success suffused its routines and practices and provided a blueprint for the running of the school. Accordingly, the chapter discusses the qualities most valued in its teaching staff, the variety of extracurricular activities organized as competitions, school policies that empowered students with great freedom and choice, discourses of "excellence" and "success" that pervaded the school, and finally, the variety of creative ways in which the school sponsored its students and promoted competitive individualism. These included multiple forms of institutional recognition that gave students the substance or appearance of success—including the naming of forty-seven valedictorians in 2003 (10 percent of the senior class). This chapter also examines the school's hiring practices to illustrate how its approach to diversity tended to be subordinate to its efforts to maintain its competitive edge.

Wilton Burnham houses grades nine through twelve; during the 2000–2001 school year, there were 1,649 students, of whom 86 percent were classified European American, 10 percent Asian American, and 4 percent African American. The school's relatively large Asian American population was attributable in part to the presence of a Honda plant in a neighboring community. During the course of the study, approximately 90 percent of Burnham's graduates attended a college, university, or technical school.

Curriculum and Teaching Staff

The Winners' Version

Overall, the school had a rich curriculum with over 225 courses, including etymology, Japanese 1–4, U.S. Political Thought and Radicalism, and Native American Cultures Studies, and art. It also offered a series of "enriched" classes for all students, as well as a comprehensive array of AP classes open to sophomores, juniors, and seniors—some of which had fewer than eight students in them. The school also had concurrent enrollment programs at several area colleges and universities, as well as both domestic and international field study programs. Seniors could enroll in an innovative joint program developed by the English and Social Studies departments called HomeB.A.S.E. Advanced Competition, in which they synthesized reading and writing on contemporary U.S. social and economic issues and participated in the building of a home for Habitat for Humanity.

Other courses, however, were very traditional in scope. For example, the content of an enriched global history/English class that we observed intensively during the first year of the study was entirely given over to Western European history, particularly, the rise and fall of various empires over the last five hundred years. At one point in winter of 2000, the social studies teacher, Neal Richards, said in class, "Let's impress our guests with how much we know about family relations and the Hapsburg line." Consulting their notes, several students then recounted some details. In a later class a student asked the teacher why they had learned very little about Portugal in the last few months. Mr. Richards replied, "You're not going to hear much about Portugal from us from here on in. You might study it specifically in college, but for us, from here on in, it just wasn't much of a part of the scene." Nuako Konadu immediately said under his breath, "So, are we against Portugal?" (Field notes 2/29/00). Mr. Richards did not respond.

Furthermore, the section of the course called "The Age of Exploration" emphasized the search for gold and, later on, colonization. There was little mention of conquest or the effects of European encroachment on indigenous peoples. In one classroom discussion regarding Cortez, David Sterling observed that he "killed the Aztec empire," and also that he "found gold." Eliza, a dark-haired child of Thai and Greek parents, immediately added, "that wasn't his." When we interviewed Sofia Rhoades's father, he expressed concern about the content of the social studies curriculum:

> I tell them differently. I say that's the way they're teaching you, but that's not the way it is. And especially in history, you know—how Indians are bad and people in other countries are not as great as people in this country. You know, that's something that I had a hard time dealing with when I was growing up, seeing cowboys and Indians on TV. I thought the Indians were bad. I thought Nazis were bad, and I thought Russians were bad. Then I grew up and I found out, after I visited a few places, that people around this world are the same as I am and they're struggling, they're raising families, and they're trying to get kids grown. (Interview 12/6/00)

Such a curriculum that emphasizes the "winners'" version of history is interpreted here as further naturalizing processes of competition, success, and failure, and as such, one of the key linkages in the school that socialized students for individualistic competition.

It is appropriate to mention that at the time of the study, the school was in the midst of realigning its curriculum to best prepare students for the new state graduation exam. As part of the state's efforts to improve school quality, the tenth-grade proficiency tests had become more rigorous. Those who were sophomores in 2003 were the first to take the test, and the district as a whole was concerned with how they would do. While the WBHS Social Studies Department wanted to offer U.S. history in eleventh grade, the district was concerned that this would be too late for students to do well on the test. Jim Greylock, an AP history teacher, said that most sophomores were not ready for U.S. history and criticized the district's plan. He explained, "The idea is to cram history down to grades seven, eight, nine, and ten, and use grades eleven and twelve for school-to-work, group think, and preparation for the workplace." Though Jim Greylock was reprimanded by an assistant principal for these remarks for not being a "team player," Greylock and a colleague ended up testifying before the Ohio State Senate on the negative effects such a plan would have on student learning. Nevertheless, the plan to teach history earlier was adopted.

Teaching Staff

The 1998–1999 Wilton Burnham "Profile of Excellence" (a one-page self-description, updated every year) described its teaching staff as follows:

> One of the keys to the school's success is its talented faculty of 134 experienced educators. Forty-eight percent of the faculty hold master's degrees and [*number missing in original*] hold doctorates. [In actuality, fewer than five teachers held doctorates.] Of those with master's degrees, seventeen percent earned an additional forty-five semester hours or more in academic studies.

In the fall of 1999, WBHS News did a story on the new teachers who had just joined the school. The student reporter introduced the segment by saying, "We wanted to find out what made them special enough to teach at Burnham."

Students generally had very favorable impressions of their teachers—especially their availability and willingness to help. Three under-achieving students praised Burnham teachers:

The teachers here make you try. (Field notes 10/1/99)

They're just a really, um, caring school. And they want the students to do well. (Interview 2/8/00; eleventh-grade European American female)

If you ever need help, we have all the help you can get—here. (Interview 5/23/02; eleventh-grade Asian American female)

In his freshman year, David Sterling said, "The great part about Wilton is that there's always someone who wants to help you. And there's tutors all around, you know, there's signs in the math room, 'Need a math tutor?' And the teachers are available in the mornings and after school and it really helps." Some teachers went well out of their way to assist students. During March and April of each year, Jim Greylock offered twenty-six out-of-school study sessions to prepare his students for the AP exam. Each session was two hours, and they were offered at 6:00 p.m. or 8:00 p.m. on school nights, so that students could fit them into their schedules. Greylock acknowledged that the sessions were a lot of work for him but said that they helped the students a great deal.

The High Stakes Cocurriculum

Wilton Burnham had close to sixty student activity groups—some of which required course work—including *Solstice,* the literary magazine; Christian Fellowship; and stock, psychology, figure skating, and sports medicine clubs. There were also several service-oriented clubs and initiatives at Burnham, including an adopt-a-child program, a walk-a-thon dedicated to raising money for Habitat for Humanity, and an annual food drive, where the school competed with its rival down the road to see which could amass the larger share of donations. There were many other charitable initiatives in the school; in 2002, there was an effort to donate $1 per student for children in Afghanistan, in response to a request from President George W. Bush.

One of the school's defining characteristics, however, was its rich and varied extracurriculum (known in the school as the cocurriculum because of its centrality to the school's mission), with award-winning programs in music, theater, and the arts, and twenty-nine varsity sports. The Office of Co-Curriculum was large and centrally located next to the administrative office. It became apparent throughout the study that competition was used as an organizing principle in all of these programs.

The Competitive Arts

The music program comprised six bands, including marching and jazz bands; two orchestras; and five choruses. The theater program shared the main auditorium (which had a full fly space) with the music groups, had a full-size scene shop, and also a more intimate "black box" theater with full lighting and sound capabilities. The theater program staged three or four major productions each year.

The school musical groups were rated by their directors as to how well they sight-read scores in preparation for regional and state competition. The most anticipated events at the school's annual Arts in Action festival were its numerous contests, such as the popular "Throw-Down"—a head-to-head contest on pottery wheels with staff judges (which Sharon Sosa won in both her junior and senior years), and a poetry slam, which promotes itself with the saying, "There are no bad poems, just bad judges." By the end of the study, the Arts in Action festival had expanded into the gymnasium, where there were foosball and inflatable jousting tournaments—with little, if any, connection to the arts.

The Athletics Program: "Learning Success through Hard Work"

A close look at the Wilton Burnham athletics program offers particular insight into the premium the school put on competitive success. Wilton Schools had a long tradition of athletic triumphs that the community attributed to local talent, strong work ethic, and a historical ability to leverage community resources to support teams. But when Wilton Burnham was first being planned, a central concern was whether or not spreading the district's athletes across two high schools would result in the same success. Bobbi Taylor, Burnham athletics director, explained in an interview.

> BT: I know that a lot of concern over the split of the high schools, they would split their athletics programs. And would we have the same success—
>
> PD: Because there had been a history of success at Wilton High School.
>
> BT: Right. Let's face it, we had a graduating class of 750 kids. It was sort of an *elitist* sort of program. We had *specialists*. We didn't have to have multiple sport athletes. We didn't have to share our athletes. We had *plenty* of athletes. . . . So, we sat down and we met as a group of coaches, and we just sort of talked about what would be important for all of us. And the one thing we said we had to honor are multiple-sport athletes. We *had* to be able to share our athletes. We had to convince a Tom Moffat [a recently graduated star athlete] that not only did he want to do soccer, which he was first team all-state, but that he wanted

to play other sports, which he has done. So that's why we had that 12 Seasons of Greatness. (Interview 5/29/02)

The 12 Seasons of Greatness was an award that the school developed to recognize athletes who played three different sports for their entire four years of high school. I then asked Taylor how she, in her role as athletics director, experienced the community's expectations for success. She began by explaining that the school was currently interviewing candidates for varsity girls soccer position and that the first candidate brought in was so unimpressive that one parent asked if girls soccer was going to turn into a "recreational program."

> I was thinking, are you or we kidding?! I said, this community would *never* stand for that. . . . I said, we will put the *best person* in that role that we can find. We owe it to this program, to this school, and to this community.

Not surprisingly, students throughout the study commented on the intensity of the athletics programs at Burnham. A senior said that he "burned out on it," because "it was too intense—the pressure to win." Another senior said that playing sports at the school was "like a job."

HARD WORK AND DETERMINATION. Virtually all of Burnham's teams in some way emphasized "hard work" in their training programs. The T-shirts the boys volleyball team had printed in the spring of 2000 were epigrammatic of local beliefs regarding effort and success: "Burnham Men's Volleyball: Learning Success Through Hard Work." Later that year the varsity baseball coach commented in an interview on WBHS News that "We feel very good about our work habits this year." The girls swim team began their preseason training in early November with hour-and-a-half practices before school and three-hour practices in the afternoon. A junior on the team commented in an interview that the team had a "hellish" Thanksgiving training. Two entries from the 2003 yearbook illustrate the attribution of athletic success to hard work at Burnham:

Failure is not an option. If you want to make your dreams come true, think it, live it, breathe it, taste it. You will make it happen.

— *Introduction to "Spring Sports" section, 2003 yearbook*

"A-ma-zing" is all that can be said about this year's boys volleyball team. Their outstanding season record shows that hard work and determination pays off.

— *Entry for volleyball, 2003 yearbook*

Such statements emphasize the extent to which Burnham coaches and students attribute their athletics success to hard work and determination.

STRONGER AND FASTER: THE BENEFITS OF THE NEW CONDITIONING PROGRAM. One consequence of the athletic program's emphasis on hard work and effort was the stress placed on weight training—which culminated in the building of the strength and power room mentioned in the previous chapter. Bobbi Taylor explained the rationale for this emphasis:

> I think the second thing we have done, and I think Bill Watson [the varsity football coach] has really spearheaded this, is that we had to be—strength training had to almost be a part of *all* of our programs. We *had* to have our athletes conditioned. In the last ten years, you've noticed that kids are bigger, stronger. We *had* to be able to compete. . . . We've always had great kids here, well-rounded kids that are highly involved, but we have to really work—we have to work on being, what I would say an optimal strength conditioning—strength and conditioning had to be an important part of our program. So I think that's really—if you look at Bob Jefferies [the boys varsity soccer coach], I think he would say that, his conditioning helped him win that state title.

Here Taylor refers to the state championship won by the boy's varsity soccer team in 2000. In the years prior to that championship, Jefferies had instituted an off-season strength training program for his players where they were expected to lift weights four days a week in the spring. The boys football team won a conference championship in 2002.

FROM LEAST SPORTSMANLIKE TO MOST SPORTSMANLIKE: THE STORY OF THE RICHARD B. THURSTON AWARD. Sportsmanship, however, had been a problem at Wilton Burnham in the mid-1990s. The extraordinary steps that the school took to polish its image suggest its highly evolved skill at what Doug Foley refers to as "impression management" (1990, 134). Burnham ranked third in the state in the number of players, coaches, and parents ejected from athletic contests during the 1997–1998 school year. The school would have led the state if ejections in non-recognized sports had been counted. The incidents included a parent who went out onto the wrestling mat in the middle of a match, verbal outbursts from a tennis player in a conference championship match, and a fight that erupted in a junior varsity soccer game. During the year several coaches were made to write letters of apology to the coaches of opposing teams. Bobbi Taylor explained that after that year the school needed to "refocus."

That refocusing manifested itself primarily in the school's effort the next year to apply for the Ohio High School Athletic Association's Richard B. Thurston Sportsmanship, Ethics, and Integrity Award. Bobbi Taylor was charged with this responsibility, and said she was "forced to do it." Indeed, the application process was elaborate. It involved the following:

- A written Board of Education policy on sportsmanship, ethics, and integrity in extracurricular activities.
- A broad-based sportsmanship, ethics, and integrity committee to coordinate the planning and implementation of a sportsmanship, ethics, and integrity program.
- Presentations throughout the school year to coaches, athletes, parents, fans, and support groups emphasizing the school's philosophy on sportsmanship, ethics, and integrity.
- An ongoing campaign that promotes sportsmanship, ethics, and integrity.
- An annual evaluation of all coaches in the areas of instruction and demonstration of sportsmanship, ethics, and integrity.
- A procedure for receiving, investigating, and acting upon complaints regarding sportsmanship, ethics, and integrity.
- A plan for dealing with critical situations such as heated rivalries, overflow crowds, and unruly spectators.
- A program for acknowledging/rewarding examples of good sportsmanship, ethics, and integrity.

Taylor said overall that this was "a *lot* of work," and during our interview she showed me a thick binder that made up the school's application. The school received the award in 1999, hung the banner in the gymnasium, and mentioned it in its next "Profile of Excellence," as well as other literature.

The story of the Richard B. Thurston Award illustrates both the community's competitive nature and its commitment to managing external impressions of itself. The fact that Wilton Burnham High School could go from leading the state in ejections to receiving the state's most prestigious sportsmanship award in two years suggests the urgency school and community leaders felt when they saw that they had an image problem, and their facility at navigating the bureaucratic channels necessary to preserve its reputation as a school in a "destination district."

Policy Permissiveness in the Service of Individual Advancement: The Logic of Freedom and Deferral

As mentioned in the previous chapter, an implicit assumption of the educational philosophy that underlay the establishment of Wilton Burnham was that granting students authority and recognition would assist them in their quest for success. Accordingly, both formal and informal routines at Burnham accorded students great freedom. Students were allowed ten minutes of passing time between classes, juniors and seniors in good academic standing could move freely within the school during their unscheduled class time, and, with parental permission, only be present in school during their scheduled classes. In addition, while the school handbook stated that students could not take food out of the cafeteria, many were allowed to, because they did not have a scheduled lunch period, in part so that they could leave school earlier to go to a job or have time to themselves (Wilton Burnham High School 1999). A new female freshman student described the school as "a more relaxed environment than any I've been in before."

One important area where students were given great latitude at Burnham was in making schedule changes. School policy stated that students could fill out "personal preference request" forms to change their schedule for reasons ranging from graduation requirements to correcting clerical errors to incorporating changes based on teacher recommendations. Most requests fit these criteria. Others, however, were filed by students to avoid particular teachers (especially "hard" or "mean" ones), to accommodate particular likes or dislikes ("I'm not a morning person"; "there is no window in third-period math"), or to free up large blocks of free time for late arrival, a long lunch, an early release, or to go to a job. The director of the counseling center estimated that his staff granted 95 percent of student requests. He explained, "Sometimes there is nothing educational about it, but we are trying to accommodate student preferences." A senior administrative assistant commented, "I went to Wilton schools twenty years ago, and we never changed our schedules the way these kids do today." Guidance counselors reported throughout the study that their capacity to advise students had been taken over by the need to manage the continuous flow of student requests for schedule changes. The effect of this co-option on the college application processes of minority students is explored in chapter 7.

Overall, these school policies that grant significant latitude to students had the effect of building up the authority that students attributed to themselves, which further prepared them for individualistic competition. This self-authority is a vital foundation for the psychological capital found among the high-achieving students in the school—which is examined in more detail in the next chapter.

The Production of Institutional and Individual Worth

From its inception, Wilton Burnham developed several ways to enhance its institutional worth—and, by association, the value of its graduates. Many of these were created by Principal Cunningham, who had a graduate degree in anthropology, was formerly a principal of a large high school in suburban Chicago, and was involved in several national educational leadership organizations. These strategies included ubiquitous discourses of "excellence" and "success," prominent displays of cultural capital throughout the school, various means of increasing the "value" of the school's diploma, and a vast student recognition program. In addition to framing student's efforts as successes, these practices all promoted a degree of competitive individualism within the school.

Discourses of "Excellence" and "Success"

The quality of a person's life is in direct proportion to his/her commitment to excellence, regardless of the chosen field of endeavor.

— *"Clubs and Organizations" section, 2003 yearbook*

As mentioned in the previous chapter, discourses of "excellence" and "success" imbued Wilton and its schools. These terms seemed to serve the dual purpose of setting a high public standard for performance and socializing students to strive to meet it. Wilton Burnham's "Profile of Excellence"—and virtually all other school literature and letterhead—included the phrase, "A Recognized School of Excellence." When Principal Cunningham welcomed the class of 2003 to WBHS in late August 1999, she told them that they were entering a school that the previous year had been named a "Blue Ribbon high school" by the U.S. Department of Education, and that it had also just won the Richard B. Thurston Sportsmanship, Ethics, and Integrity Award. She then said, "Welcome to an outstanding national treasure." She continued:

> You have come to an important school. But no school gets where it is without excellent students. You are the best prepared students we have

ever had. Today we will be asking for 100 percent of your effort. If we had only 99 percent of your effort, then, for example, two planes a day would not land successfully at O'Hare; tens of thousands of letters would not be delivered to the correct addresses from the post office. . . . Think about the Four P's: Purpose, Plan, Passion, and Persistence. (Field notes 8/24/99)

She ended her remarks by leading the class in a groups cheer: "Go '03!"

Many of the high-achieving students in the school internalized this discourse to a striking degree. The President of the Class of 2000 included this phrase in her farewell address to her classmates in the WBHS newspaper's senior issue:

For some of us, the next phase of our lives may be college, and for others as full-time job, but whatever our future holds, it is different new, and exciting. It's a chance to excel and an opportunity to make our own choices. (Whittier 2000)

Constructing Institutional Capital

The school both displayed and produced various kinds of symbolic capital. The Commons had flags from nations around the world draped from the ceiling, with the school's Blue Ribbon banner featured prominently in the center of them. Throughout the school's hallways, framed artwork adorned the walls, and classical music emanated quietly from speakers.

When the class of 1999 graduated, 86 percent of the students received a "Certificate of Excellence," and all received a WBHS keychain and a wallet-sized copy of their diploma, which stipulated, "Bearer entitled to all rights and privileges" of being a WBHS graduate. For the school's tenth anniversary, Principal Cunningham commissioned an original composition from a professor of music at a nearby university; the piece was mentioned on postcards of the school that were printed to mark the occasion. In chapter 4, I relate how Principal Cunningham sought to remedy the school's chronic cheating problem in a way that would also build institutional capital.

Some students expressed some cynicism about these sorts of efforts. During one interview I asked Sofia Rhoades if she thought Burnham was a "really competitive school." In terms of academics, she said:

They want us to be the best, so they can be the best in Ohio. . . . At the beginning of the school year, when the principal was talking to us, she was saying, "oh yeah" we're the best at this and that and that and that.

I'm just saying, yup, it seemed like she was telling us that we need to be the best at this so that our school can get recognized more in some way. (Interview 6/2/00)

These examples all show how the school self-consciously constructed its own symbolic capital, which, by association, would enhance the worth of its students. The most direct means of enhancing the worth of Wilton Burnham's students, however, was through the school's vast array of recognition programs. Through the course of the study I came to call these "technologies of recognition" to reflect the creative work they accomplished in terms of enhancing students status in both figurative and material ways.

Technologies of Recognition

The WBHS Planning Committee decided early on that "the achievement of each student is important and should be recognized." It was this philosophy that led the school to develop so many recognition programs. These included:

Honor Roll
Student of the Month
Academic honor awards (Bronze Key, Silver Key, Gold Key)
Award of Merit
Honors Diploma
Junior Book awards
Senior Recognition Program
Key Club
Socratic Society
National Honor Society
Scholar Athlete Award
Celebration of Excellence Medal
12 Seasons of Greatness
Hall of Fame

Most of the winners of these awards were on display in the Commons, along with photographs of National Merit finalists. Farther on, toward the athletics wing, were plaques and photographs commemorating the accomplishments of teams as well as individual athletes. (Parents could buy space on the Athletic Wall of Fame and mount a plaque with their child's photograph on it if the student had attained some sort of distinction in interscholastic competition.) Students could also receive individual recognition by being featured as a "Stellar Senior" on the WBHS News broadcast or in the "15 Minutes of Fame" column in the WBHS student newspaper.

High-achieving and "high-profile" students in the school valued these forms of recognition and were generally keenly aware of the criteria for receiving them. One day in 1999, the enriched global history/English class mentioned above watched a WBHS News announcement regarding the posting of names of students who had received merit awards. One white female student said to another, "There it is! How do you get it?" After ascertaining that none of the students sitting near her knew, she went up and asked the teacher.

Indeed, there was a pattern of high student expectations for recognition throughout the study. One of the "Stellar Senior" segments on WBHS News began, "This week's Stellar Senior is someone who doesn't always get the recognition they deserve. Let's take a look on why Sandy Morton is this week's Stellar Senior." This student had actually received the school's Scholar Athlete award for lacrosse for four years in a row, won the Academic All-Ohio Girls Lacrosse Award, was a member of the Key Club, and was a perennial honors student.

The rationale for the Student of the Month award offers further insight into the centrality of individual recognition in the philosophy of the school. One teacher explained the origin of the award as follows: "Because some students may not get any recognition. But if a teacher catches a student doing something good, then they can give them that recognition." Another teacher explained simply, "We always pick someone who is just doing their job."

Photographs of pupils who had been identified as "Student of the Month" along with the staff nominations were also featured in the Commons. Some examples of these nominations include:

> Kari is a delight to know! She is a conscientious hard worker who brings a ready smile to cheer those around her. We appreciate her good use of the library and all she brings to our school. (6/01)

> Vijay has made a complete turnaround from the first semester. He has exhibited diligence and commitment to success. (6/01)

A WBHS alumnus commented that Student of the Month "was kind of a joke, because, like, everyone ends up getting it."

As the Sterling family related in the first chapter, these extensive technologies of recognition were most visible around graduation time. The school had three special events before graduation: the Celebration of Excellence, where students who had received recognition outside WBHS in athletic, arts, and music competition were given a Celebration of Excellence Medal (in effect, an award for receiving an award); Senior Recognition Night; and Academic Signing Day. At graduation, in addition to being inducted into the National Honors Society or being on the honor roll, students could receive gold, silver, or bronze keys; an award of merit; and an honors diploma.

On the evening of May 23, 2002, Carol Shipton, director of co-curricular activities welcomed a full auditorium to Senior Recognition Night in the following way:

> Tonight we're going to recognize 231 of the 414 students on the graduate list. These are some of the awards they are going to receive: 117, Presidential Academic Fitness; 153, Gold Key [for 3.5 or better]; 141, National Honor Society; 161, Honors Diploma (they get a tassel with white on it—so whenever you see that, you know that's an honors student); 42 students—a record number of students—maintained a GPA of 4.0, they are our valedictorians; 118, Celebration of Excellence Medals—students who contributed countless hours to our cocurricular program. Examples include getting a superior rating at a state solo ensemble context; earning a superior score in the National Mathematics Contest, Lacrosse 2nd team all-district, Marching band. (Field notes 5/23/02)

Notably, during the four years of data collection, a pattern of recognition inflation began to emerge. Forty more seniors were invited to the Celebration of Excellence in 2002 than in 2001, though the classes were the same size. Several students who were not on the program appeared at the event with the expectation of receiving an award. An administrative assistant recalled that the situation was "awkward." In addition, while the membership in the school's prestigious Socratic Society swelled from 1998–2000, in 2001 far fewer were selected for membership. A WBHS News reporter stated, "Because of this change, students said it was a lot more meaningful. A student who had been selected said, "I think it restores the honor of the award, and it makes it a lot more flattering to be inducted when there are so little people, and it makes the award more personal. It's a lot more personal" (WBHS News 10/25/01).

FORTY-SEVEN VALEDICTORIANS IN THE CLASS OF 2003. Finally, the school had another way of recognizing students that bordered on credentials fraud: school policy dictated that all students who graduated with a 4.0 or higher GPA were to be named valedictorian. Because the school, and so many others like it, assigned "weighted" grades to AP courses (where an A = 5.0 points), every year there were many students who graduated with GPAs above 4.0. Thus, the WBHS Class of 2000 had twenty-eight valedictorians, the class of 2001 had forty-one, the class of 2002 had forty-two, and the class of 2003 had forty-seven—10 percent of the class (students and teachers alike attributed the rising number of valedictorians to grade inflation). School administrators were aware that this policy was a kind of sleight of hand. When I queried the director of the counseling center about it in the middle of the study, he made a small smile and said, "All these schools that offer scholarships to valedictorians; they might think we're double, triple, or quadruple-dipping. But no one has called us on it yet." (David Sterling was one of those forty-seven vale-dictorians in the class of 2003 and received a Valedictorian Scholarship to a selective university.)

During the last year of the study, the director of the counseling center told me that the school was planning to eliminate reporting class rank. He explained, "Having forty-two valedictorians last year was great, but what does that do to the student who has a 3.98 GPA? Their class rank is forty-three—they get penalized. Most highly competitive high schools have done away with ranking, so it makes sense that we do as well." An administrative assistant later told us that a representative from an Ivy League school had actually questioned the school on the valedictorian policy several years earlier. He had asked, "How can you have twelve number ones?"

Wilton Burnham students certainly benefitted from the institution's assiduous and creative effort to enhance its and ultimately their value. The ubiquitous discourses of "excellence" and "success" and the variety of tech-nologies of recognition in the school certainly have been developed with these purposes in mind. It is important to point out that while all forms of recognition bestowed by the school contribute to students' self-worth and further socialize them into a culture of individualistic competition (such as Celebration of Excellence medals, and, for the less cynical, Student of the Month), not all can have the market value, for example, of being named a valedictorian. The data suggest that during the study, students were for the most part well aware of the value of different forms of recognition available within and outside of the school. This was certainly related to their keen awareness of the education and employment markets for which they were preparing themselves—which is taken up in chapter 4. Next, however, I turn to some of the deleterious effects of the school's hiring policies.

Institutional Practices Related to Diversity and Racial Exclusion

The final section in this chapter examines how institutional practices related to diversity articulated with the school's efforts to maintain its comparative advantages. Some recent history is relevant here: the Wilton School District was sued twice for racial discrimination between 1997 and 2001. The first was filed by an African American teacher in Robert Wilton High School (the other high school in Wilton) who claimed she had been the victim of racial discrimination and the recipient of racially offensive hate mail. The suit was settled out of court. The second was brought by the parents of two African American elementary school students who claimed that administrators had allowed the racial harassment of their children. A settlement was reached in that suit after the first day of hearings in federal court. As part of the settlement, both Wilton High School and Wilton Burnham High School were required to diversify their administration. In the spring of 2001, Burnham hired a new African American assistant principal—James Welkes.

Wilton Burnham's policies and practices related to diversity were somewhat spare and reflected a tendency to address diversity on the school's own terms. The student/staff/parent handbook included a statement on the "prohibition of harassment" (including on the basis of race), and the WBHS Student Code of Conduct specified grounds for suspension, expulsion, or other disciplinary action in the event of "discriminating and/or racist acts." The school regularly held an assembly for Black History Month and had a club that discussed multicultural issues. In addition, several teachers, particularly in the English Department, explicitly dealt with issues of race/ethnicity, equity, and even white privilege in their classes.

However, students differed on the extent to which they believed Burnham was a "multicultural community." On the survey, 79 percent of white students answered affirmatively, compared with 66.2 percent of minority students. Certain students' responses were illuminating:

White middle class—you tell me? (ninth-grade European American female)

It is, but in the least multicultural it can get away with. (ninth-grade European American male)

I don't know but I know I'm really sheltered. (ninth-grade European American female)

Every culture is here it feels like, but I don't understand why Africans get "Black History Month" while Caucasians get nothing except President's Day and they also get Martin Luther King Jr. Day and stuff. It's so *unfair*! (ninth-grade European American female)

Sophia Rhoades responded simply, "Kinda sorta."

White parents we interviewed seemed to have little awareness of how the school handled issues related to diversity and multiculturalism. When we asked in interviews how they thought the school did in dealing with issues of diversity, Julie Rice's mother said of her daughter, "To be blunt. . . . Her circle of friends has never really included a child of another race, I don't know. To be very honest with you, I really don't know." Kevin Madsen's mother said, "I think we have a statement that we support diversity. I think we try to do some things, uh culturally, to celebrate diversity." For her part, Sharon Sosa's mother worried that many people in the community didn't know "real black people."

Principal Cunningham herself was much more explicit in her assessment of how the school fared in terms of multiculturalism. In the spring of 2000 she told me, "This institution is profoundly racist." A more in-depth examination of the school's treatment of diversity and of the experiences of its minority students is in chapter 7. I want to note here, though, the likely effects of the teaching staff's racial composition on the educational experience of African American students, and in particular their confidence and predispositions to self-advocate—two components of psychological capital discussed in the next chapter. During the first year of the study, there were three African American teachers at the school; for the next three years there were four, plus the new assistant principal, Mr. Welkes. Two of the original three African American teachers were male and approximately the same age and height—they told us they were repeatedly mistaken for each other by their white colleagues during their early years at the school.

Both black students and black parents mentioned the deleterious effects of such a paltry representation of African American staff members. One African American male student said in his senior year that having more black teachers would "give you more confidence." Sofia Rhoades' father said:

It's a sore spot because people are going to complain because you picked a black person to teach and there's other qualified white people to teach. But you've got to have the mix. You've got to have the mix. Yeah, you're going to step on some toes and you're going to cause people to be upset, but if you have a school that is mixed and if you don't have the same type of mixture in your teachers, then it's going to hurt. (Interview 12/6/00)

During the 1999–2000 school year, the school sought to fill an opening in its Social Studies Department, which at the time was made up entirely of white teachers. One of the applicants was Brian Stanton, a European American male who was completing his student teaching assignment at the school. In April 2000, when we asked the chair of the Social Studies Department about the opening, she said that Mr. Stanton actually had a very good chance of getting hired: "We would like to diversify our department, because we are all the same. But he is so strong on content, and there is no substitute for that" (Field notes 4/13/00). Mr. Stanton was hired later that year. Such a decision exemplifies the school's approach to diversity when left to its own devices. More specifically, it illustrates the privileging of certain goods over others—in this case, strength in "content" and its value to a school keenly focused on its own comparative advantages over the diversification of a departmental teaching staff and better meeting the needs of minority students.

Conclusion

Wilton Burnham High School is typical of suburban schools that are seeking to prepare their students for competitive education and employment markets. In addition to its rich curriculum and dedicated teaching staff, the school is notable in its ability to leverage institutional resources to sponsor its students and instill in them the habits of competitive individualism. The school's paramount emphasis of preparing students for competitive success led to the devaluation of other goods, which are discussed throughout the book. Part of this chapter discussed the school's lack of urgency in meeting the needs of minority students.

The chapter explained that the local emphasis on the maintenance of self-worth and the preparation for individual competitiveness seemed to lead the school to develop policies geared toward ceding control to young people and empowering them with choice. It also showed the variety of ways in which the school sponsored students, from its continuous emphasis on "excellence" and "success" to the countless means through which it formally recognized students. I suggest that these expansive recognition programs make up a process of *hypercredentialing* at Wilton Burnham: the production of artificially high credentials intended to strengthen students' positions on education and job markets. A related form of hypercredentialing practiced at the school, the production of artificially high assessments, is taken up in chapter 5.

This chapter pointed out that while not all of the school's forms of recognition had exchange value on education and employment markets, most of them, aside from those whose value had been inflated, had the effect building up students' self-worth. Most importantly, these discourses of excellence and technologies of recognition seemed to function as feedback mechanisms in this system of educational self-advancement, in terms of what students believed about the purpose of schools, their activities there, and their futures: they made competition appear to be a natural social process, and contributed to the construction of these students as adult-successes-in-the-making. In all of these ways Wilton Burnham resembled the schools recently criticized by Currie (2004), which, he said, were "concerned with enforcing conformity to the constricting norms of an increasingly competitive middle class" (p. 273).

Logics of competition also imbued the school's rich and well-resourced cocurricular program—including the arts. The success of the athletics program was attributed in part to the community and school's commitment to mobilizing resources. The previous chapter discussed the local importance of experiencing winning in Wilton; the athletics program, as described in this chapter, was dedicated to making this possible for as many students as possible. At Burnham, there was little evidence of Kohn's twenty-year-old critique of the ill effects of competition in schools (1986) or his more recent book on "the praise problem" and how young people could actually be "punished by rewards" (1993).

The chapter also pointed out effects of the school's approach to diversity—specifically in the racial composition of its staff. The hiring of Mr. Stanton represented the school's understandable valuation of faculty with strong content knowledge. However, the school did not go to great lengths to recruit a minority teacher who might also have been "strong on content." As such, the episode represents a privileging of the school's commitment to maintaining its comparative advantages regarding the teaching of content over better meeting the needs of its minority students.

Part Two
Student Identity and Practice

Chapter Four Identities for Control and Success: The Acquisition of Psychological Capital

You are *who* you *choose* to be.
— *Sign on door of WBHS Co-Curricular Office*

It's all to do with self-control.
— *"Dilapidation," a student poem*

As I mentioned in the introduction, I had studied student identity previously in the urban United States, and Manus, Papua New Guinea, and several events early on in the study made it clear that students at Burnham were different. One of these occurred in October 1999. Jill Lynch was observing an English class where students were giving speeches that dealt with "success" in some way. They had been asked to refer in their speech to some sort of item they brought with them that was related to "success." One of the speeches that day was given by a white male sophomore who was on the Burnham wrestling team. He brought in a framed greeting card with a printed message of support about success and learning from failure. He explained that his mother had given it to him his freshman year when he had first started wrestling on the varsity level and was losing a lot of matches. He began his speech by holding up the framed card and saying, "I love my mom, and I love success, so I love this." Soon after Jill shared her notes on the class with me, I realized that Manus youth, who struggled to accommodate their personal ambitions within a historically egalitarian social system, would probably think that to love success as one loves one's mother, was an exotic—if not crazy—thing to say.

But achievement-oriented[1] Burnham students had actually developed a whole suite of identity characteristics that were geared toward success— and control. These were no doubt shaped in part by the emphasis placed on competitive success by the community of Wilton, parents, and the school. This chapter describes how achievement-oriented students at Burnham were constructing their selves to exert control over their educational experiences and acquire the psychological capital they would need for their futures. These students had a sophisticated understanding of market forces, extremely strong beliefs in their own agency, deeply held attachments to personal advancement, and highly specific aspirations. They were predisposed to advocate for themselves, and they self-consciously managed their impressions on others and cultivated their work ethics. They also struggled to habituate to stress and fatigue. Throughout the study we learned about gender and racial differences in these identity characteristics, and these are related throughout.[2] These differences are attributed in part to larger factors associated with the neoliberal context, such as how the school's efforts to meet the needs of minority students were subordinate to its broader goals of remaining competitive.

Middle-Class Identity and Educational Advantage

There has actually been relatively little research that has examined how middle-class student identities contribute to academic engagement and ultimately to educational advantage. Two notable exceptions are the work of Peshkin (2000) and Howard (2008), which were discussed in the introduction.

From an anthropological perspective, the models of self described in this chapter are linked to the Western notion of the "free-standing, self-contained individual" (Strathern 1991; Peshkin 2000), and also reflect distinctly American attachments to individual growth and development. Scholarship on social change and identity in the West suggests that since the Enlightenment, there has been an "increasing desire for self-conscious improvement" (Knauft 2002, 7) and that under conditions of Western modernity, as affiliations beyond the family grow, individuality grows, such that "opportunities for individualization proliferate into infinity" (Simmel 1964, 151). Giddens has observed that under such conditions the self faces a "puzzling diversity of options and possibilities" and thus becomes a "reflexive project" characterized by incessant efforts to exert control (1991, 117). Moreover, given the unprecedented pace, scope, and profoundness of social change, Giddens holds that modernity is a risk culture: individuals must think in terms of risk and risk assessment more or less constantly as they attempt to "colonise the future for themselves as an intrinsic part of their life-planning" (p. 125). Beck observes more specifically that under such conditions "the *perception* of threatening risks determines thought and action" (2000, 213; original emphasis). Foucault's theory of governmentality (1972, 1983, 1988) is central to Giddens's formulation of the risk culture, particularly how power, as expressed through the structures and discourses of modernity, subjects the body to the "internal discipline of self-control" and how "bodily discipline is intrinsic to the competent social agent" (1991, 57).

Neoliberalism, as a current moment of Western modernity, has further implications for the development of young peoples' identities. Neoliberal market reforms involve the disciplining of nation-states by markets and emphasize privatization and ultimately individual competition. Michael Apple recently argued that neoliberalism demands "the constant production of evidence that one is in fact making an enterprise of oneself" (2001, 420) and can demonstrate what the biological anthropologist Emily Martin refers to as, "earnable competence" (2000, 140).

In this view, I see these achievement-oriented Burnham students' identities, in part, as adaptations to the neoliberal context: as attempts to allay their anxieties over futures characterized by acute competition, declining social support, and uncertainty. The voices and experiences of these students show that they are self-consciously fashioning themselves to be marketable—and even enterprising. I argue that components of their identities represent new forms of what Sherry Ortner calls "psychological capital," which forms the basis for "the production of the kind of social self a person emerges with from childhood . . . the things that make for different social effectiveness" (2002, 13).[3]

There were certain socializing influences in Wilton that seemed to shape the selves of the majority of young people there—not just high-achieving students. These influences—namely, permissive parenting styles, intensive involvements with electronic and commodity culture, and extensive experience in "democratic" classrooms with "student-centered" pedagogies—all shared the characteristic of deferring to students' experiences and judgments, and thereby according them significant authority. I mention this here because the authority that students in general attributed to themselves was a prominent theme in the study as a whole: it seems to be a product of this broad array of socializing influences and is a specific consequence of them—as is the entitlement that Lareau (2003) writes about. This pattern is explored in more detail elsewhere (Demerath 2007). Most importantly, this self-authority seemed to function as a kind of reflexive feedback mechanism that justified and reinforced students' identities and practices, including their aspirations and achievement orientations.

Self-Construction for Market-Driven Contexts:
The Centrality of Psychological Capital

Achievement-oriented students' awareness of what personal qualities would lend them competitive advantages was likely related in part to their generation's substantial experience with consumer markets. Many students demonstrated fairly sophisticated consumptive identities as early as ninth grade. One had set up a mutual fund with her previous summer's earnings, and another watched a financial news channel regularly to keep up with his investments. The survey indicated that 17.2 percent of ninth graders and 56.68 percent of eleventh graders held jobs that they went to either after school, on weekends, or both. As Paul Willis (2003) recently pointed out, these experiences and opportunities seemed to provide particularly attractive resources for student's self-construction; at the conclusion of an interview during his ninth-grade year, Nuako Konadu said, "Here's my card," and handed me a non-personalized card with the imprint of the video store at which he worked.

We also noticed that throughout the study that students used business and military language to describe their academic challenges and triumphs. They sometimes referred to their academic work as "product," had a keen eye for where "cheap A's" could be had, and if not, "battled back," "reinforced," and closely monitored their course progress until they had an A in "lockdown." Such language use suggests the extent to which they saw their education as a high-stakes, commodity-based venture. Jim Greylock, the AP history teacher, characterized the school culture as a "business culture."

Awareness of Local and Translocal Competition

Like their parents, achievement-oriented Burnham students were acutely aware of being in competition with others—in their school and beyond. When I asked David Sterling how his sophomore year had started, his comments were framed by competitive concerns.

> DS: Last year my first nine weeks killed me. Not killed me, this is Wilton, I got three B's my first nine weeks and that set me back, but I had like a 3.6.
>
> PD: Yeah, it seemed like it killed you.
>
> DS: It really did though, because I know a senior who has a 3.8 and he's seventy-second in his class. He's not even top 10 percent with a 3.8.
>
> PD: Wow—

DS: Wilton is such a competitive place, and Burnham is such a competitive school, that those three B's hurt and they hurt a lot. . . .

PD: Do you think you were prepared for that?

DS: I think when I went into the school I was sitting here last year, I'm not sure I understood how competitive it was, but it just didn't hit me that, you know, there are going to be thirty-some valedictorians in my class. And high school is a gateway to college and if you don't do well in high school, you're not going to get into a good college. And things like grades and rank in class are kind of important. And I don't think that I really understood that until I came to high school and I saw that all these people were not just smarter than me, probably some of them are smarter, probably a lot of them are smarter than me, but they worked harder than me and got better grades than me. And it was, this year I came in and I was familiar with the people and I was familiar with what they did to get these grades. And I knew that if I want to get into a good college, there are a lot of good colleges, but if I want to do the things that I want to do, I'm going to have to knuckle down and do this. And familiarity with the competition that I have to go up against, and the teachers I had, and the material, greatly helped me this nine weeks so that I didn't have the downfall that I had last year. Actually it was four A's and three B's. Not bad.

PD: Oh.

DS: But in as competitive a school as Burnham is, that's not good. It's not bad, but it's a great perspective on how good a school Burnham is to have somebody sit here and tell you three B's and four A's is bad. (Interview 11/31/00)

In this interview David reflected on what he had to do to compete effectively at Burnham. His comments about the number of students with 4.0 GPAs, the number of valedictorians, and the actual class rank of the upperclassman signal a keen awareness of the academic competition at Burnham—and the way in which he constructed what school was about.

As a sophomore David told us, "I'd like to get a 4.0, that's something I'd like to do. I would like to end high school with a 4.0." He elaborated:

Getting a 4.0 would be more difficult for me in college and it would put me in more difficult classes, make me work harder in college. But once I get to the workplace, I would take it as a ladder. I would be higher up on a ladder than someone who . . . let's say I go to Notre Dame. I get a 4.0 and I go to Notre Dame, get good grades at Notre Dame, and leave Notre Dame. I'm going to be higher on a ladder than if I would have gotten a 3.6 going to Miami [University in Ohio] and done well at Miami. (Interview 11/31/00)

As a freshman, Nuako Konadu, whose father was originally from Ghana, was concerned about his ability to compete for college scholarships. He said he knew his parents would not have money for him to go to college. At the time, he was getting mostly A's in his classes and was an extremely lively participant in the class discussions we had observed. He was also on the JV football, basketball, and track teams, and worked ten to fifteen hours a week outside of school.

> PD: Do you want to go to college?
>
> NK: Of course I want to go to college, but I just have a 3.8 and mostly 4.0 kids get college scholarships and stuff. And that's kind of scaring me. I definitely don't want to go to the army and use my body and stuff. Really I just want to be something when I grow up. Like getting a PhD or something would be great and going on to a profession where I could, like, interact with people would be great. Really, I don't want to have a profession like bus driver or janitor. Not saying that those are low-class jobs or anything. Like, my dad told me that when he came over, he's told me this story, like, many times to influence my learning . . . When he came over from Ghana he had no money and he had to be the school janitor to pay for his schooling at IU [Indiana University]. When he finally finished he had to go back to being the school janitor until he found an accountant job in Alaska. He had to work his way up. He always tells me that I've been given a chance to get a good education because he got his education in Ghana. He doesn't want me to waste it. (Interview 2/7/00)

Nuako's perspective on the competitive landscape in and beyond high school was influenced by his father's experience. As a high-achieving Burnham student with an immigrant parent, he had a unique insider-outsider perspective on the tenuousness of his position—and future. The quotes above from David and Nuako give a sense of how they, like other achievement-oriented Burnham students, tended to see their selves as ongoing projects. They were also ambitious.

Attachments to Personal Success

Several students said openly in interviews that everyone's goal was to excel, succeed, or to be "the best." An English teacher said, "I think there's a tremendous amount of pressure on them. And it just seems to be increasing, increasing, increasing, particularly the pressure to be successful." Student voices from the study, including that of the wrestler with the framed greeting card, illuminate strikingly deep attachments to personal success. Sharon Sosa explained that this came partly from her parents:

ss: And they've always, since I was young, I've been like a straight-A student, I've always gotten A's so they expect it out of me now. And when your parents expect something, you don't care as much about it. so it's like when I get straight A's, you're not proud of me because I always get straight A's. . . .

PD: So, how does that make you feel, those expectations?

ss: I don't really mind because I expect it from myself also, you know, and strive for it, getting all A's and being like the top. (Interview 10/19/00)

Furthermore, many students articulated aspirations marked by success, and some expressed particular desires to not have to go through the same class struggles as their parents. Nuako said, "I just don't want to have to start on the bottom like they did and have to work up. I feel like, they've worked up, so I have to . . . start up, and continue from there." Indeed, when asked on the survey to describe the qualities of a "successful person," responses commonly mentioned achievement:

4.0 + good at sports. (tenth-grade European American male)

1600 SAT, 4.0, medical school. (ninth-grade Asian American female)

Someone who can balance schoolwork, out of school activities, and also free time. To achieve at both ends. (eleventh-grade European American female)

Other students responded in less idealized ways:

Leads good happy life with little stress. (tenth-grade European American male)

One not in depression. (eleventh-grade Asian American male)

Achievement-oriented students in Wilton seemed to be most animated when discussing their own accomplishments. Grades in particular seemed to define their emotional states in certain ways. Occasionally when one of us asked our student participants how they were, they would answer with an unsolicited remark on their academic progress: "I'm fine, I got an A on my algebra test." Julie Rice's self descriptions frequently made reference to her academic accomplishments—and occasional trials. The meeting we had shortly after her maxillofacial surgery (see the introduction) was typical. For example, I ran into her in the hallway one day when she was a junior and asked her how it was going. She breathlessly told me, "Actually, I'm having a *really* good day today. This morning I found out that I was selected for a ten-member all female *a cappella* singing group, and then I got a 9 on my DBQ in history." (The DBQ is a document-based question used to prepare for the AP exam; Jim Greylock, her AP U.S. history teacher later told me that 6 was the average score and that it was "almost impossible to get a 9.")

Conversely, an English teacher told me that she had once asked her students to write an essay about "loss." Several boys wrote about how, due to past behavior, they had "lost" their opportunity to get a better GPA and attend the college of their choice. These cases all illustrate the extent to which achievement influenced these students emotional states and ultimately self-regard.

Female students seemed to have more deeply internalized attachments to personal success. Julie's single-minded focus on her school achievements as related at the beginning of the book certainly exemplified this. One high-achieving student who won a scholarship to a prestigious arts school noted on the survey that she was "stressed out . . . all the time"—a theme explored in detail in chapter 6. She explained:

> Junior year was a lot of pressure. Like everyone would talk about how like junior-year grades count the most towards college and stuff? And that was just—there was just so much going on, it was just a major juggling act like, getting all your work done [she was working forty hours per week at a job at the mall). Like keeping your grades up. Like there was never any pressure at home for me to like do good, or, like it was never—it was my own work ethic coming out, just always trying to do my best, and . . . it was just me not being able to like, let up, you know. Just like, I'm my own worst critic. Just like—if you don't turn in this homework, it will screw up your grade, and . . . I just *cannot* do that. So I just—I always did my work, and tried my hardest, and—I was like an overachiever. Because that's just how I am. Like I—I do my—I put my all into everything. (Interview 7/9/03)

This student's admissions that she could not "let up" and that she could not let herself "screw up" her grades illustrates the depth of her own attachment to individual success. In the next chapter I present survey findings that show that female students tended to be more deeply immersed in the culture of competition in the school.

The Press for Control in Self-Authorship

There were several ways in which the exertion of control was required for these achievement-oriented Burnham students to realize their ambitions.

Control was central to their beliefs about the role of effort in determining life chances and the development of self-confidence, self-advocacy, and the highly specific aspirations they formed early in their high school careers.

Students at Wilton Burnham were exposed to a constant flow of messages that emphasized the primacy of their own efforts in shaping their future lives. One sign that hung on the door of the Co-Curricular Office read, "You are *who* you *choose* to be." In addition, at the welcoming assembly held in August 1999 (see chapter 3), the Class of 2003 was told by the then senior class president, "The staff works very hard to set you up for success. . . . Life is 10 percent what happens to you and 90 percent how you react to it." Finally, in 2002 at a talk sponsored by Bears Inc., a former local college football star told the students, "It's nice to have others, but it depends on *you,* because everything in the world depends on *you.*" He concluded his talk by advising the students that, "You don't ever want to stop progressing."

Many students seemed to internalize these sentiments. One of the survey items asked students to rank the following influences in determining a person's future: individual effort, parents' background, social support, and quality of education. Effort was ranked at the top by 71.5 percent of students. Indeed, in a lively discussion on the origins and perpetuation of social inequality in an enriched social studies class, two European American female students made the following comments:

> TIFFANY: Our parents have worked very hard to send us to good schools, but some of them haven't tried as hard.
> SUSAN: Some of them don't have the will. (Field notes 11/30/99)

The importance of exerting such control seemed to shape many students' sense of self-efficacy, as illustrated in the next section.

Confidence and Empowerment

When Principal Trent took over at WBHS in the fall of 2000, she expressed surprise at "how empowered the students were." Indeed, 75.5 percent of surveyed pupils described themselves as a "confident student." Strikingly, in responding to the subsequent question, "If yes, where does this confidence come from?" a number of students referenced themselves (several simply said, "me" or "myself"):

> This confidence comes from me. I don't care what anybody else's opinion about me is, except for mine. (ninth-grade European American male)

My confidence comes from the satisfaction I get from getting good grades. (ninth-grade European American male)

It comes from my drive to be successful and get what I want. (eleventh-grade European American female)

When we asked Dianne Heinlen, an achievement-oriented white female freshman, where her confidence came from, her response was grounded in her family history and how she envisioned her own gender role. We had been talking about her social studies class and she was explaining why she admired Queen Elizabeth I:

> DH: She's just incredibly manly, I guess, in a way. She took on a man's role in government, and she held her own, you know, in society. . . . And she was like, "I am the master, and I am not going to let anyone rule over me."
>
> RICH MILNER: And why is that important?
>
> DH: I don't know. I think maybe because my parents are divorced and my mom sort of like plays both roles—mom and dad. She fixes things and everything. She sort of takes on both roles. I sort of picture myself that way. It took me ten years to become the person I am today and I'm not going to let anybody rule over my life except maybe my mom because she does stuff like make me get off the phone or whatever. . . .
>
> PD: Where does your confidence come from?
>
> DH: I sort of developed it myself, because fifth grade was once of the worst years of my life. My mom taught me that it doesn't matter what other people think about you. You need to stand strong and go on and not really worry about what other people think about you—just go with your goals. (Interview 3/29/00)

Dianne Heinlen's commentary is instructive in several ways. Grounded in her family history, she makes reference to her own goals and her desire, as a young woman, to be in control of her own life. She self-consciously attributes her present state of being to her own efforts. It is not surprising that such a young person would see Elizabeth I as one of her "heroes."

Certainly the school itself bore some responsibility for instilling confidence in many of its students. In addition to the policies and forms of recognition mentioned in the previous chapter, the Counseling Center occasionally showed students a video entitled, *Confident for Life: Kids and Body Image.* In it, a white female student comments:

> When you see someone who is confident about themselves, they start to look . . . beautiful. I think that when you project the sense of confidence

and passion about something, people automatically want to be around you. They want to be near you, because you convey a sense of happiness with yourself, and everyone wants to be a part of that.

On the other hand, of the minority of students who reported not being confident, many of them reported deleterious effects of the in-school culture of competition:

> I constantly need reassurance that I am doing well. I constantly doubt myself. My lack of confidence comes from my low self-esteem that I have from being in Burnham and Carlisle's [a middle school that feeds into Burnham] social climates from the past 4–5 years. (eleventh-grade European American female)

> I feel that I have to be the perfect student, straight A's, the perfect weight (110 pounds), the perfect size (6) and the perfect fashion googoo. (ninth-grade European American female)

Bryan Bowen said that he knew many students who were not confident, which he attributed to their circumstances at home. He said:

> I think there's a lot of students in this school who aren't confident. They don't really know . . . I think some people are stressed out, have a messed up life at home and stuff and they don't really know they're not confident. Their mom or dad doesn't give them much love, you know, and they're not that confident. I know a few people like that. My mom shows me love and I show my mom love, so I mean that makes me more confident personally. (Interview 4/11/00)

Sharon's confidence was an issue for her, in part because there were so few other African American students in enriched and AP classes—her experience is explored in more detail in chapter 7. It is not unsurprising, then, that after their first two months of high school, when we asked the focal students what advice he or she would give next year's incoming freshmen, the first thing Sharon mentioned was "be confident."

Predispositions to Advocate for the Self

In addition, achievement-oriented students generally possessed impressive self-advocacy skills, perhaps a product of the "concerted cultivation" they experienced at home. A senior administrative assistant commented, "These kids today aren't afraid to advocate for themselves." Study data suggest that these students' predispositions to self-advocate had a basis in a measure of confidence, as well as entitlement. Many of these high-achieving students became highly skilled negotiators, in part due to the leeway offered them in many of their student-centered classrooms. Referred to by Eckert as "adult handling skills" (1989, 116) these abilities enabled some students to develop potentially exploitable relationships with other people—including their teachers and counselors. These are recounted in more detail in the next chapter.

This, however, was one of the most important areas of contrast between white and black students in the study. In interviews, more than one of the African American focal students expressed either bewilderment or frustration as to how it was that they 1) were marginalized in their classrooms and 2) received inadequate advice from their guidance counselor regarding the college application process. These differences are discussed further in chapter 7.

Colonizing the Future: Precociously Circumscribed Aspirations

The achievement-oriented students' powerful compulsion to exert control over their lives was especially apparent in their aspirations. Beginning as freshmen, these students had strikingly precise ideas about what they wanted their future lives to be like—and work, jobs, and achievement were central to them. A ninth-grade white female student explained:

> Some of us, like, think really far ahead. You know, like, if I don't do this assignment, then my grades are going to go down and my GPA's going to fall, and then I can't get into the college I want, or whatever. (Interview 12/14/99)

Throughout the study college-bound students referred to their major in the present, rather than the future tense—even as underclassmen. In the "Stellar Senior" segment on WBHS News, a typical question was, "Where do you plan to go to college and what is your major?" As a freshman, Sharon said she was planning on "minoring in culinary arts later down the line as a side career to enjoy."

Students were also highly specific in imagining their future careers and occupations. As a ninth grader, one female student said, "My sister has tried like five different careers right now . . . It would just be a lot easier to, like, find what you want, first." When asked on the survey what they wanted their "future life to be like," most students responded with great specificity, both in terms of their expectations, and their strategies for realizing them:

I want to be an architect or fashion designer so I will do whatever is necessary. (tenth-grade European American female)

Become a pilot, save up some money, open a microbrewery. (eleventh-grade European American male)

I want to go to OSU [Ohio State University] and major in vet tech with a minor in equine business management. (eleventh-grade European American female)

The school also played a role in reinforcing the compulsion to form early and specific occupational aspirations. In spring of 2000, the Counseling Center sponsored a series of information sessions where seniors could share with sophomores what they had learned about the college preparation process. In one of the sessions a white female senior told the sophomores, "If you don't know what you want to do out of college, and end up doing a job you don't like, you're basically screwed."

There were, however, students who resisted this pressure to form early and specific aspirations. Later in the same session, a white male senior panelist told the sophomores that he disagreed with the previous speaker, and that it was "perfectly OK if you don't know what you're going to do." He told them his advice was to "Keep your options open." Indeed, on the survey there were a small number of negative cases, some of which were quite forthright.

No idea—I'm 15 and I don't know yet—I just wish people would back off about this. (ninth-grade European American female)

Nevertheless, most achievement-oriented students we spoke with at Burnham demonstrated a strong compulsion to predict, foretell, or, in Giddens's terms, to "colonize" the future. It seems reasonable to conclude that these were subconscious attempts to allay uncertainties and anxieties about their future lives. Such total efforts could produce somewhat dizzying effects at times, such as when Julie Rice told me during her sophomore year, "I am a lot more focused on what I need to be focused on and I need to be focused on that."

Impression Management: Adopting Politically Correct Ways of Speaking

In addition, achievement-oriented students at Burnham exhibited the sorts of social or "people" skills desired as cultural capital in the corporate world.

Throughout the study we were struck by the extent to which they seemed to be conscious of the high personal cost of social miscues; they adopted politically correct ways of speaking about individual "success" and people from other ethnic groups. In this way, they were demonstrating an "instrumental style of communication or impression management" that Foley found in his study in Texas to be portrayed as the "cultural ideal" (1990, 134).

First, students commonly referred to individual success as doing "well." In our interview with David Sterling's father, he explained how he had taught his sons the importance of speaking appropriately about personal success. He said he wanted them to understand that "not everyone feels wonderful about your success because some people feel bad that it's not their success." In his freshman year, David indicated that he had internalized this lesson. He said, "No one wants to admit that they're better than anyone else. I think people in this school try not to talk about it because we don't want to seem better than anyone else." As a senior, David had further developed this skill. When we were discussing what school was for, he commented:

> It's, you know, learning how to interact with people who may be different from you, or who learn differently from you. Because when you're in the work force, not everyone's going to work in the same way you do. Not everyone's going to be successful in the same ways that you are successful. (Interview 5/12/03)

Second, a notable feature of the student culture was the degree to which achievement-oriented students from different social locations and groups got along, supported, and even socialized with one another in school. Students seemed to value being able to move fluidly between groups—proclaiming with pride that they had different kinds of friends, especially as they moved through the grades. One female European American student said as a senior, "I've got a lot of connections to a lot of people." During the first year of the study, Rich Milner asked an achievement-oriented white female student whether she thought everyone in the school was "treated the same," regardless of race. She responded, "I treat everyone the same because I have a lot of friends who are black or Asian, or whatever."

As a freshman, David talked about what he was learning from being in school with classmates from different religious and ethnic backgrounds:

> DS: I have friends who are Buddhist and Muslim and Jewish, which is, probably, not [like] the majority of Burnham, but it's nice to learn

about them and it makes you a better student. Just culturally and ethically.

JILL LYNCH: What are some ways that you think it makes you a better student?

DS: Well, it helps in part of the classroom in understanding, because a lot of times, at least, what I do, I just yell out something, and I don't really think about what other people are thinking about. . . . So if I get other people with different ideas and from different places, then I get their views also. And I think it's helped me, a little bit, to take time before I yell something out and think, "Well, what do these other people think? And what might they do if, you know—" Everything has a consequence and I don't want to say anything that would either offend someone or, you know, get people mad at me, so if I know where people are coming from better, it helps me stay away from those topics that are more touchy. (Interview 5/11/00)

Self-Conscious Cultivation of Work Ethic

Another component of psychological capital that was central to these students' identities for success was the self-conscious development of an extremely strong work ethic. The consensus was that most Wilton students worked very hard to get good grades. Several of the high-achieving focal students mentioned staying up until 1:00, 2:00, or even 3:00 in the morning in order to study for tests. One student said of the enriched social studies/English class:

We have tons of projects going on at once, but I feel like it makes your work ethic stronger. And it makes you realize that, you know, this is how life's going to be from now on. (Interview 3/28/00)

These beliefs were summarized in an exchange between two male students in the Commons where one said, "I hate geniuses. They get an easy break. They don't work for it."

As David Sterling moved through Burnham, he learned about what it would take to succeed in such a competitive environment. As a sophomore he reflected on what he had learned his freshman year:

People work hard at Wilton. There's never a dull moment. I don't know if it's from the backgrounds they come from, but people don't rest. And if you rest, you're going to get burnt. I rested my first nine weeks last year here and I found out I can't do that anymore because there are so many people and there are so many people that want to get into a competitive college that they're work hard and they really do.

He went on:

> We have the work ethic, because we've had to have it. If we didn't have the work ethic, we weren't going to get into this college that we want to go to. We were not going to do the kind of things we wanted to do if we didn't have to work hard. So when I get into college and when I go into the workplace, hopefully I'll already have this work ethic because I've had to work like this. Because everyone's goal is to be the best. (Interview 11/31/00)

David later described his strategy for recovering from that first marking period and reaching his goal of graduating with a 4.0 GPA: by taking AP classes (which reward an A with a 5.0). Over the next four years, he cultivated his work ethic accordingly. David accomplished his goal, and in the spring of his senior year said:

> I told myself long ago that, you may not be the smartest guy, you may not be the fastest runner, but if you work hard, there's a lot of people who you'll go past. (Interview 5/12/03)

The deep-seated adoption of this work ethic, or "inner drive," married to the success orientation seemed to be behind the constant compulsion of the achievement-oriented students to be, or do something, "productive." When, as a junior, we asked David whether he was able to have time to have fun, he replied, "It depends what month it is. . . . That's what the summer's for." Later in that interview I asked David what he had done the night before:

> DS: I had no homework last night. And so, I mean I just—I don't even know what I did last night. I should have done something productive. I didn't [chuckles], but—
>
> PD: What do you mean, something productive?
>
> DS: I should have read a book. I should have worked on my vocabulary for the SATs. I should, you know, I should have done something that's going to help me in the long run. Now, I mean granted, you know, my brother and I, we went out and played baseball in the back yard, and, you know, shot baskets, and—I guess that's productive in the sense that I'm building a deep relationship with my brother, but—it's not—not academically or anything like that. (Interview 5/24/02)

It is striking that a seventeen-year-old like David was aware of whether he was being productive on an evening at home with his brother at the very end of his junior year. Work ethics are nothing new, but the degree to which these young people rationalize them and self-consciously cultivate them may be.

Conclusion

In this chapter I identified elements of an accelerating competitive individualism among these youth as they attempt to maximize their appeal on higher education and employment markets—and at the very least, remain in the middle class. These identities for success were fostered in part by Wilton's pronounced expectations for personal advancement and the school's emphasis on competitive academic success. The components of psychological capital exhibited by achievement-oriented students at Burnham included strong agentic beliefs in students' capacities to influence the kinds of people they were and would become, affective attachments to personal success, precociously circumscribed aspirations, predispositions to self-advocate, highly developed social skills, including politically correct means of speaking, and the self-conscious development of a strong work ethic resulting in a habitual proclivity to be "productive."

Neoliberalism may be seen as an "amplification" of the core market mechanisms of late capitalism (Stambach 2007; Weiss 2004), and as such, the identity constructs found among these Wilton youth themselves seem to represent an "amplification" of many of the components of the competitive Western model of personhood reviewed at the outset of this chapter. What seems to be new among these young people is the extent to which their total selves are oriented toward personal success and the management of risk, and their seeming awareness that particular identity characteristics had value as psychological capital.

Some of the components of psychological capital discussed here likely have a basis in Lareau's "concerted cultivation" middle-class parenting strategy, and as such, suggest that its consequences are more far-ranging than mere entitlement. In addition, the conception of psychological capital in this chapter takes Ortner's initial description beyond the family into broader social environments—especially the landscape of intensifying individualistic competition.

The study also uncovered important differences in the distribution of psychological capital across different groups of students in the school. White female high-achieving students exhibited virtually the same psychological capital as white male students. However, they seemed to have deeper attachments to personal success, and, as the next chapter relates, be more immersed in the competitive culture and routines of the school. Perhaps the most important element of psychological capital that these students struggled to acquire was the ability to habituate to more or less ever-present levels of stress and fatigue. This finding, and the significant gender differences associated with it, is taken up in detail in chapter 6. Racial differences in students' confidence and their abilities to self-advocate are attributable in part to the ways in which the school handled diversity—specifically in the racial composition of its staff. The role of race in student experience at Burnham is explored further in chapter 7.

Most broadly, the class cultural identities of these achievement-oriented youth are guided by an astute consciousness of the competitive landscape, sophisticated understanding of market forces, and constant rationalization. In view of Giddens's argument regarding the predicament of the self in the risk culture of modernity, it seems clear that these young people are deeply involved in the management of risk. At the core of this logic of self-authoring is the constant evaluation of whether particular practices and experiences will lead to its betterment and advancement. In this way, these young people have become "strategic manipulators" (Gergen 1991, 147). In the next chapter, I turn to the implications of these identities for everyday practices of schooling. I show how these student selves, in concert with the school's commitment to institutional advantaging, led to an instrumental approach to learning.

Chapter Five Teaching the "Point-Hungry" Student: Hypercredentialing in Practice

★ ★ ★ ★ ★

Grades are everything. You have to realize it's the only possible way to get into a good college, and you resort to any means necessary.

> — *Tenth-grade European American male*

Our job is to get these kids into the best college they can possibly get in to.

> — *Neil Richards, social studies teacher*

In early January 2000, Jill, Rich and I filed into Neal Richards's enriched ninth-grade global history class. This was one of several classes we had been attending every week since the beginning of the school year, and was typically taken by students who expected to take AP social studies and English classes in the coming years. The class was "blocked" (two periods, or ninety-six minutes, long), and Sharon, Nuako, Julie, and David were all in it. We fanned out in the classroom, took our seats, greeted the students around us, and asked them what we would be doing that day (our favorite conversation opener). I was told that today was "Monk Day."

Neal Richards, a white social studies teacher who was in his seventh year at Burnham, got the class started with a reminder of some upcoming quizzes and tests, then explained that "Monk Day" would simulate their being monks in Middle Ages Europe. All students would start out with forty points at the beginning of the activity, but would lose two points each time they spoke or used sign language. He then told the students to wait in the hall with Rich while Jill and I helped him and his student teacher, Mr. Stanton, set up the activity. We set up four stations: a "scriptorium" for illuminated writing, a "dormitory" to nap, a "music/prayer room" to listen to Gregorian chants and meditate or pray, and a "workroom" to pick up trash (simulated by crumpled up pieces of paper). Once we had things set up, the students came back in, divided themselves among the stations, and began the activity. Neal had asked me to supervise the work room. In addition to enforcing the no talking/signing rule, I was supposed to empty the contents of the wastebasket back onto the floor each time the students filled it up.

I immediately noticed how seriously the students approached the activity. Several pupils in the music/prayer room had their eyes closed—presumably mediating, and the students in the workroom worked quickly to pick up the trash and put it in the wastebasket (apparently not realizing that the faster they worked, the more trash they would end up picking up). Midway through his time in the workroom, David figured out that by laying the wastebasket horizontally on the floor, they could all more easily sweep the trash into it. At the end of the activity Neal asked the students to take out a piece of paper and write about what it was like for them. While the students were writing, he passed back a map worksheet he had just graded. Julie's neighbor, another white female student, very quietly and politely asked her what she had gotten. Julie mouthed, "A-plus." Her neighbor said she had gotten the same thing. Across the room, David exclaimed, "Whew!" and pumped his fist beside him. Overall, student attention seemed to be more on the graded work they had just been given back than on their current writing assignment. Several students soon asked Mr. Richards about how he had graded their work; one asked if perhaps he had "misread" how she had done her assignment, and another wondered why points had been taken off for a certain mistake. After the class, we asked students what they thought of Monk Day. The responses included "OK," "boring," and "pointless." Julie Rice said, "I liked it. I got all the points."

This class was typical of enriched courses at Burnham. Learning activities were tightly linked to assessments, which in turn powerfully shaped students' perceptions of the class itself. Lightfoot brought these emerging trends to light twenty five years ago in suburban Chicago. The students she observed at Highland Park High School expressed an "early concern for educational excellence" (1983, 129) but rarely revealed a "burning educational curiosity" (p. 145). As mentioned in the introduction, more recently researchers have pointed out that intensified market-based competition has given rise to increasing educational credentialism in the United States and elsewhere (Labaree 1997; D. K. Brown 2001). Labaree likened academic credentials to commodities and said that many schools are in the process of adapting themselves to "meet the demands of the consumers" who seek to acquire them. Overall, Labaree's work described the socioeconomic forces that promote educational credentialism and commodification and argued that they privilege social sorting over teaching and personal advancement over learning.

At Burnham, these were logical consequences of the community's concern with individual advancement, achievement-oriented students' unwavering focus on future markets, and the identities they were developing to succeed within them. A science teacher referred to such students as being "point hungry." In Denise Pope's terms (2001), they had already fallen into the "grade trap" and were simply "doing school:" they believed that the point of school is to get "good grades" and adopted a mechanistic approach to their education. This was certainly true of most of the high-achieving focal students in the study. But many teachers, who saw their primary role as enabling students to compete, contributed to this emphasis on credentialing as well. In our first interview, Neal Richards said, "Our job is to get these kids into the best college they can possibly get in to."

This chapter provides a glimpse into how educational credentialism is perpetuated through the everyday practices of students and teachers. It begins by discussing students' preoccupations with the grades they "needed" and the strategies they adopted to "get" them. These included applying mighty effort to their schoolwork; negotiating with their teachers for extra points, easier assignments, or extra credit; judging the utility of their classes; personalizing their relationships with teachers; and cheating. All of these student practices involve the exertion of control over educational experiences, and as such, are predicated on the identity characteristics discussed in the previous chapter. Throughout, the chapter relates the range of ways in which teachers and administrators complied with or resisted achievement-oriented Burnham students' fixation on grades and academic credentials.

In order to provide context for the ensuing discussion, I include statistical differences in academic achievement between several groups of students based on analysis of survey data and GPA. These should be considered in addition to those differences in academic achievement related to parental background reported in the second chapter: 1) female students had significantly higher mean GPAs (2.67) than male students (2.31)[1]; 2) students who identified themselves as being "involved" in the school tended to have higher GPAs than students who were not "involved" in the school[2]; and 3) students with jobs tended to have lower GPAs.[3]

Students' Preoccupation with "Getting the Grade You Need"

As related in the previous chapter, achievement-oriented Burnham students were acutely aware of competition both in and out of school. For most of them, this resulted in a strong preoccupation with "getting" good grades, or the grades they thought they would "need" to reach their future goals. A white special education coordinator in her forties reflected on how high school had changed since she had been a student: "I think it's a lot, it's push, it's think about college, think about your career, and high school is just a—a means to an end. It's not a process in life anymore! You're not growing here." Students received messages about getting good grades throughout their years at Burnham. In Principal Cunningham's welcoming speech to the Class of 2003, she said she fervently hoped that theirs would be the first class to get straight A's the first marking period. Shortly thereafter, the president of the senior class advised students to "take risks" and to "work hard," because "it is worth it, especially if you make varsity, get a band solo. Getting the grade is worth it." At the end of her senior year, one achievement-oriented student told me her approach had been to "work, have fun, and just get the good grade." When Sharon Sosa was a senior, I asked her what advice she would have to incoming freshmen. She said:

> I tell freshmen, get good grades, keep them, because that's your foundation. You know what I mean? That's what's going to be what carries you the whole way through. People who have that—you know, if you can have that—faith in yourself, that you can perform to your best ability, then that's what you're going to—you're going to feel good at the end of the year, when you have the grades you want, the lifestyle that you want. (Interview 6/2/03)

Kevin Madsen said his approach was simply, "You come here; you get the grade you need."

Students' preoccupation with grades dominated their approach to classroom activities. We frequently saw students ask teachers if they had graded their tests or if they would stop what they were doing to grade their tests. We also saw students using calculators to rework their averages after receiving tests back in class. A science teacher told us, "They're very grade conscious, yeah, I've noticed that. Everything revolves around points and grades for the most part."

One day in April 2000, in his enriched science class, Nuako Konadu and his group partners listened to the teacher give instructions for a major large group project. The teacher explained that this project would be worth 360 points—virtually all of their points for the final grading period of the year. The teacher then said they could take a few minutes to look over some projects from previous years that had been set out on tables in the classroom. Nuako and his group partners, two quiet European American boys, and a South Asian boy named Krish with a zeal for the class, moved over to inspect the projects. Krish and Nuako proceeded to criticize many of them. Krish pointed at one and said, "Look at this—colored paper. It looks like a fifth-grade project." Nuako pointed toward another, and said, "Look at this one, guys, he's got a four point [4.0]. Look at this one. We know it's good." Krish found more projects that received high grades and repeatedly said, "Nuako, Nuako, look at this," all the while quickly scrawling notes on what they should and shouldn't do on their project. After several minutes the students returned to their seats and the teacher went over the grading criteria in more detail. When the teacher said that each group would be assessed on how well they worked together, Nuako turned to Krish, almost as a matter of reflex, and said with a broad smile, "I love you, man."

High-achieving Burnham students were also generally conscious of the requirements for successful college applications. For example, as a freshman, Sharon expressed an awareness of how working at the local science museum would look on her college application. Student responses to the survey question, "What are you doing to gain admission to the college of your choice?" were telling:

Working on grades, extracurriculars. (ninth-grade European American male)

Trying really hard to get good grades and do stuff that would look good on a resume. (ninth-grade European American female)

I am building my resume with all-around strength and involvement in numerous activities outside of school. (tenth-grade European American male)

Trying really hard to get good grades and do stuff that would look good on a resume. (ninth-grade European American female)

Doing my best at what I feel I'll need. (ninth-grade European American female)

The last quote is perhaps the most succinct example of the achievement-oriented Burnham student's instrumental approach to school. All the quotes illustrate how students often regarded their extracurricular activities as things they "needed" to do, and at which they had to "work." Upperclassmen even gave advice to underclassmen on building resumes, such as at the information session in spring of 2000 sponsored by the Counseling Center mentioned in the previous chapter. During that session when a when a student volunteered that he was interested in theater, the same white female senior who had told the sophomores that they would be "basically screwed" if they left college with no plan for their dream career said, "So at a small school, Brad can use that as an extracurricular activity."

Teachers and students alike acknowledged that there were a lot of "resume writers" at the school. One student who reviewed another's resume questioned how "devoted" the student was to all the activities she had listed. Even as a freshman, a white female student noticed, "Like, tons of freshmen are joining Key Club and SSAP [Students Substance Abuse Prevention Program] and all that just to have it on their transcript, for their applications to college, so they'll look good."

Grim and Mighty Effort

Nevertheless, study data indicated that most high-achieving students worked very hard to get good grades. As mentioned above, they had strong work ethics and proclivities to be "productive." Students routinely told us about staying up very late to study—especially before tests. Sharon reported staying up until 3:00 in the morning at least once a week during her first two years of high school. When I asked Catherine Walters, the student with the highest average grade in Neal Richards's class, whether she had played outside over a rare snowy weekend in late January 2000, she said, "No, I wanted to, but I had to do homework." Nuako told us about his efforts to prepare for an enriched science test freshman year:

> If you could see the look on kids' faces when we're taking exams, everyone is stressed out, especially in science. Every kid who walked in that door was like freaking out because she is the hardest teacher at this school. I literally spent six hours on her test alone, and I only got a B on it. I took all the time up on the test studying for it and I still got them wrong. The nervous breakdown part is when you realize that you have no time left and then you think you haven't studied enough but you have . . . like you think you need more time. So, a lot of people, especially freshmen, it's like the first time we've taken exams here and we're stressed out. People who really care about their grade are like really freaking out. It's like you become a different person you're so stressed out. And like lack of sleep . . . everyone's tired. (Interview 2/7/00)

After getting three B's his freshman year, which set him back in his goal to graduate as a valedictorian like his brother, David Sterling adopted a highly methodical way of studying for exams so he could "keep getting A's." In the middle of his junior year, he shared his approach:

PD: Well, so how much time do you spend now on your schoolwork, outside of school?

DS: It depends if it's a test night. If I have a test—like, Wednesday, I have a math test, so I'll probably end up studying an hour, an hour and a half, alone, on Wednesday night for the math test, then probably half hour, forty minutes of French, and then, probably an hour for all the other stuff—

PD: So—if you have a test, you might be studying as much as three hours, three-and-a-half hours.

DS: Oh, usually, it's probably about that much. Now if I don't have a test, I won't study the hour and a half for math.

PD: Okay, and weekends—it depends?

DS: Weekends, yeah, it really depends on what I have due the next—I mean weekends for me is the time I use to get long-term stuff done. If I have a project due on Friday, I'll get it done over the weekend so I don't have to worry about it during the week. Let's see, I have a French test next Wednesday, so I will study for that over the weekend. And I will study Monday and Tuesday, but it's just—with things like French and math, that need constant reinforcement, I will study a lot of days in a row, so hopefully I will do well. And that's something I have learned—from high school, is that I used to just be able in middle school to fit everything in one night, you know, I had a French test the next day, I'd study for forty minutes and get an A. You can't do it anymore. You actually have to take time in successive days to study and reinforce things. (Interview 5/24/02)

David explained in subsequent interviews that the courses that tended to need "reinforcement" were the ones like math and French where he was not either "high A" or "solid A" (meaning, in his words, "I'm going to get an A").

One of the hardest-working students we learned of during the study was a Japanese girl named Yuki Kato. She was one of several Japanese students at Burnham; most of whom had a parent that worked at the nearby Honda plant. Yuki's father was an executive there, and she had come to the United States at the beginning of her freshman year for high school. Due to a change in plans, she was going to have to return to Japan earlier than expected, so she completed her coursework in three years. She took summer school classes and seven to eight academic classes each semester of high school. She typically came home from school at 3:30, had English tutoring until 5:30, went to a *juku* (a special school to prepare for the Japanese college entrance examinations) until 10:00, then came home and started her homework. Yuki said she typically got to sleep around 2:00 or 3:00 in the morning, and then slept until "five minutes before the bus comes." She said she caught up on sleep on the weekends and sometimes in her classes, but that overall the year was very stressful.

The rationale for these students' grim and mighty efforts can sometimes be seen on T-shirts in suburban American high schools today: "Hard Work Beats Talent When Talent Doesn't Work Hard." However, other, more instrumental approaches to school work were clearly evident at Burnham, which students adopted to, as one senior said, "get the best grade with the least amount of work." These included contesting grades, negotiating with teachers for easier assignments and more extra credit opportunities, and cheating.

While teachers responded to this student expectation and push for grades in a variety of ways, as detailed below, the widespread adoption of these strategies throughout the school was due to the fact that so many of them, like Neal Richards, saw their primary work as credentialing, and emphasized assessment in their classes. In this way the practices of "point-hungry" students in assessment-dominated classrooms make up another feedback process in the school that set students up for individual success. The result is another form of hypercredentialing.

Inside the Assessment-Dominated Classroom:
Self-Advocacy, Negotiation, and "Adult-Handling" Skills

Typically the first ten minutes or so of Neal Richards's classes were taken up with providing information and answering students' questions about assessment. For example, one morning in mid-April 2000, Mr. Richards said at the beginning of class, "You don't get full credit for homework if you didn't add notes on what we discussed in class." Then he said, "Tomorrow you will turn in everything you have for points. Then, in class, you will have another opportunity to earn points on worksheets." These explanations of assignments and assessments frequently became a kind of negotiating session where students bargained for "easier" assignments, partner quizzes, and extra credit.

On the first day back in school after a holiday weekend in February 2000, there was confusion among the students as to when various parts of a homework assignment had been due. Because of the long weekend, about half of the students had forgotten it. A discussion ensued with the teacher about whether the entire assignment would be due the next day (Wednesday), or the day after (Thursday). Neal Richards announced that because so many students had forgotten the homework that he would make it due the next day. Ashleigh, a white female student, was visibly distressed by this. She turned to David Sterling and said, quite audibly, "That's not fair. I did my homework during *my* break, and I didn't have to." Nuako, on the other side of class, then quickly said, "Can we earn extra credit if we turn it in today?" Richards then agreed to give extra credit for those students who had finished the assignment on time. Ashleigh sighed, and told David, "Okay, now I'm okay with this." She and David gave their papers back to the teacher so that they could receive their extra credit.

As mentioned in the previous chapter, many of these achievement-oriented students were highly skilled negotiators, likely in part due to the leeway offered them in Wilton's student-centered classrooms. A science teacher explained:

> They're big negotiators. They want everything for extra credit. . . . And they want this to be worth lots of points if they do well, but they don't want it to be worth very many points if the didn't do well. . . . And usually when they see they haven't done quite as well as they had hoped, then they start all their angles, trying to get points. (Interview 5/23/00)

Overall, such students' "adult handling skills" (Eckert 1989, 116) enabled them to develop potentially exploitable relationships with other people—including their teachers and counselors. When we asked one high-achieving student how she had managed to negotiate a senior year schedule of two courses per semester—well below the district minimum of five—so she could work at her job forty hours per week, she responded:

> You build rapport with people over time, and then you can work things out, you know? You scratch my back and I scratch yours, just like in the business world, you know? (Field notes 6/5/03)

Indeed, Jim Greylock characterized the school culture as a "business culture."

ADOPTING INSTRUMENTAL RELATIONSHIPS WITH TEACHERS: FROM CRITIQUE TO PERSONALIZATION. As achievement-oriented Burnham students moved through their high school years, another skill many seemed to acquire was developing personal relationships with teachers. It seemed to take these students time to realize the value of such relationships, and as such, this is one trend in the study data that we saw clearly develop over time.

When many of these achievement-oriented students first arrived in high school, their first impulse seemed to be to question their teachers and their teaching methods. Earlier in their high school careers, several students told us that they had "issues" with some of their teachers and the way they taught. These students frequently shared these criticisms with their teachers—in class. One teacher said her students questioned "everything." We observed several of these events in Neal Richards's class, such as the time when, in the middle of an activity, a white male student raised his hand and said, "I don't think this is a lesson that is helping our class." Six or so students then raised their hands and said that they agreed. We observed another incident when a white female student commented, "This is so stupid," in the middle of a class discussion. Sharon described one the teaching style of one of her teachers her sophomore year by saying, "It's just the way she teaches sometimes, it's not how we want to be taught." An English teacher commented in an interview simply, "It's like they know more than you."

Most broadly, these student judgments about the effectiveness of their education (whether it was providing them with what they thought they needed to know) can be seen as further attempts to exert control over their present and future lives. They are also evidence of the authority these students attribute to themselves that was mentioned in the previous chapter. Finally, these judgments are a part of the development of a valuable kind of cultural capital that Bourdieu (1984) referred to as critical discourse. He argued that the process of "becoming critical" was one way in which middle class children begin to distinguish themselves from others and socialize themselves into class membership.

However, study data suggested that as students moved through high school and learned what was required for academic success, they tempered these critical comments of teachers and teaching. We observed fewer critical comments about teachers and teaching in classes with upperclassmen in them. What we did notice were more student attempts to personalize their relationships with teachers. They talked about the importance of having good relationships with teachers and tended to cite personal qualities or characteristics of teachers in their evaluations of them. One student replied as follows to the survey question "Do you think you know better than your teachers how you ought to learn?"

I used to think so, but more recently I have struggled more with my grades and need to listen to them. (ninth-grade European American female)

This tendency to personalize relationships with teachers seemed to be motivated by two trends: First, some students may have had few meaningful relationships with adults in their lives, and turned to their teachers to fill important supportive roles. Second, many students signaled an awareness that having friendly relationships with teachers had instrumental value and could help them get better grades. Certainly this was another example of how their middle-class "adult-handling skills" could benefit them.

Several students said their favorite teachers were the ones who "knew them well." As Sharon described a favorite teacher, "She's like a great teacher—a great person." Other students nicknamed their teachers. Most telling were the focal students' responses to an interview question during their senior year that asked what advice they would give incoming freshmen regarding their relationships with teachers.

I would tell them definitely to build a strong relationship with your teachers, because even when you get into college, having a relationship with a teacher—it can even give you better grades. (Sharon, Interview 4/30/03)

Be nice . . . talk to them . . . I think teachers are some of the most *fascinating* people ever. I *loved* getting to become friends with my teachers . . . Because then you get to understand where they're coming from, and why they—like grade things the way they do, and why they like—take certain things higher than—other things. (Sofia, Interview 7/9/03)

Don't be a smart aleck! . . . If you *try* to get on with your teachers, you're going to get such better results . . . Just be nice to your teachers . . . they'll help you out, they really will. (Julie, Interview 5/12/03)

Instead of becoming friends with everybody else and becoming that popular kid, become friends with your teachers, because they're the ones who are going to get you through. I mean, your friends aren't going to get you a good grade, your *teachers* are going to give you the good grade by your talking to them, instead of your friends. (Kevin, Interview 5/14/03)

Teachers responded to this push for personalization in a variety of ways. Some teachers commented on how students had "so many things going on" in their lives, that many of them were "very needy," with "really serious issues." Some teachers capitulated to this student push for personalization, and used it to engage students in their classes. Others commented on the added pressure it created for them. One said, "You have to like them and then if you like them, they'll decide they like you and then they'll learn. If they don't like you, they put up a wall."

Researchers have commented on a historical trend whereby students and teachers in particular kinds of classrooms establish a kind of "conspiracy of the least" where they allow their social interaction to create "a facade of orderly purposefulness" (Sizer 1992a, 156). Stout refers to the new teacher-student relationship as "let's be friends" (Stout 2000, 152). What seems to be new here is these students' explicit awareness of the instrumental value of personalized relationships with their teachers.[4]

Sources of Grade Inflation: "Building Up" and "Padding" Assessments
Burnham students and teachers alike acknowledged that there was grade inflation at the school and agreed that it was especially common in higher-level classes. A senior male named Jeff Kalmakoff reported that it seemed to be expected that the majority of students would get A's and B's in their classes: "And, like, if the average on a test was a D, then they'll [the teachers] automatically give, like, extra credit."

I interviewed Jeff Kalmakoff during the first year of the study, and it quickly became apparent that he had a critical perspective on such issues in the school. He talked about how students constantly exerted pressure on teachers, how many teachers were "intimidated" by "high-profile" students, and how, consequently, teachers "built up" their grades.

> JK: I just think teachers are afraid to give bad grades anymore. I don't think bad grades are given . . .
> PD: I know. I wonder if it's also because the teachers want to help students get into college?
> JK: It's almost, like—and a lot of this stuff kind of ties into that as far as the cheating and everyone joining clubs and the reason why discipline isn't taken—people violate the drug and alcohol policy is because it's kind of like kids are trying to get into college and that's why they're in high school, kind of like teachers recognize that. (Interview 5/23/00)

During his senior year, David Sterling attributed the growing number of valedictorians each year of his high school career to grade inflation.

> I look at our classes that I'm in, and, you know, I've got a lot of classes where the lowest grade's an 83 percent. And, you know, I don't mind—our

GPAs look good. It's just, that's not how it is real life. In real life people fail, you know. So that's what I think it's a sign of. I think it's also a sign that we have some really, really bright kids here. (Interview 5/12/03)

EXTRA CREDIT. Extra credit was a major source of grade inflation and most courses allowed students numerous opportunities to earn it. One science teacher gave each student three bathroom passes for each nine-week marking period. If the passes went unused, the student could turn them in at the end of the marking period for extra credit. Other teachers gave extra credit for attending school athletic events and participating in certain prosocial activities, such as the school food drive. Even so, students seemed to constantly desire more. This was especially true in science, where one teacher told me that "students want extra credit for everything . . . they always ask for extra credit, they want to do more work than was originally assigned to try and make up points." At the beginning of a German class, we observed a student exclaim, "Frau, me and Rob spoke German at the prom!" Another student immediately interjected, "You're just trying to get extra credit." One of many ironic moments of the project came when a female senior student offered to share a paper she had written for her science class categorizing students at WBHS; her teacher had suggested she discuss it with me for extra credit. The adroitness with which they identified openings to argue for extra credit opportunities to teachers, such as the quote from Nuako when he argued for extra points in Mr. Richards's class, suggest the extent to which they saw their education as a commodified venture, and extra credit as a credential on sale. These students' market orientation meant that they were very good at spotting—and negotiating for—bargains.

Survey responses to the question, "Is extra credit important to you? Y/N If yes, why?" were illuminating in several ways. First, 74.5 percent of students answered affirmatively. Second, a striking number of the positive responses mentioned "need":

It helps if you need a better grade. (ninth-grade European American female)

Because it helps to "fluff" up your grade at the end of the quarter to get yourself where you need to be. (eleventh-grade European American female)

Because it is imperative to receive good grades. (tenth-grade European American male)

It keeps me from having to worry about my grade because it "cushions" my grade in some classes. (tenth-grade African American female)

In some classes, I need to raise my grade quickly. (eleventh-grade European American male)

Because if I mess up on a quiz or test I would like to try and earn back some points. Also it keeps me busy and I feel so good about myself when I accomplish a lot of work without having to do it. (tenth-grade European American female)

I'm serious about my grades. (ninth-grade European American female)

This last comment succinctly captures these high-achieving students' overwhelming orientation toward assessment and grades. Other students exhibited a more cynical attitude towards extra credit. A student who replied that it was not important explained:

Because I view it as a form of making up for not doing the work the first time. Much like cheating. (tenth-grade European American male)

Most importantly, the survey revealed significant gender differences as to how students regarded extra credit. Female students were far more likely than male students to say that extra credit was "important" to them (81.6 percent compared to 66.1 percent). This gender difference is likely related to many female students' deeply internalized expectations for individual success discussed in the previous chapter, and consequently, their greater immersion in cultures of competition in the school and beyond. This theme is elaborated in the next chapter.

GENEROUS CURVING AND ROUNDING. Many Burnham teachers adopted generous test curving and rounding practices, which also artificially inflated student grades. These teachers reported that students frequently asked them whether or not they "rounded up," and if so, under what circumstances. While the social studies department's assessment software program automatically rounded up grades of .5, several teachers admitted that they would, under certain circumstances, round up grades of, for example, 89.1. I asked Neal Richards to give an example of those circumstances.

If a student would have an 89.1, let's say, and this is my philosophy, there's really nothing that says I can or can't do this, I tell them it's at my discretion. If they've consistently done all of their homework, which is not a problem in the enriched class, if they do their homework, they tried, you know, what I tell them, if they're not a pain in the butt, the colleges look at an A— a lot higher than they look at that B+. (Interview 2/8/00)

At the end of a marking period in January 2000, Neal Richards showed me the grading sheets for the enriched global history class, which he had just turned in. I pointed to the grade of Stephanie Johnson, a white female student, which was printed on the sheet as 89.4: B+. But the B+ had been crossed out an A— had been written in.

PD: What's this here?

NR: Now here, I rounded this one up to an A—. The computer automatically rounds up with a point-five. But this is a point-four, and it probably comes from a couple of points that she didn't get on an essay during the quarter. But this kind of grade difference makes a big difference to the colleges. So I rounded it up. (Interview 2/8/00).

Nuako's family moved to Toledo in the middle of his junior year so his father could take an administrative position at the University of Toledo. I went to Toledo at the end of Nuako's senior year to hear his impressions of the differences between his urban high school there and Burnham.

PD: Okay, now let's move back. You have class rank as ninth [here]. Does that make you a valedictorian?

NK: No, it doesn't. Valedictorian at our school is only the first place person, and the salutatorian is the second place person. Burnham had, like, twenty?

PD: Forty this year.

NK: There's forty this year?

PD: Forty.

NK: Forty above a four-point?

PD: Forty.

NK: [Laughing.] That's ridiculous! . . . Because at Burnham, there's like, everyone can have above a 4.0, if you really—I wouldn't have even bothered going to school. But valedictorian's just that one person, that's the way I think it should be. I don't think it should be like the top forty [chuckles again] people in the school.

PD: Right. Well, let's talk about that for a minute. Um, I mean, did you notice how the teachers—talk about some of the extra-credit opportunities at Burnham.

NK: Oh, they really padded you up there.

PD: They padded you?

NK: Yeah. Really. I don't know if it's because I haven't had any extra credit at this school at all. Like, Burnham, like I said, they'll help you with the A, if you really want. . . . I mean, like there's extra credit for if you don't go to the bathroom. . . . And I remember, like, a hall pass, if you never use it, you'll get your A.

PD: Do you think the teachers were more lenient?

NK: They were a lot more lenient. It's like—the grade. Like they curved a lot more too, I remember that. (Interview 5/19/03)

Burnham teachers' "leniency" was also a product of the pressure they often endured from parents and administrators to change grades, as mentioned in chapter 2. A science teacher said that she had adopted an approach where "You have to remain consistent, but you always have to be willing to be flexible. And I don't know if that makes any sense." In sum, students' push for good grades and the teachers' accommodations mentioned above made up another kind of hypercredentialing in Burnham's classrooms. Even with this sort of institutional support, however, many Burnham students cheated.

Cheating

Cheating was a serious problem at Burnham and the staff struggled to deal with it. One social studies teacher said of students, "Cheating is instrumental in getting what they want." Another said, "They cheat and they are open about it. They need the points. They need to get in. They need to get into college." A third commented on the kinds of students who tended to cheat the most in school, "It's the four pointers that are cheaters. We've got valedictorians that are cheaters."

The most common cheating practices included directly asking students who had just taken a test about its contents; hiding formulas or answers in scientific calculators and bringing them into a test; and plagiarism (most typically copying and pasting from the Internet). We learned of students purchasing prewritten high school essays on a variety of topics from Web sites such as schoolsucks.com (pricing ranged from $19.97 for prewritten essays to $59.95 for custom-written college essays, with $10.00 for each additional page). We also observed numerous instances of students copying off of each other's tests, worksheets, or homework assignments and accusing each other of cheating.

An anonymous school survey administered by the Student Forum during the 1998–1999 academic year revealed the following:

77 percent of students in the school admitted to having cheated.

65 percent of students said that it was not dishonest to witness someone cheating and not report it.

55 percent of students said that if Burnham had an honor code, they would sign it.

35 percent of students said that if they signed the honor code, they would still cheat.

Student comments on the survey included the following:

"An Honor Code and Burnham are contradictory words."

"Cheaters always win. Bending the system is what makes the human race the most advanced."

"Cheating is real life. People who are rich and successful lie and cheat every day."

These data certainly reflect national trends. Academic cheating by students in the United States is at an all-time high (D. Callahan 2004). Eleventh graders were much less likely than ninth graders to say on the survey that cheating was a serious problem at the school (32.8 percent compared to 44.9 percent). It is possible that many of them, after two years of high school, came to the conclusion that it was a legitimate way to help them achieve their aspirations. As Jeff Kalmakoff said, "It's because they don't want to work for their grade and they want to get the best grade they can, which is natural."

However, cheating was also common outside of academics. Notably, 3 percent of students in the Wilton City Schools recently reported taking performance enhancing substances such as ephedra, glutamine, or creatine—a number sufficient to field two football teams (Education Council and Drug-Free Schools Consortium 2003). Pupils outside of the Student Forum and Student Council expressed concerns about cheating in the extracurriculum (such as lying about golf scores in varsity try outs) and athletes violating the school's drug and alcohol policy. Jeff Kalmakoff described the policy, which athletes had to sign as a "joke." He elaborated:

> JK: One thing that has changed since I was a freshman or sophomore and right now when I'm a senior, I can understand some of the corruption that goes on here as far as like with teachers and just with everything. And it's kind of like a lot of this school doesn't make sense and it's, like, frustrating for me.

PD: What do you mean, corruption?

JK: As far as. . . . It almost seems like, the values, no one seems to, I don't know, how much values, I mean, the people here, or how much the right thing to do means to people here. It's kind of like, the honor code when students were considering doing that. We put out, the student body put out the survey and the numbers that came back for the amount of people that cheated.

PD: Yeah. I saw that.

JK: It's just disturbing. And it's kind of like, everyone cheats as well even though, they know it's wrong to cheat. . . . And it's sort of the same with the drug and alcohol policy and over the years there has been, like, numbers of teens and tons of individuals who have been caught abusing the policy, grossly abusing the policy. But yet nothing is done because, oh they're athletes and you know what would happen if on a Friday night half the football team didn't show up for the game. Then the newspapers are going to report it, they'd probably make a big story out of it, and our school would get a bad rap. . . . I mean, it's a known fact we've had a good football team here for the last couple of years, this year they're, like, really good. I mean these are guys I know, not really close, I mean I'm not personal friends with anyone in particular, but it's just like common fact that the football team, they all party every weekend and drink. (Interview 5/23/00)

Students like Jeff commonly criticized the school's handling of cheating and violations of the drug and alcohol policy and bemoaned the number of student "hypocrites" who were able to thrive in the school. A white female senior recalled a mandatory pep rally where the school gave honors out to athletes, and an administrator told the student body that these people were their "heroes" and that they should "look up to them." She recalled, "And I was just stunned. I was like, you know, half the people up there are drunks. And—you know, they're fuck-ups. And that just made me shake my head. Like them telling us that we should live up to *them*."

ADDRESSING CHEATING. Most of the school staff acknowledged that they needed to do something about the cheating problem in the school. Some took great pains to eliminate opportunities for cheating in their classes. In addition, the grassroots community organization Partners for Citizenship and Character sought to raise awareness of ethical and character issues in all Wilton. Principal Cunningham devoted several staff meetings to discuss the cheating problem and appointed an Integrity Committee to develop solutions. The day before the first meeting, in January 2000, a teacher sent a memo to the rest of the staff regarding the cheating problem. The memo argued that an honor code would not work because it was "superficial," was "wholly unenforceable," and smacked of "McCarthyism." It advocated turning to more authentic assessments and eliminating extra credit and participation points. It concluded:

> If administrators were really serious about the issue of cheating, they would spend much more time learning how students are assessed in this school, and they would actively encourage and facilitate the use of authentic, performance-based assessments.

During the meeting, Principal Cunningham said, "I don't know of anything that is more at the root of our job than this." An assistant principal pointed out that the Student Council hoped to have some sort of honor code by finals, but then a female teacher observed that that both the Student Forum and Student Council were made up of a "select group" of students who probably wouldn't cheat, but that the rest of the school was different.

A social studies teacher encouraged his colleagues to come up with "authentic consequences" for cheating. Rather than being given Saturday school for cheating (a behavioral consequence for an academic offense), he advocated assigning a student an F for a marking period for the first offense, and an F for the course for the second. Principal Cunningham responded that they could run into resistance from parents. She said she thought many parents would be in favor of such a solution "up to the point where it impacted their child," then, if their child was caught, they would be against it.

Four months later, Principal Cunningham told teachers in a staff meeting to report all instances of plagiarism to the school administration. She explained that she had registered the school with the Web site plagiarism. org, which allowed all teachers access to the site, which detects plagiarism in student papers. She explained:

> It strengthens us as a school to deal with these issues this way. *Don't* deal with it on your own. We are also going to have plagiarism.org available to all teachers. No other school is doing this—only the University of California system. This will add to the value of our diploma. (Field notes 5/15/00)

Principal Cunningham's last comment suggests her awareness that her approach to dealing with the plagiarism problem would also build institutional capital—as such, it was certainly consistent with the Wilton Way.

At the end of the 1999–2000 school year, Jim Greylock lamented, "The problem here is that we should just be able to say that cheating is wrong. But where is the *virtue* here? Why isn't this conversation about what is right and wrong?"

Effects of Hypercredentialing on Classroom Learning: "They're Engaged, but There's Something Funny About Them"

Finally, it became clear throughout the study that emphasis on credentialing interfered with students' engagement with course subject matter. Several teachers worried about the educational effects of students being so "grade conscious." There were many times in Neal Richards's class, as in the instance above, where he tried to initiate a substantive discussion about a historical topic while handing back student tests, quizzes, or papers. His students' attention, however, was invariably on the graded work. In an interview Richards discussed what it was like to teach achievement-oriented students who were so motivated by grades: "I am blessed in that my freshmen . . . are motivated by grades. And no matter what you throw out to them, they are going to do it because they want a good grade. You get increased engagement." Other teachers tapped into student preoccupation with grades in various ways as well, such as the science teacher who, in his introduction of the requirements for a new project, advised students to "start thinking about what kind of grade you're looking for."

However, our observations indicated that students were frequently more engaged with assessments than with subject matter. We observed many instances where once the assessment dialogue was over, and Neal Richards was discussing a historical event or topic, he would be interrupted by a student with a question about assessment. For example, when the class was in the midst of an intense discussion about why, according to Nostradamus, Napoleon was the first Antichrist, a white female student raised her hand and said, "Um, are you going to check our homework?" Neal Richards lamented this kind of student behavior in an interview:

> You'll be in the middle of what you think is this great idea, fifteen minutes into class, you'll get this hand up, and you'll think, oh! comment! good! You know, you'll call on them, and [adopting a high pitched whiny voice], "Are you giving homework tonight?" (Interview 1/22/01)

Such non sequiturs illustrate how many of the achievement-oriented students were in their own little worlds—fixated on assessments in the midst of content-based classroom discussions going on around them. More broadly, they illustrate disjunctions between processes of learning and credentialing.

Many students in this highly competitive class complained when Mr. Stanton, the student teacher, tried to enrich a unit on Napoleon by telling stories of the ruler's personal life, and generally eschewed "touchy feely" activities ("we're wasting time"). In such cases they admonished the teacher to "just give us the notes" (or "information") that they would be tested on. Two white female students shared their approach to the class, which certainly seemed, in Denise Pope's terms (2001), "mechanistic:"

> I never remember anything from the class. I just memorize for the test, and then don't remember any of it at all. (Interview 12/14/99)

> I like that class 'cause I've been acing it all year. . . . Get the notes over with and not listen to the stories. . . . All the information, they want it, get that down! Take the test! Get it over with! Forget about it! (Interview 3/28/00)

Other learning preferences were occasionally evident, however, such as the time a white female student remarked, "I think we should learn an interesting fact about all of these people, like when William the Conqueror's casket was closed and he exploded in pus. It will help us learn everything else better." Nevertheless, Neal Richards lamented his students' lack of intellectual curiosity:

> I've had kids in the past that—just want to learn, you know, like—oh tell me more about that story. Tell me more about that time period in history. Nobody asks that. It's kind of like the class is [changing tone of voice], "Are we done yet? *Please* don't make us learn anything else." And it's odd, out of thirty-nine kids, that *nobody* wants to know more. (Interview 1/22/01)

It is striking that Neal Richards expresses no awareness here of how his own privileging of credentialing over learning contributed to his students' lack of intellectual curiosity. His colleague, June Carroll, commented on what this focus on credentials meant for students in the class: "They're engaged, but there's something funny about them."

Countering Credentialism: Struggles to Preserve Ideals of Teaching and Learning

Several teachers at Burnham expressed concerns to us throughout the study about students' focus on grades and how this affected their overall learning. During the first year of the study a science teacher shared with us her worry about students' preoccupations with grades: "Personally I think there's too much emphasis placed on a letter grade, because a lot of these kids walk away not knowing anything. They worked really hard and they got that A, but they can't apply it." Another science teacher, Sarah Fusako, talked about the differences among students that she saw:

> SF: It's our kids, you know, like I told you about the point hungry enriched kid, there are some that are there because they really want to learn the stuff, and that's so refreshing, and that's a shame that I feel that way.
>
> PD: Yeah.
>
> SF: Because, like, this year, I nominated one of the students for Student of the Month because he's very bright, but when he misses a point, he doesn't argue for the sake of getting a point, he asks how he can understand that better. And I think, gosh, that's really nice. Then I thought, no, that's not right. Because it should be the exception, the kid who just argues, argues, argues over a point for the sake of a point. But it's not that way. (Interview 5/23/00)

Finally, an art teacher explained that she frequently had to deal with "competitively minded" students who came into her classes and want her to tell them exactly what she wants so they "jump through the hoop and get the A." She said she routinely told such students, "Well, this approach is not going to get you there because I want you to think."

Some teachers took steps to counter the school's emphasis on credentialing. For example, the English department had regular conversations about the perils of overemphasizing grades and credentials and developed innovative programs to instill in students a "love" of reading and fluency in writing. At the end of each school year, Jim Greylock gave those students whom he felt demonstrated true intellectual curiosity T-shirts with Aeschylus' epigram, "Wisdom through suffering."

David Sterling's parents themselves expressed concerns in an interview about the school's overemphasis on credentialing. Susan Sterling said, "Despite the fact that our kids are really good students, we're not driven by grades." Michael Sterling added, "I think my focus has been more on not on 'you have to get good grades,' because there's so much pressure, because I think the kids feel so much pressure to get good grades. But we really do lose track of what sometimes we're trying to learn." David's parents recounted an exchange with one of David's middle school teachers to illustrate their concern. They had noticed that David was struggling to make connections between concepts in his algebra class, so they made an appointment with the teacher. They said the teacher's response, in effect, was, "Well, he's getting an A, what's the matter?"

We also spoke with several students who had skeptical view of hypercredentialing at Burnham. One white female AP student said, "I was pressured to take enriched chemistry, like, 'colleges will be looking for it.' I think the whole point is to take what you're interested in, but you have to do all this other crap for your resume. It's frustrating." All of these people expressed concerns about the emphasis on competitive success in Burnham, and struggled to find ways to preserve ideals of teaching and learning.

Conclusion

The practice of hypercredentialing at WBHS is a logical local response to an intensifying global academic arms race. It is a practical outcome of the community's emphasis on individual advancement and the school's policies of institutional advantaging, parent's proprietary relationship toward the school, students' identities for control and success, and teachers' conceptions of their work as preparing students for higher education markets. Achievement-oriented students' push for "good grades" and the accommodations teachers granted them through ample extra-credit opportunities and generous rounding and curving practices make up another key linkage that further integrates the cultural system as a whole.

These students' highly developed abilities to "get the best grade with the least amount of work" suggest an economic calculus of cost-benefit. Accordingly, one available metaphor for understanding students' preoccupation with extra credit is shopping. "Thrift" is central to an anthropological logic of shopping in the West (see D. Miller 1998), and in this view, extra credit is essentially a credential on sale—a "bargain." As shown in the chapter, many achievement-oriented Burnham students were expert at maximizing their opportunities to obtain such bargains.

In their aptly titled book, *Fraud and Education: The Worm in the Apple*, Noah and Eckstein observe that as the "frontiers of the credentials society" have expanded, so has academic fraud (2001, 17). David Callahan asserts that in the United States, the rise in cheating and fraud reflect "deep anxiety and insecurity" (2004, ix), and is one way "not to be left behind" (p. 224). Most importantly Callahan chronicles the prevalence of cheating at Horace Mann High School and Stuyvesant High School in New York, where distinct cultures of cheating and a "new ethical calculus" had emerged. Indeed, according to the Josephson Institute of Ethics, high school students rank "getting a high-paying job" above being "ethical and honorable" (Josephson Institute of Ethics 2002). The extent to which cheating has increasingly become accepted among certain kinds of students in the United States is illustrated by a quotation from a focus group interview conducted by Donald McCabe that is quoted in Clark's recent book (2004). An adolescent student said:

> I think times have changed. Cheating is kind of considered, I don't know, just a kind of daily thing that's out there, almost kind of acceptable. Teachers know it and students know it. . . . I think grown-ups have gotten a little bit more with-it in terms of knowing that you're just going to kind of cheat. . . . It's almost a big deal if you don't cheat . . . People cheat. It doesn't make you less of a person or worse of a person. There are times when you are just in need of a little help . . . I think people are going to cheat so it will help them to get into an Ivy League school. . . . You can't change that; you can't change people wanting to get an A or whatever. If cheating is going to get you the grade, then that's the way to do it. (p. 153)

In addition to understanding the extent to which cheating has become "naturalized" among students, we also need to understand how widespread hypercredentialing is, and the different forms it takes, because issues of fairness are involved. The net effect of hypercredentialing is that the value of an A from an institution like Burnham may not be equivalent to an A from another institution where hypercredentialism is not as prevalent. Inequities in access to institutions of higher learning could result.

Hypercredentialism can promote poor pedagogy and interfere with students' engagement with learning. Neal Richards's comment that students' motivation by grades meant that they would be engaged "no matter what you throw at them" raises questions about the quality of teaching promoted by hypercredentialism. Regarding the effects of credentialism in general on students, Alfie Kohn asserts that, "We shouldn't be worried that too many kids are getting A's. We should be worried that too many kids think that the point of school is to get A's" (1999, 1). It is noteworthy that according to several teachers, students who did not "play the game" of credentialing were in the minority. Many of them, as chapter 7 shows, disengaged from learning altogether. Next, however, I turn to one of the most important effects of Burnham students' orientation to personal advancement: stress.

Part Three
Costs of Personal Advancement

Chapter Six "Generation Stress" and School Success

✯ ✯ ✯ ✯ ✯ ✯

People need to know what's happening to these kids.
  — *WBHS art teacher*

Student stress has become an increasingly prominent feature of schooling in the United States. David Elkind wrote about pressure for "early educational attainment" over twenty-five years ago in *The Hurried Child*. More recently, Lareau described first graders whose parents were heavily involved in their schooling showing signs of stress. She reported that teachers were noticing more and more students with "nervous problems" (2003, 159). The "successful" students Pope studied lived in a "constant state of stress" (2001, 3). In a recent piece on the pressures to succeed in upper-middle-class America, Sontag described a culture of "ambition but also one of high anxiety that is shaping a kind of generation stress" (2002, 2).

I was aware of some of this literature when I began the research in Wilton. But, like Clark in his study of adolescents near Los Angeles (2004), I was surprised at the prevalence of stress in these young peoples' lives. This book could actually have become an ethnography of stress. That is where the voices, experiences, and concerns of so many of these upwardly oriented young people in Burnham led us. The 2003 WBHS yearbook opened with a two-page frontispiece devoted to student stress. Titled "Stressed out Bears," it read:

> We are all overwhelmed with schoolwork, lack of sleep, and sports. Stress is a natural reaction, but at some point, enough is enough. "Not only do we have to go home and deal with family and friends, but we also have to worry about our homework, projects, and competitions," said junior Erica Thompson. Too much stress can cause many problems now as well as later in our lives.

On the survey, 70.2 percent of students reported that they were stressed out "frequently" or "all the time." Study data clearly showed that these achievement-oriented students' unceasing attempts to control their educational experiences, get good grades, and acquire competitive credentials exacted a high cost in terms of stress and fatigue. There were significant gender differences in terms of reported stress, as female students were much more likely to report high levels of stress. These are explored in detail below.

This chapter attempts to paint a comprehensive picture of stress in the lives of achievement-oriented Burnham students. It discusses sources of stress, how students experienced stress, and the successful and unsuccessful ways they attempted to cope with it. It also discusses how these coping responses changed them, both psychologically and physiologically, and even led to a new anxiety disorder among some students, which the school counselors referred to as "school phobia." Overall, the chapter concludes that habituating to more or less ever-present levels of stress and fatigue was the most challenging component of psychological capital for Burnham students to acquire.

Fatigue

It would not be an exaggeration to say that most of these high-achieving students lived overscheduled lives (see Rosenfeld and Wise 2000). Many juniors and seniors "loaded" the front of their school schedules so they could get "early release" and begin working at a job in the afternoon. The difficulty some students encountered in balancing school and work is illustrated by the following exchange between two ninth graders, which occurred just after their teacher had given them a heavy homework assignment:

> [Audible groans throughout the classroom.]
> TOM: It's high school, guys.
> ASHLEIGH: Tom, shut up. You probably don't have a job. (Field notes 1/25/00)

However, while many of these students said they "had" to work; they often could not articulate what it was that they spent their money on. Some said they "wasted" their money; others spoke of consumer goods that they "needed." One black male senior said, "It's real tough because when you don't have money, it's like there's so much stuff you need."

As a ninth grader, Nuako Konadu told us how he went about balancing school, sports, his job, and his family: "I don't get home very often." For her part, Sofia Rhoades expressed frustration with some of her friends' schedules: "I try to do something with you, I try to like have a good time with you, and you're either at *work,* or you're doing your *homework,* or you're sleeping. You know? . . . It's not worth it." While students had varying degrees of success in coping with such heavy schedules and expectations, fatigue and especially stress were mentioned throughout the study. Many students told us how tired they were throughout the four years of the study. One student in an AP class advised me, "We're tired every day. Ask it on your next survey."

Julie Rice reached a point with her schedule during her senior year where she wrote an editorial about student fatigue, which she sent to the Wilton schools superintendent. In it she argued:

> The teenagers of today lead excessively busy lives. We attend school and complete homework, hold down part time jobs, participate in extracurricular activities, and manage to fit in time for family and friends. Somewhere in our busy lives we must find time to sleep, and recent studies show that the amount of sleep the average teenage student receives is declining steadily.
>
> Recent research conducted at Northwestern University shows that the sleeping and waking patterns of teenagers change dramatically as their "body clocks" (which tell them exactly how much sleep they need) adjust to adulthood. This means that while the average teenager receives five to six hours of sleep per night, they need nine to ten. As a result, many suffer from moderate to severe sleep deprivation, a problem that may result in behavioral and/or mental problems, and academic difficulties including lower grades and shortened retention and comprehension.
>
> It is essential that the school district take note of this problem and remedy it, namely by starting school later.

Social Sources of Stress

When asked on the survey to identify "which of the following stress you out the most," students responded as follows:

40.6 percent	schoolwork
16.4 percent	social life / relationships with people in school
13.8 percent	things at home / family
13 percent	the future / reaching aspirations
5.4 percent	extracurriculars

While students' overscheduled lives brought them fatigue and stress (as explored below), there were other, more social and relational sources of stress that students reported as well. First, the survey findings strongly indicated that isolation seemed to be associated with experiencing high levels of stress.

Aloneness

Certainly as Americans we are accustomed to a degree of independence and "personal space." One late afternoon in Manus in 1995, I was sitting on the rickety bridge going out to one of the outhouses perched over the lagoon. It was my favorite spot to take a break from the intense social bustle of village life, collect my thoughts and watch the sun set over the Bismarck Sea. After a few minutes I saw one of my friends from the village, Pwendrilei Pondraken, approach along the beach. He paused when he saw me, and greeted me, "Matamareila, Peter!"[1] I called back, "Matamareila, Pwendrilei!" He looked at me a moment, seemingly puzzled, then said, "Peter, on dro wian?" (Are you all right?) I replied, "Em nau, yon dro wian. Mi scalim tingting bilong mi tasol" (Yes, I'm all right, I'm just scaling my thoughts). He furled his brow a little, shrugged, and continued down the beach. When Pere men needed to get away, they generally went to sea in their canoes. I think for Pwendrilei it was a little strange to see a person choose to be alone in the village. But I was accustomed to some amount of time alone, as were most of the students at Wilton Burnham. What the study pointed out, however, were the negative effects of too much of it.

Students who spent more time alone during school days were more likely to report high stress levels,[2] as were students who ate dinner with their families infrequently.[3] These findings extend current understandings of the life space of U.S. suburban adolescents. Several researchers have recently commented that the most important characteristic of these young people is their "aloneness" (Csikszentmihalyi and Schneider 2000; Hersch 1998; Nichols and Good 2004). Adolescents in one study reported spending, on average, a quarter of their waking time alone—an amount that can lead to stress (Schneider and Stevenson 1999) and that, according to Csikszentmihalyi and Schneider (2000) would be "not admissible" in many cultural groups. Indeed, the amount of "total contact time" American parents spend with their children has dropped 40 percent over the last thirty-five years (Hewlett 1992); according to one study it is white children from affluent families who spend the largest number of hours on their own each week (Richardson et al. 1989).

Relationships

Several of the focal students told us about stress they were dealing with from home and from various social relationships in and out of school. Nuako Konadu's father and mother worried during his freshman year about his efforts to "fit in" at Burnham. Their concern was that "he might overdo it to the point where it leaves . . . emotional and mental scar[s]." During her sophomore year, Sharon Sosa went through a difficult period with her best friend, broke up with a boyfriend, and continued to struggle to fit in with her mother's side of her family back in the Bahamas. She explained, "They grew up together, so they know each other and they have, like, the close bond, close-knit relationships, while I'm a stranger to them. And they treat me like that." The focal student with the most difficult home situation was Cindi Criswell, whose parents were divorced and ultimately were unable to have her live with them. Cindi's struggles with her home and family life certainly affected her school work, and are taken up in the next chapter.

There was a significant gender difference in students who attributed most of their stress to social life and relationships in school, though not as large as might be expected (18.4 percent of female students and 14.4 percent of male students said their social life and relationships in school stressed them out the most.[4] When we asked one high-achieving student what stressed her out in school, she answered dryly, "There are people here who I find stressful."

Competitive Awareness and Pressure to Succeed

As mentioned in chapter 3, two of the components of psychological capital found among achievement-oriented Burnham students were a keen awareness of competition and deep attachments to personal success. The survey provided evidence that such attributes were associated with high reported stress levels. Students who reported high levels of stress were more likely than those with low levels of stress to report that they were "very much" in competition with other students in and outside the school.[5] Open-ended responses to "other" as a source of stress included the following:

Pleasing myself with my performance in life (ninth-grade European American female)

Not being good enough compared to others. (tenth-grade Asian American female)

All my work and needing 40 plus hours all the time. (tenth-grade Asian American male)

Will I succeed in life? (ninth-grade Asian American male)

Just having time. (ninth-grade European American female)

More specifically, there were also significant relationships between high reported stress levels and several survey questions that were designed to assess the extent to which students were immersed in the culture of competition in school. Students who reported high levels of stress were also more likely to say that extra credit was "important" to them;[6] that Burnham did not have enough ways of "recognizing students;"[7] and that cheating was a "not very serious" or "somewhat serious" problem in the school.[8] A physical education teacher with an abiding interest in overall student wellness expressed concern over the stressful effects of students' constant press for good grades: "You give them a worksheet to do in class, and they say, 'Is this for points? What do I get out of it?'" In addition, students who reported that they "often knew better than their teachers what or how they ought to learn" were more likely to report high levels of stress.[9] This last finding may suggest the stress involved in students' attempts to exert control over their educational experiences by rendering critical judgments of their teachers and their teaching.

The focal students' most stressful time was during their junior year (when the survey was administered). Sharon circled "all the time" on the reported stress item, and when I asked her about it, she said:

ss: Let's see. This year has been the worst year ever in high school, I can tell you that! [slight laugh.]
pd: Yeah?
ss: Normally, freshman year was hard, but it was challenging hard to the point where I worked hard, had long hours, and, like, the product was good. And then this year, it's, like, two steps up. You know, you're a junior and it's not really just one level up, it's like two levels up. And no matter how hard I work, and how many long hours I put in, it's like the product's just not good. . . . I just had my report card and everything, my semester grade, I got a 3.3. And I never, I've never done that before. It's, you know, difficult going from a like a 3.8 or a 4.0 to a 3.3.
pd: And that's what you had, coming into this year? 3.8, 4.0, in there?
ss: Yeah. Yeah, that's what I had coming in. I mean, I didn't expect to do just as good, but I didn't expect it to be as hard. And this is college year, so I'm just worried about, you know, getting into college. I mean, I

know I'm going to get into college, and I don't have to worry about applying until senior year, but, it's just, you know what I mean? This is the
year that they're going to look at, and it's so stressful . . .

PD: Would you say that you're fairly stressed, or anxious, um, do you have
a lot of friends that are? Talk to me about some of that. About how
students—how you and other classmates are responding, in terms of,
you know, just sort of overall well-being?

SS: Me personally? . . . I get to a point where I get really stressed out and,
like, anxiety is just at an all-time high. I can't sleep at night. I'm just
worried about where I'm going and what I'm supposed to be doing. . . .
And I know that I'm doing what I have to do, then, then I just have
to keep checking, you know, the product, and hopefully I'll do better.
(Interview 5/23/02)

Several teachers said that they thought student stress levels had risen over
the last several years. One said, "But now I'm seeing really good students,
you see how stressed out they are. I just wonder, what are we doing?"

Gender Differences in Immersion in Culture of Competition and Reported Stress

Previous chapters have reported on gender differences in orientation to
competition: female students had higher GPAs than male students, seemed
to have more deeply internalized expectations for personal success, and
seemed to be more immersed in the school's competitive routines. This
achievement orientation is likely behind the fact that female students experienced a great deal more stress related to academics. They were much
more likely to report being "stressed out" either "frequently" (64.9 percent of females; 45.5 percent of males) or "all the time" (17.9 percent of
females; 12.3 percent of males) and to identify their schoolwork as the
most important source of stress (48.3 percent of females; 31.6 percent of
males).[10]

The expectations achievement-oriented Burnham female students had
for their own academic performance and their incessant efforts to realize those expectations certainly seem to partially explain these findings.
Being "unable to let up," even in the face of significant stress, suggests
an inner drive and mentality that we are only beginning to understand.
Contemporary writers and researchers have recently turned their attention to the experiences and inner worlds of such achievement-oriented
girls in different domains of activity. Michael Sokolove (2008) recently
reported on the stunning evidence that female athletes are five times more

likely than male athletes to rupture their anterior cruciate ligaments when playing similar sports (such as soccer and basketball). He attributes the difference in part to the "warrior girl" mentality found in many of these athletes—their propensity to play through pain to the point where they put themselves at risk. This is an important area for further research and interpretation (see chapter 8).

Embodied Effects of Stress: What Stress Does to Students

I first became aware of how deeply Burnham students were affected by stress at the 2000 Arts in Action event. As mentioned in chapter 3, this event was held mainly in the Commons, and while most students focused their attention on the "Throw-Down," poetry slam, and the live performances of the jazz band, along the east wall there were dozens of pieces of student artwork on display. I spent most of my time that day, and at subsequent Arts in Action events, looking at these. I couldn't help but notice how much of the visual art powerfully expressed themes of anxiety, stress, failure, loss, desolation, and emptiness. There seemed to be a deep compulsion in these student artists to express their struggles with these issues. Soon after that first Arts in Action event, I interviewed Monica Stabler, who had been teaching arts in the Wilton schools for twenty-four years and helped to design the arts wing of Wilton Burnham. I asked her about a particularly disturbing self-portrait I had noticed. It depicted a disfigured and barely recognizable human face, and was called *Stress Caused by Mr. Street*. She explained that the student had done the painting after being up three nights in a row doing a project for which her teachers apparently didn't give her enough time.

> MS: I'm seeing real pain come out of some of these kids. It's showing itself as, some of it is frustration. Some of it is, they have spoken about feelings of the world being chaotic because of how much is loaded upon them academically. So I went ahead and put the name tag on one of the paintings, it was *Stress Caused by Mr. Street*.
> PD: Yeah.
> MS: Which is a real, now that's a bold thing for a student to do.
> PD: Yeah.
> MS: And for me not to edit it, I wasn't going to chop that up or go back and say, now don't you think you ought to? I was very supportive of the point being expressed. Because people need to know what's hap-

pening to these kids. So I've taken spontaneous painting activities and her painting is one of them, and. . . . we were just starting a conversation about how much we load kids up with assessment all in the same day.

PD: Uh-huh.

MS: Or whatever vehicle that's going to be delivered in. And at a staff meeting I unrolled a [different] canvas and said, what I'm going to show you is a spontaneous painting activity that really taps the subconscious because they don't have time to analytically think through this process. He [the student artist] had come into class having taken three exams in a row. I want you to look at this. There were gasps—horrendous.

PD: Really?

MS: Horrendous. I saw no eyes, the blankest expression on the face, but it was a face. And the colors were all muted and dark, they weren't dark, they would be dulled, like their senses had been dulled. And they were in control of their colors and mixing and what they made that image into. (Interview 6/1/00)

Much of the student artwork displayed at Arts in Action and published in *Solstice,* the school literary magazine, also expressed deeply felt senses of stress, angst, and ennui.

In the previous chapter, Nuako said that in studying for science tests, "It's like you become a different person, you're so stressed out." During the study, we actually learned of two young women whose body chemistry had been affected by high stress levels. One was Julie Rice.

Because of what we had been learning about the prevalence of stress in the school, when I interviewed the focal students during the spring of their senior year I included a question about their overall wellness. I asked them how they were doing in terms of their mental, spiritual, and physical health. Julie said her mind was good, and that she had been reading a lot more, which she thought calmed her down, because things had been so "crazy" that spring. She said, "Things were just so stressed out, with college and everything, that I really didn't have time to do things for myself." She explained that the stress was worst when she had begun working as a waitress at Bob Evans, a regional family restaurant chain, on Mondays, Thursdays, and Saturdays from 5:00 p.m. to 9:00 p.m., mainly to cover the insurance for the car her parents had recently bought her. She explained that her stress was the worst in January and February when she was also involved in two school plays, *Cinderella* and *Steel Magnolias.*

JR: I would come home from play practice, do my homework, eat, maybe get online for half an hour, and then go to bed. And I was getting to bed at, like, 11:00, 11:30 every night, and I was tired all the time, and I had so much to do, getting to classes.

PD: Getting up at 6:30 still?

JR: Getting up at 6:30, not getting a lot of sleep. I had a lot of projects to do for Government [class]. So, I would say that January and February my stress was really high . . .

PD: Okay.

JR: Uh . . . do you want to know this? I don't know. It's kind of weird. Um, I had to go see the gynecologist.

PD: Uh-huh.

JR: Because of all the stress, my period was—really weird.

PD: Really.

JR: I was having it—I'm still having it every three weeks.

PD: You're having your period more frequently?

JR: Yeah. I've had it six times this year already.

PD: And what did the gynecologist say?

JR: She said it was—she said it was probably due to the stress. Just—due to all the stress. So I'm on the pill now! [nervous laugh.] (Interview 5/12/03)

Julie explained that her gynecologist had prescribed birth control pills to try to normalize her cycle. She said that the pills made her feel hungry, but she couldn't eat a lot because they also made her feel sick. Overall, Julie, who was a devout Christian, said she thought that the remedy "added to the stress."

Anna Norquist, a white female recent graduate of WBHS, adopted a raw foods diet in college, in part because of what her body had gone through in high school. She said her body had been "really taxed" at Burnham because of her schedule (she was a high-achieving student and very involved in sports) and her diet (she drank lots of coffee—two of the cafeteria cappuccinos per day). When she got to college, she said, her "adrenal glands were just shot," and she "couldn't handle stress anymore." So after consulting with several doctors as well as people at the health-food store where she worked, she decided to go to a raw foods diet, " just to detox." She said that other than a juice fast, it would be the "fastest way to get all pollutants" out of her system.

Julie's and Anna's experiences point out the profound ways in which their bodies bore the costs of the overscheduled and high-pressure lives they led while at Burnham. The attempts of young people to cope with such stress in their lives is taken up next.

FIGURE 3 Callie Herman, drawing of a skeleton (2003).

FIGURE 4   Clarke Buchanan, "Screaming Man" (2003).

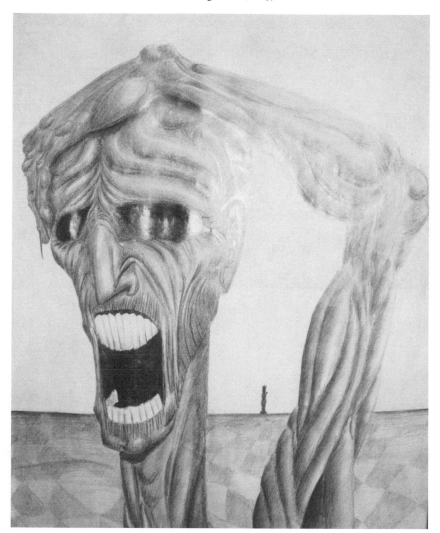

FIGURE 5 Nikki Sorrick, drawing of a woman (2003).

FIGURE 6   Marissa Houk, painting of a woman on her back (2003).

FIGURE 7 Georgina Vanegas-Hernandez, "American Dream" (2003).

FIGURE 8 Maria Stasko, drawing of a girl (2003).

FIGURE 9   Liz Cross, Untitled (2003). Published in *Solstice,* vol. 12.

Attempts to Habituate to Stress and Fatigue

When asked on the survey, "If you do often feel stressed out, how do you cope with it?" students responded in a variety of ways. Many said that they couldn't, which is discussed in the next section. Common coping strategies included talking with friends, listening to music, being physically aggressive (a surprising number of students—both male and female—referred to their punching bags at home), crying, sleeping, and taking medication (such as antidepressants):

> Beat things up. (ninth-grade European American male)

> Punch my punching bag. (eleventh-grade European American female)

> I usually take a time out and read or go outside and run or play soccer or basketball aggressively to help reduce it. (tenth-grade European American female)

> Praying, crying. (eleventh-grade European American male)

> Smoke weed [marijuana]. (eleventh-grade European American male)

> I go to my counselor (not at school, though). Plus I take medication for it too. (ninth-grade European American female)

Most notable were the coping strategies that alluded to a conscious or unconscious ability to adapt to more or less ever-present levels of stress:

> Stop, breath[e], recover, continue. (eleventh-grade European American male)

> It really doesn't matter how I cope. I have a life to live, and things to do. So there isn't much time to "cope." (ninth-grade European American female)

> I don't, I just keep going. (twelfth-grade European American male)

> I deal with it by playing sports and filling my need for competition because it relaxes my mind. (ninth-grade European American male)

> I try to just take a few minutes to remind myself why I have to do well and that it will be easier soon. I will try to do one thing during that time that

I enjoy. For example, try to go to bed early, listen to music, watch a TV show, or something like that. (eleventh-grade European American female)

Julie exhibited another means of coping with stress when she breathlessly told us during her junior year, "I made Allegro [a select choral group]! That was a nice relief of stress. Because sixteen people tried out, and they only took seven." Such a quote suggests that one way to relieve stress was to achieve further. As a junior, David Sterling expressed impatience with fellow students who complained about being stressed out:

You have to learn to deal with stress. Because stress is going to be a part of your life . . . You are always going to have the project that needs to get done . . . the speech that you're going to need to make in front of your co-workers, or in front of your boss . . . There's always going to be stress, you need to work through it. (Interview 5/24/02)

But most students struggled to adjust to the stress of the Burnham environment and the pressures of their internalized (self-imposed) expectations. A sample of their survey responses follow:

I have been trying. Nothing works. I try hard but if I don't "get" to where I'm supposed to then I try not to let it bother me. The things that stress me out put too much pressure/judgment on me. (ninth-grade European American female)

I have a difficult time dealing with my stress based on the fact that I run every day in track, which over-exercises my body, making me more stressed, then I go home and do homework. So the only way I could deal with my stress is to take a break from it, but I can't because I'll either get a bad grade or be kicked off the track team. (ninth-grade European American female)

Look at people who have it worse than me and I feel better about my life. (eleventh-grade European American male)

I tend to not handle my stress the right way, it continues to get at me and it makes myself sick. I just recently started this year going to a counselor to deal with what's troubling me right away. (ninth-grade European American female)

Every day, I cope by eating or working out. (eleventh-grade European American female)

I don't. Skipping school is my only escape. (tenth-grade European American male)

The physical education teacher quoted earlier in the chapter said that when she asked students on informal wellness surveys how they "managed" stress, a common answer was "drugs"—specifically, marijuana.

The 2003 Primary Prevention Awareness, Attitude, & Use Survey, an anonymous questionnaire administered to 4,772 students in the Wilton schools every four years, indicated that alcohol was the most popular drug used by students (23 percent of ninth and tenth graders and 40 percent of eleventh and twelfth graders reported that they drank regularly [at least once a month]), followed by marijuana (used at least once a month by 12 percent of ninth and tenth graders, and 21 percent of eleventh and twelfth graders) (Education Council and Drug-Free Schools Consortium 2003). Several students, however, estimated that between 50%–75 percent of their peers regularly drank or used marijuana several times a month. During the study, students and teachers also reported on the rising use of ecstasy, as well as the common selling and purchasing of Adderall a frequently prescribed drug for ADHD. Finally, school-sponsored attempts to help students deal with stress were not always well conceived. In February 2003, students were given a document titled "Stress Hurts," which explained "effects of stress" and "common methods to reduce stress." The first example of "negative stress" listed was "getting poor grades," followed by "death of a parent or loved one," and "illness or surgery."

Chronic Mental Health Problems and "Stress Disorders": The Appearance of "School Phobia"

As in virtually any high school in the United States, there was a population of students at the school who struggled with mental health problems of various kinds. What was notable about Wilton Burnham, however, were the number and kind of mental health problems that the school psychologist and counselors attributed to adjustment to stresses within the school environment.

Aside from the high numbers of ADHD-diagnosed students (see chapter 2), the school psychologist said that the most common mental health problems she saw in the school were depression and anxiety. Most striking, however, were the rising number of cases of "school phobia" that the school psychologist and intervention assistance team coordinator had seen in recent years. The intervention assistance team coordinator could not tell me where the term "school phobia" came from, but said that she and her colleagues used it to describe the condition where students "can't be here. They'll come in and they'll have an anxiety attack." She said that they had had kids "who literally could not get in the door. If they got in, they left. They could not make it a whole day." The school psychologist described students "so severely stricken with depression or anxiety that they're unable to attend school." The school psychologist said that the condition led many parents to seek a doctor's referral for home tutoring. She said that during the 2001–2002 school year, she had received seven referrals for home tutoring, five of which were for students with diagnoses of depression and anxiety. Clearly more research is needed on "school phobia"—its prevalence, as well as the origins of the debilitating depression and anxiety that characterize it.

Conclusion

The emphasis on competitive success in Wilton, in Wilton homes, and at WBHS, made for a pressure-filled environment. Accordingly, achievement-oriented Wilton youth, especially young women, struggled to adapt to more-or-less constant levels of stress and fatigue. This chapter attempted to paint a comprehensive picture of the sources of stress in the lives of young people in Wilton. For example, the survey brought to light evidence that spending an inordinate amount of time alone or without regular family contact is stressful—a finding potentially of interest to professionals in adolescent development, social work, and family social science. Interpreted in light of the book's cross-cultural perspective, this finding raises the question of whether adolescent youth in this sort of suburban U.S. setting have adequate meaningful social contact with their families and caregivers.

More importantly, the survey suggested that students who assert greater control over their schooling and are more immersed in competitive routines of the school experience higher levels of stress. In other words, students who do many of the things that are expected of "successful" students are likely to experience high levels of stress. The voices, experiences, and artwork of students struggling to cope with stress suggest that some of them feel trapped by their circumstances.

Recent research on stress using the experience sampling method and collection of cortisol in one upper-middle-class community found that high school students had the highest stress levels in the community. In looking at cortisol values across the day, the study found that high-stress teens do not get adequate hormonal recovery at the end of the day, which can affect levels of thought and emotion (Schneider 2003).

In addition, it could be the case that these young people have not reached a stage of cognitive development sufficient to enable them to handle their pressure-filled, overscheduled lives. Recent research on the adolescent brain has shown that the prefrontal cortex, a center of judgment, is still undergoing such rapid change into late adolescence that Laurence Steinberg, a leading adolescence researcher, likened the situation to one in which "one is starting an engine without yet having a skilled driver behind the wheel" (2005; see also Giedd 2004; Thompson 2000). While more research is needed to adequately understand linkages between adolescent brain development and behavior, it is possible that young people at this age are not cognitively equipped to temper their efforts or trim their schedules in the interest of their overall well-being.

This may be especially true of young women. Lyn Brown (1998) recently wrote of the struggles of girls from different class and racial backgrounds to discern what it meant to be a "good girl." She said that many of those with a somewhat privileged background conceived of success in terms of "radical individualism," and the "embrace of competition" (p. 205). We certainly need more measures of how males and females experience physiological stress differently, so we can get beyond differences in how they talk about stress.

While it is clear that habituation to stress and fatigue is an adaptive trait in this environment, it is possible that the implications are more far-ranging. The biological anthropologist Emily Martin (2000) recently argued that current cultural shifts associated with neoliberalism are forging new conceptions of "fitness" that are aligned with changes in the kind of person and worker that is seen as desirable in today's rapidly changing and fiercely competitive corporate world—including "continuous flexibility" (p. 136).

Achievement-oriented young people may be increasingly aware of how such "fitness" is required for success. David Brooks concluded the following from spending time with students at Yale:

> The system does encourage students to exert themselves. Actually, it demands it. As one student at the Yale political union astutely noted, the system doesn't necessarily reward brains, it rewards energy. The ones who thrive are the ones who can keep going from one activity to another, from

music, to science, to sports, to community service, to the library, and so on without rest. To get into a competitive school, you need a hyperactive thyroid as much as high intelligence. (2002, 4)

Wilton Burnham's awareness of the importance of this sort of "fitness" was evident in the Student Wellness Strategy it developed during the study. One component was to open up the new four-thousand-square-foot strength and power room to all students and to make a strength coach available to them. The director of the Co-Curricular Office explained the decision as, "This is leave no kid behind. We don't want any kid feeling uncomfortable coming to Burnham."

As Varenne and McDermott (1998) showed in their work, such success for some is predicated on failure for others. The next chapter shows how many students responded to Burnham's competitive environment in negative ways: by disengaging from their academics, being uncivil to their classmates, and becoming marginalized.

Chapter Seven Alienation, Marginalization, and Incivility

Any description of a culture of competition would be incomplete without including the experiences and perspectives of those who do not succeed. As mentioned in the introduction and at the end of the last chapter, American education has been criticized for its historical commitment to a system whereby the success of the few are contingent on the failure of the many (Henry 1963; Varenne and McDermott 1998). Several years ago, the Spindlers (1998) called for investigation into the perspectives and self-definition processes of students who do not succeed in competitive contexts such as Wilton, as well as the extent to which such programming for success raises possible psychosocial costs.

This chapter looks beyond the experiences of achievement-oriented students in an effort to understand other educational and social effects of the culture of personal advancement at Burnham. The voices and experiences of lower-achieving Burnham students point out three entrenched problems related to the school's emphasis on personal advancement: their alienation from learning, incivility, and the marginalization of minority students. Study data suggested that many average and under-achieving students seemed to connect their academic disengagement to the competitive emphases of the school, feeling "defeated," "alienated" from the school, and ultimately deciding not to "play the game." This chapter describes the problems of student harassment and vandalism that intensified during the study and suggests that they were linked to the frustration many average and below-average students felt toward the school and its hierarchical ranking system. Finally, the chapter discusses the social and academic marginalization of African American students within the school—their struggles to "fit in" and the specific ways in which their academic needs went largely unmet.

This chapter draws on the experiences of the four focal students who were identified by teachers in their freshman years as "under-achieving:" Sophia Rhoades, Bryan Bowen, Cindi Criswell, and Kevin Madsen. It also includes numerous other data sources, including results from a bullying and harassment survey with which I assisted the school in 2003.

Barriers to Effort: Academic Disengagement at Wilton Burnham

Under-achieving Burnham students identified multiple factors that shaped their approach to school including their own lack of effort, family circumstances, classroom climate, and the intense culture of competition within the school.

Student Awareness and Explanations

In interviews, Cindi, Sophia, and Kevin all acknowledged that they were not trying their hardest in school. Kevin got very poor grades his freshman year. During his sophomore year, I asked him if he was still not trying as hard as he could.

> I don't know, I totally don't study for tests. . . . If I study more I could get A's on the tests, I could maybe end up with a 4.0, but I really don't feel like doing that all the time. I just . . . school's not my thing at all. Not at all. (Interview 2/9/01)

During his junior year, Kevin said, "school's just school," and in his senior year, he said he was looking forward to "just getting out of here, getting on with my life, what I've always wanted to do, just get a life to myself, basically."

Sophia Rhoades never strived to be an A student. She said that when she received tests with a B back, she would say to herself, "Okay, I got a B. That's good. I never really was like, 'Oh! I have to get that A! I have to do that.'" She explained, "I think in my mind, if I know that I can do something, I don't really need to like—prove it, half the time. I just do it." Sophia's last statement certainly suggests the authority she attributed to herself as arbiter of appropriate effort and academic performance.

Despite the school's emphasis on competitive success, there were all sorts of students that were not dialed into its competitive routines, or even the college admissions process. During a WBHS News segment titled "How much do WBHS students know?" a reporter asked students what "SAT" stood for. One white male student looked momentarily blank and then responded, "Uh . . . students attending a test."

Lack of Social and Family Support

Other students more explicitly attributed their academic struggles to unstable, distracting, or harmful family circumstances. Bryan Bowen, for example, had a very difficult family situation. His father died in 1995, and he had twenty-one half brothers and sisters, none by his mother (with whom he lived). Most of his brothers lived in Detroit and other cities in Michigan, where some of them had been involved with gangs. One was nearing the end of a prison term for murder. Bryan said he worried about gangs getting in the way of his schooling. Even though Bryan said he was not in a gang, he said everyone he hung around with was "Crip-affiliated":

> Blood is red, Crip is blue. You'll never see me with red on, all my friends would be like, what are you doing, blah, blah, blah. . . . Like my brother was in a gang, but I ain't going that route. I just hang with people, I mean I talk to them and stuff and play basketball with them. But as far as, I mean, you know, being in a gang, it's not me because I've seen where it got my brother and I'm not trying to be there, you know. (Interview 4/11/00)

Cindi Criswell endured the most difficult family problems that we encountered during the study. As mentioned in chapter 2, over the course of the study Cindi's parents divorced and she moved three times. Her father could not afford to have her live with him, and her mother kicked her out of her house during her junior year for fighting with her younger brother and threatening her twin sister with a knife (Cindi acknowledged having a "violent side"). Cindi's appearance could be described as goth (slang for "gothic"). She always wore black clothes and adorned herself with various chains and bracelets, many of which had spikes on them. She had multiple piercings visible on her ears and face, always wore very dark eye shadow, and sometimes had dark designs on her face.

Cindi worked several jobs during her years in high school and moved frequently between the houses and apartments of her mother, father, and several friends. At one point, she said, "I'm exhausted, every minute of every day." When we shadowed Cindi during her freshman year, she frequently had her head down on her desk in class and did not participate in class discussions. She failed all of her classes that year. During her sophomore year, her relationship with her mother became increasingly strained and her father was evicted from his apartment for not paying rent. When we asked at the time her how she was doing, she said these family problems were affecting her approach to school: "No, I'm not doing very well. Because of all the stress in my life, like, personally it's really reflected in my school because I can't concentrate in my classes." The following year she said:

Because I move around so much, it's very stressful for me—to be in school. And actually a lot of people are surprised with how much I do move around, that I'm actually still in school right now. . . . With everything going on in my life right now, it's too stressful for me to have to worry about school, and I've been working so hard, and all of my teachers just keep screwing me over that it—well, it drives me more to a point of insanity, because I'm working so hard for something and no one is acknowledging it at all. (Interview 5/29/02)

Bryan's and Cindi's unstable family circumstances certainly distracted them from their schoolwork. However, certain teachers explicitly mentioned how the school itself was culpable for the disengagement of many students.

Alienation from Learning: The Turnoff of Competitive Academic Success

One notable pattern that emerged from the data on under-achieving students was how many of them seemed to connect their own academic disengagement or underperformance to the competitive emphases of the school. A science teacher told us about a student who was "smart as a whip," but had failed every quarter because "she just doesn't want to play the game." Two teachers perceived a decline in the academic engagement of average students during their tenure at Wilton Burnham. One said, "I'm seeing more apathy than I saw in the first ten years that I taught." The African American teacher of marketing education (one of the vocational education programs in the school) told April Peters:

They are aware of the competition but they choose not to participate in the competition. The funny thing about my students is they don't mind a D or an F. D is *passing*, and for *them*, D is *fine*, because they are indeed passing. If it's an F, oh well, they'll deal with that. You know, their main concern is mom and dad at home, and if mom and dad are sometimes okay with an F, because they're at least coming to school, that's fine. Again, I deal with those at-risk kids who are not doing school well, so academics are not really that important to them. (Interview 5/4/01)

The marketing education teacher's use of the term "doing school" (the title of Pope's book [2001]) indicates how integral academic competition is to the education provided at Burnham.

Interviews with members of the Counseling Center suggested that the competitive emphasis of the school diminished the motivation of special education students. They referred to a pattern of special education students refusing to come to them for help. The intervention assistance coordinator explained how these students seemed to interpret the rules of competition:

> For some reason the kids I work with feel like they have to do it themselves: "I have to do this alone." I think there's something about the competition that leads to the idea that they have to do it alone. Like they think that "I'm competing against," you know, those who are competing. When you're in competition, you do it by yourself. (Interview 6/5/02)

A special education teacher suggested that seemingly as a result of the school's emphasis on competition, "there are a lot of kids here that feel very defeated." Such students will "back away," she said, because, "they've been defeated so many times, why should they go up and get defeated some more, you know, get beat against that wall?"

This trend, and particularly the use of the word "defeated," suggests the extent to which even lower-achieving students were unwittingly caught up in the school's system of competition. In 2005, Nicole Gnezda, an art teacher at Burnham, published a book entitled *Teaching Difficult Students: Blue Jays in the Classroom*. Drawing in part on her experiences at the school, she wrote, "Competition in the classroom may motivate some students to excel, but it also motivates many to give up" (2005, 61). The self-portrait in figure 10, displayed at one of the school's Arts in Action events, shows the centrality of "failure" to this white male student's sense of self. Further effects of the school's emphasis of competition on average and lower-achieving students, including how they regarded they regarded their classes and their peers, are discussed in the pages that follow.

"Passive Noncompliance" and Other Distractions in the Disengaged Classroom

Several teachers commented on the extent to which students in their mainstream and lower-level classes seemed withdrawn or disengaged from learning. When I asked Gene Foster, a math teacher who had been at Burnham since its opening, whether he had noticed any changes in students over the years, he said, "Ah! I have . . . and I've given it a name: "passive noncompliance." He elaborated:

> They basically withdraw from the work or they may do enough work to get by with a passing grade . . . But as far as extending themselves, or being challenged or motivated by learning—that doesn't exist. (Interview 5/10/00)

FIGURE 10 Clarke Buchanan, "Failure" (2003).

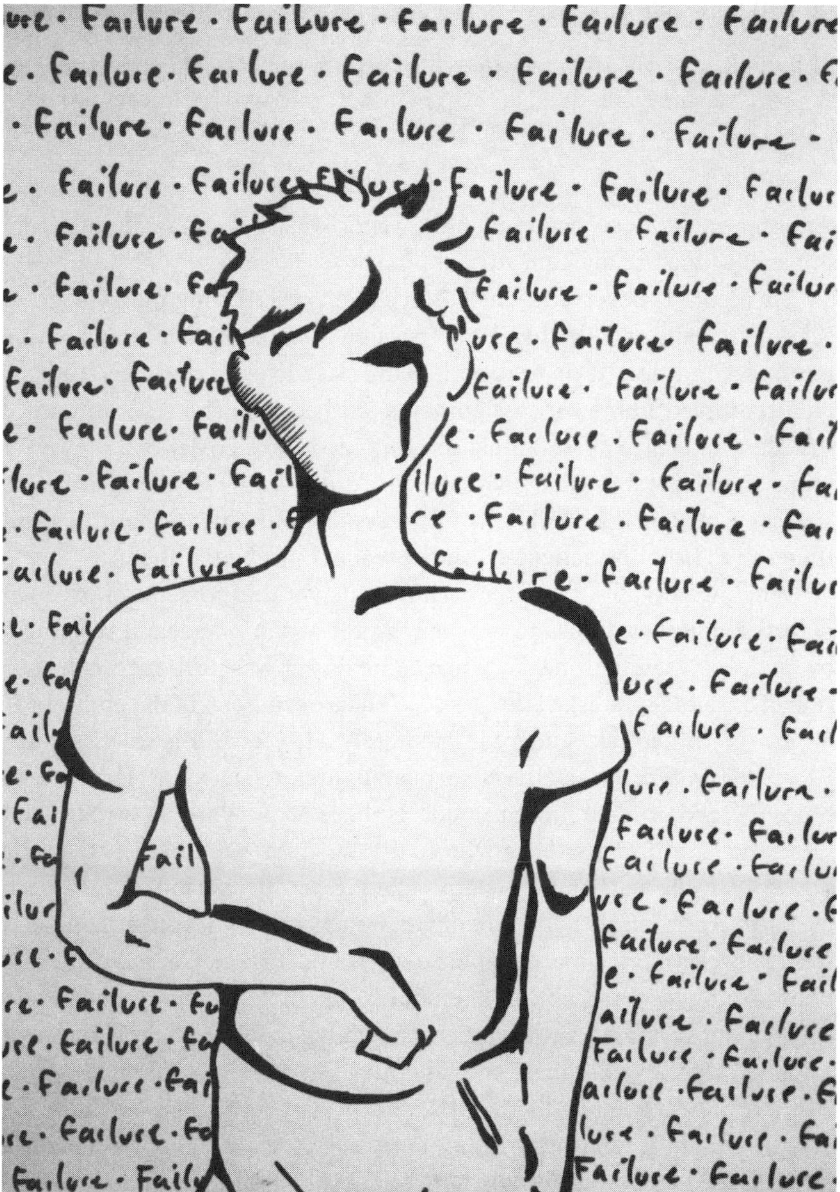

When I recounted Gene Foster's term to a science teacher, she picked up on it immediately:

> I think passively noncompliant is the best way to put it. They're not outwardly being disruptive, but they're not doing what I, as a teacher, would hope or expect them to do. . . . They're like, "What's the point?" (Interview 5/16/00)

Another science teacher commented, "There's a lot of that really, just kind of passive, don't-really-care attitude" in those classes.

We regularly observed Gene Foster's math class during the 1999–2000 school year and saw firsthand the "passive noncompliance" to which he referred. Cindi and Kevin were both in the class. Every day we saw students fail to complete homework assignments (and be open about it), announce that they had failed a test or quiz, announce to Gene Foster that they were going to fail a test or quiz because they "didn't know jack shit." We also saw students engage in all sorts of horseplay to distract each other and themselves from the activities that the teacher put before them.

What was notable, though, was how much of this horseplay was laden with sexual undertones, and how much of it was initiated, and sustained, by boys. For example, one day when Gene Foster was introducing the notion of binomials, he asked the class, "What are examples of the prefix 'bi'?" One large white male student immediately answered, "Bisexual." As Mr. Foster then tried, amidst the ensuring laughter, to steer the class back to binomials, the student mused aloud, "Is there such a thing as a trisexual?" Other boys, especially those who had long since been banished to the back row by the teacher, incessantly called each other various names, such as "turd tickler," and "butt sniffer." Girls participated in this discourse as well. I observed one draw a graphic depiction of oral sex on her dry-erase board—only to visibly shrink in embarrassment when she realized I had seen it. But the vast majority of the sexually laden banter was initiated by boys. As one white male special education student explained to me, "They're always bugging them [girls] and stuff." One English teacher even caught a male student masturbating in her class. She reported that he finished the task before complying with her demand to stop.

The sexually-laden climate of many mainstream and lower-level classrooms at Burnham certainly interfered with the learning of students who wished to engage with the subject matter. Toward the end of the year, Gene Foster had taken to posting student test scores on a wall of the classroom as a "motivational thing—just to get a little competition going." He said that it seemed to have little impact.

The Discourse of Degradation

The other notable feature of the in-school lives of lower-achieving and less involved students at Burnham was how much they verbally degraded one another. In contrast to achievement-oriented students' cultivation of their "people" skills, these students— male and female, and mostly European American—commonly told each other to "shut up" and frequently pointed out how much of the world and their experiences in it "sucked." Students often unconsciously used this language in talking with me. One Monday when I asked a white male student in Gene Foster's class about his winter break, he replied matter-of-factly, "It sucked. I didn't do anything. Well, I went to a DMZ concert, and my friend got busted for having pot." A white female student similarly replied, "It sucked—I worked the whole time."

We were also struck by how often, in their everyday conversations, students told each other to "shut up." When I asked Kevin what it meant, he said, "It's like, you shouldn't be talking [slight laugh]. Something like that, I guess. Just . . . they [other people] don't really care what you're saying, so just keep your mouth shut." Several teachers said that even though they thought many students did not see it as rude, that they themselves were bothered by it. A science teacher pointed out that "the kids that are the rudest to each other" were the ones in her class who "struggled the most." She added, "But I find that has really been on the rise, just the things these kids say to each other." In Mr. Foster's class, we once saw a student complain about noise coming from an open window during a test. A white male student suggested, "You could just shut the window." Another white male immediately said, "You could just shut your mouth." A science teacher worried about the effect such harsh comments had on students' participation in their classes, "And I think also some kids kind of shut down because they just feel it's not worth putting the effort out, you know, if they've been, you know, if they say things and the kids cut them down."

It is likely that much of this negativity can be attributed to student frustration and even anger at their performance in school. As reported in the previous chapter, a striking number of students reported that they relieved stress by using punching bags. Many students told us about being angry at certain grades they had received—One said she "took her anger" out on the clay in her ceramics class. During Kevin's freshman year, after he failed a math test, he "vented" his anger on the soccer field by knocking out an opponent during a fight. He received red cards (ejections) in his first two games.

In this way, the anti-academic, sexually charged classroom climate, largely established by boys, and the harsh speech directed by students at each other seemed to function as additional feedback mechanisms in the cultural system of the school. Likely originating in these students' awareness of their location in the school's status hierarchy, and amplified by the well-known thrust of peer influence (Harris 1995), they seemed to reify negative impressions students may have had of themselves and the school, and made it easier for them to rationalize disengaging from their classes and contribute to the negative climate themselves. We did see students turn these negative comments on themselves, such as the instance when a white male upperclassman was criticized by his peers for not objecting during a mock trial in his law class. He hung his head and said, "I suck."

A Gendered Tendency Towards Harassment and Vandalism

The school's incivility problem was not limited to harsh speech between students. During the final year of the study, Wilton Burnham experienced a marked increase in reported incidents of student harassment, as well as vandalism and theft. I had been aware of the increasing seriousness of these problems, largely through interviews and observations. This is not to say that we did not learn of many genuine instances of student compassion for others and assorted prosocial behavior. We did. One of the special education teachers recounted a time where she had observed a female senior lecturing several freshman whom she had seen making fun of a special education student with autism. She apparently said to the freshmen, "We don't make fun of people here that have learning disabilities. I'm a senior, and you're freshmen. And you might not know this, but we don't make fun of people." The focal students shared with us their own experiences and aspirations regarding the importance of helping people. During the summer before his sophomore year, Kevin went to South Carolina for a work camp with his church group and helped build a house for a family in need. Julie Rice aspired to become a teacher/missionary and establish a school in an underdeveloped country. During her junior year she served as a mentor for a seventh grader in her church. In general, Julie said, "It's really important to help people and to be a good person."

Harassment and Bullying

Nevertheless, in the winter of 2003, Burnham's harassment and bullying problem reached a point where one of the assistant principals asked me to help the school design a survey to assess the nature and extent of it, and to suggest means of addressing it. The school provided funds for me to hire a doctoral student in my department to design a survey on harassment and analyze the findings. I also put the school in contact with Penn State psychology professor Jeff Parker, a leader on developing anti-harassment and bullying programs in U.S. schools. Jeff Parker came to Wilton in the spring of 2003 and met with WBHS administrators to discuss ways of addressing the school's problem.

The results of the harassment survey were telling: nearly a third (32.8 percent) of surveyed students reported having been bullied or harassed at the school during the previous four weeks; nearly a quarter (23.9 percent) reported having been physically attacked. There were also significant gender differences in the ways in which boys and girls understood and experienced bullying. Notably, boys were almost twice as likely as girls to opine that victims of bullying "bring it on themselves."[1] Also, boys were more likely than girls to believe that bullying makes people tougher and were less likely to believe that bullying hurts people very much. Harassment could take on more subtle and even class-inflected forms in the school. A librarian reported, "We've even had quarters superglued to shelves."

Just after data collection for the study was concluded, the 2003 Primary Prevention Awareness, Attitude & Use Survey was released in Wilton. It revealed important differences in school climate between Wilton middle schools and high schools. It indicated that 62 percent of middle school students and 47 percent of high school students in Wilton agreed that "students in this school treat each other with respect" (Education Council and Drug-Free Schools Consortium 2003). This decline in civility as students move up through the grades begs the question of how students learn to treat each other in this environment.

Vandalism and Theft

Data from the study suggested that student disrespect for school facilities increased from 1999 to 2003 and seemed to intensify during the last two years. When Principal Trent assumed her post in the fall of 2000, she announced at one of the first assemblies that there would no longer be close-in designated spaces for seniors in the student parking lot. The seniors booed her off the stage. Shortly thereafter, seniors urinated through the open window of one underclassman's car and scratched a swastika on another's.

Kevin participated in one of the most dramatic displays of vandalism during the spring of his senior year: He, along with approximately thirty other male students, defecated in a single toilet without flushing. He said he and his friends called the stunt "Poopapalooza." He explained, "That's one of those immature things I've got to be in on. The only reason we got caught was because we were dumb enough to have a sign-in sheet, and we left it on the door of the stall, and then signed it." During the 2002–2003 school year, the school's vandalism and theft problems escalated significantly. The March 2003 issue of the student newspaper detailed rising incidents of theft from student lockers, over $500 worth of library books stolen or vandalized (with pages cut out), fifteen mouse balls taken from school computers, and the destruction and theft student artwork—including an elaborate painting needed for a student's scholarship to an elite art school. There was also a marked increase in the amount of trash on the floors of the Commons and in the locker bays on the second floor. The director of the Counseling Center commented that students showed "no respect for the building," and David Sterling, who by that point was president of the Student Council said "It's pathetic . . . it's all about respect, and they don't respect our school."

The Marginalization of African American Students

The study makes a sociological distinction between voluntary minority students (those who have become minorities of their own free will, e.g. through immigration), and involuntary minority students (those who have become minorities against their will, e.g., through colonization or enslavement; see Ogbu 1978). One of the limitations of the study is the lack of representation of the voices and experiences of Asian American students.

Academics
While the survey analysis did not reveal ethnic differences in academic achievement, it should be kept in mind that the sample of minority students was comparatively small. One clear pattern was that African American students were consistently underrepresented in enriched and AP classes. David said during his senior year:

> I can go through my day and not see an African American kid . . . There just aren't that many African American kids taking high-level classes. And I, I think it's kind of sad. In our AP calculus class, we had forty kids take the [AP] exam. One was black. One. (Interview 5/12/02)

While the African American students we spoke with did not commonly mention discrimination in their classes, qualitative data suggested that they may have been disadvantaged in more subtle ways. When we asked Sofia what it was like to be an African American student at Burnham, she paused, and then said:

> It's kind of strange, I think, because you look around your classroom and there's not many people that are black. You look at the teachers and not many teachers are black either. So you kind of sit there. I think one day in English we were doing something and the teacher never called on me. I don't know why. It was kind of odd. (Interview 6/2/00)

More specifically, study data suggested that some African American students did not adopt many of the same instrumental strategies oriented toward individual advancement as their white peers—especially the "adult handling" and self-advocacy skills that could serve as effective negotiating tools. Sharon Sosa's experience was particularly illustrative of this pattern. During her junior year, for example, she said that her math teacher seemed to always teach to the same small group of white students, who had an ability to continually make themselves front and center in the class. "He would always pick on the same people," she said. She also thought the teacher might have had lower expectations for her and other African American students in the class. She struggled in the course.

Sharon also had difficulty fitting into her AP classes at Burnham, which seemed to take a toll on her in terms of stress:

> And it was so uncomfortable for me. If I'm in an AP class, everybody kind of looks at me like, you know, if I talk, they say, "Does she really know what she's talking about?" And even if I do know what I'm talking about, you know, they give me that look like, you're not one of us. And I'm just so tired of being stuck in that point. (Interview 6/2/03)

College Application Process

There also seemed to be differences in the college application experiences of black and white students; especially in their use of the Counseling Center and their preparation for standardized tests. Again, Sharon's experience was telling. She graduated with a 3.6 GPA but scored a 940 on the SAT. Sharon said she felt "really unprepared" for the college application process, and it is reasonable to speculate that better test preparation might have brought up her SAT score. She did no explicit preparation for the SATs and actually said in an interview that "you have to be rich, you know," to take test preparation courses. The school's Counseling Center likely bears some responsibility for this misconception—it certainly did not serve Sharon well. Sharon felt that the Counseling Center did not provide adequate academic support or help her with her selection of colleges. She said of her counselor, "She would go in and listen to what I was telling her, and she would shake her head, and say, 'Well, I'm sure you'll find a way to fix it.'" She added that the Counseling Center did not give her good advice on what to look for in a college. She said, "They don't tell you good things to look at, as far as class size, or for me, since I'm a minority, the diversity of the school." When we asked Sharon to grade them on how well they prepared her for the college application process she gave the Counseling Center a C−. In his last interview David commented that the Counseling Center "is good for people who don't really understand the system."

"Fitting In"

Several African American students commented on how their ethnicity shaped their experience and status in the school. Sofia Rhoades said that sometimes she felt like she didn't "fit in." Some expressed their frustration that European American and higher SES students thought they were "better" than they were. Bryan Bowen was very aware of this sort of hierarchy at Burnham. He explained to Rich Milner and me:

> BB: When I came here I didn't like it because there are all these rich folks and I'm not that rich. And they're all wearing all these expensive clothes and they think they're higher than people because they've got more money than people. But I just, I try to compete with them, do better than they can because they think they're higher just because they've got more money.
> RM: You try to do better?
> BB: Yeah, like at sports. (Interview 4/11/00)

Other African American students also lamented their collective social status within the school. One told us, "It's the popular people that count here, and we are not popular." Others said they were "tired of being the authority on all black folk," and that it was "hard to mesh" with other students in the school. They also expressed frustration that their music was not played enough at dances and that attendance at a black history assembly had not been required for all students in 2002, given that the school had had a number of incidents of racism that year. African American cultural styles, meanwhile, were freely appropriated by white students, as indicated by peer groups known as the "White Gangsta Rappas" and the "Wiggers."

Achievement-oriented African American students mentioned tensions concerning striving for success in the school while maintaining favorable relationships with other black students: One such student was called "a punk bitch" by his black peers. The African American teachers also had ongoing concerns about their place in the school. Two of them wondered aloud to us if they would "ever see a black person" up on the WBHS Hall of Fame (there were none over the course of the study, and the most recent inductee in 2002 was the director of Co-Curricular Activities—a white woman).

There were occasional incidents of racial discrimination that occurred during the study, and the way the school handled one of them in the spring of 2002 is instructive. During that year there had been a number of incidents involving racial harassment of black students. In May, after several white male students learned that an African American student was dating a white student, they informed the black student that they were going to bring the Ku Klux Klan to the school. A group of African American students met with administrators and staged their own protest in the school by congregating by the railing at the top of the stairs in the Commons—a location where "high profile" and almost entirely white students usually stood. I recall walking through that hallway between classes on that day and seeing a lone African American student sitting in a chair right at the top of the railing. He had a defiant look on his face. Meanwhile, when several African American parents heard about the threat of bringing the KKK to the school they immediately demanded to meet with the school administration. They were granted a meeting with Mr. Welkes. During the meeting, in response to their concerns he commented, "You better get used to it, because we're all niggers out here." The parents were infuriated.

This statement, taken with Sharon's difficulties fitting in to upper-level classes, suggests how race can continue to be hauntingly relevant to the social mobility of African American students and parents. For Sharon, these social and academic stresses built up to the point where during the spring of her senior year she told me, "To be perfectly honest with you, if I had to stay in school much longer, I probably would have had a nervous breakdown." She said that she did not even want to go to Commencement.

Conclusion

The study indicated that the emphasis on competitive academic success and personal advancement at schools like Wilton Burnham has its costs. In addition to the student stress and fatigue described in the previous chapter, other costs seem to include the disengagement of many students from learning, student incivility, and the marginalization of involuntary minority students. These problems raise the question of whether public schools like this one are best meeting the needs of all their students. More specifically, the chapter described the experiences of many students who, seemingly discouraged by the school's competitive emphasis and their position in its resulting status hierarchies, reduced their own academic effort and approached school with an attitude of "passive noncompliance." The climate inside some of the mainstream classrooms seemed to contribute to student academic disengagement, and in this way functioned as a feedback mechanism within the school. The sexually-laden comments, largely from boys, were clearly a distraction in class; and the degrading comments students directed at each other may inhibit their participation in classroom dialogue. Some of this discourse might be seen as a male-dominated, sexually charged, and highly negative version of what Margret Finders (1997) referred to as the "literate underlife" practiced by the "Social Queens" in her ethnography of hidden literacies in a Midwestern U.S. junior high school. More specifically, as Eder (1997) observed in her ethnography of a junior high school that such language use may contribute to the maintenance of power differentials between male and female students.

Cindi dropped out of Burnham at the end of her junior year with five credits (the minimum requirement for graduation was 21.5 credits). At the time she told us, "I'm not a school person. I don't do well in school." Such a statement begs the question of just what a "school person" is, and the extent to which a public high school ought to be able to ensure that all students can be one. In his recent book, *The Road to Whatever: Middle Class Culture and the Crisis of Adolescence,* Elliott Currie (2004) attributed the boredom, anger, and disengagement of many students to their schools' embrace of "neglectful individualism." He argued that such an emphasis "helped confirm their sense of themselves as failures, screw-ups, or outsiders" (p. 192). While more research is needed in this area, it is certainly possible to conclude that the competitive emphases of Wilton Burnham alienate some average and under-achieving students from learning.

The degrading comments students directed at one another were part of a larger incivility problem at Burnham that intensified throughout the study. This chapter described the prevalence of harassment, bullying, and vandalism that became of increasing concern to school administrators. It is possible that these incidents were related to the frustration and anger many average, under-achieving, or low-profile students may have had with their status within the relative ranking system that predominated within the school. In Milner's recent research on high school status relations (2004), he explained student cruelty toward and harassment of one another through the nature of status as a relative ranking, where the total amount of available status within the group is fixed. This may have contributed to an atmosphere at Burnham that led Jim Greylock to say simply, "Civility is dead here." Certainly this incivility, along with the stress and "school phobia" mentioned in the previous chapter, are the sorts of "psychosocial costs" with which George and Louise Spindler (1967, 1998) were concerned.

In the introduction, I mentioned that in Manus in 1995, high school students who openly tried hard in school, spoke a lot of English, wore new Western-style clothes or makeup, and aspired to jobs in town or in the cash sector were ridiculed for acting "extra." I think this criticism was based in students' own frustrations and anger over how school was sorting them into an increasingly class stratified society; those who would gain white-collar employment and live in a town or city, and those who would return to their villages and make their living from subsistence fishing or agriculture.

Over the last thirty years anthropologists and sociologists have shown how such marginalization and sorting practices in schools lead to the disengagement and resistance of many students, and ultimately the reproduction of existing social inequities (Fine 1991; Fordham and Ogbu 1986; Fordham 1996; P. E. Willis 1977; Foley 1990; Levinson, Foley, and Holland 1996). Twenty-five years ago Wexler argued that such student responses were based on their social alienation by schools that were so clearly sorting them to assume lower-status positions in the social structure (1983, see esp. 130–31). In *Becoming Somebody,* Wexler (1992) explained that these students' identities were largely formed in response to the lack of meaningful ties to their school or broader communities. In this view, the discourse of degradation might be seen as an expression of these average and lower-achieving students' senses of self. They might also be seen as "scripts of resistance" which express the anger and frustration many experience in school—as they see themselves getting left behind (Gallegos 2005, 115).

The chapter also pointed out the continuing salience of race for many African American students at Burnham. These students reported difficulties in "fitting in" to the social environment of the school, and struggled to develop the same confidence and self-advocacy skills (components of psychological capital) as their white peers. They also seemed to suffer from the Counseling Center's approach to preparing students for the college application process. In chapter 3 I suggested that some of these difficulties were attributable to ways in which the school handled diversity—specifically in the racial composition of its staff.

More specifically, however, it is possible minority students in particular were ill-served by the school's assumption that ceding control to students and accommodating their preferences would help them succeed. This well-intentioned means of supporting student success positions the student as the arbiter of judgment with regard to how to go about garnering the credentials and distinctions necessary for educational and occupational success. In the case of African American students, such a logic presumes that all students have an adequate familiarity with the explicit and implicit rules for academic success. Sharon clearly did not. Delpit (1995) called these well-intentioned assumptions into question several years ago. Overall, the voices and experiences of these African American students and parents show how race can continue to be hauntingly relevant to their education.

Chapter Eight Conclusions

Two years after the focal students in the study graduated, Jim Greylock invited me back to the school to share findings with his AP U.S. history students. Jim had been an enthusiastic supporter of the project from the beginning and had just taken a class with me at Ohio State. I immediately agreed, eager to share some of what I'd learned and to see what the students would make of it. It was also a chance to conduct something of a "member check" with a slightly different group of pupils. Jim obtained the consent of the students and we agreed that before the meeting they would read the final report of the study that I had given to the school that spring, as well as David Brooks's *Atlantic Monthly* article, "The Organization Kid" (2001).

We met on a school day in the early evening in Jim's history classroom. Nine students were present: three Asian American females, two European American females, and four European American males. All but three were sophomores. Two of the boys had two-liter bottles of Mountain Dew on their desks. When I asked about the soda, they shrugged, half-smiled, and one mumbled, "Long night last night." I explained the purposes and methods of the study to them, some of the preliminary findings, and then we opened things up to a general discussion. First, Richard, a sophomore, responded to my comments about cheating in the school: "Grades are everything. You have to realize it's the only possible way to get into a good college and you resort to any means necessary." Brad, also a sophomore, added, "In middle school you could get a cheap A, as long as you played the game. As long as you figured out what the teacher wanted." When I asked what a "cheap A" was, Lydia, an Asian American sophomore, explained that is was an A "you don't have to work for. You just have to sit there. It's what some people sign up for." Paul, also a sophomore, added, "In easy A classes, teachers still think we're little kids—afraid we'll be hurt if we don't get A's." The students agreed that some classes "bring down standards for

A work," so they felt like they didn't get very much out of them. Libby, also a sophomore, mentioned a government teacher who would give students free points or would borrow points from another quarter if students were in danger of failing.

Next the conversation turned to stress. Paul explained that the "peak" of stress was the week leading up to AP exams. Brad added that things for him started getting more difficult in all of his classes during the second semester. He said, "Tons of homework, late nights. I would fall asleep doing homework, and I would have a pop whenever I needed an extra hour of perkiness. It helped." Sarah, also a sophomore, then said, "I'm a big believer in caffeine pills. . . . I'm a huge perfectionist. I had to get everything done, and it had to be done perfectly. Some nights I didn't sleep. . . . I would take caffeine pills, stay up to 3:00 or 4:00, then take sleeping pills." Paul added, "I'd rather sleep than have a sit-down dinner. I'll eat cereal as I'm writing my paper." When I asked them what they did with their free time, the room filled with an outburst of surprised laughter. Over the din I heard one student say, "Free time? What free time?" Another said, "Sleep!" Once the laughter had died down, Richard explained, "A lot of students here are used to being tired. It's rare when we're not." A little alarmed by this, and realizing I hadn't asked about fatigue on the survey, I asked how often they were tired. Sarah immediately said, "Every high school student is tired, always." Another added, "We're tired every day. Ask it on your next survey."

Then I asked, "So what drives you—to work so hard?" Lydia responded, "It's harder for our generation to live the same lifestyle as our parents do." She went on to say, "A lot of us are looking to the future . . . others won't get as far." Greg, a junior, explained that for him, part of it was "inner drive." Richard then said that over the years he too had developed an "inner drive." He explained it by saying that smart students were the "ones that really push themselves to get better." The conversation then turned to parental pressure for a few minutes, and Paul said, "I started with parental pressure, but now I don't care what they think. It's all about going to West Point. What I think is, will this, this, this, or this, help me get into West Point?"

After more discussion about drive and expectations, I asked them to share their ideas of what made for a successful person. Brad immediately said, "Being successful is living up to half of what my brother was. He is the smartest person I've ever met, and my parents compare everything. They took my interims [quarterly grades] down from the fridge when my brother came home [from college]. I can't do anything to fill his shoes."

Sarah then said, "I know exactly what I want and that's to be successful in life. And I know the only way I'm going to get it is to compete with the Mark Westphals of the world [a particularly high-achieving recent graduate of the school]. You *have* to compete. My goal is I want to be a lawyer and major in political science. I know there are going to be ten Mark Westphals competing for that spot at the law firm and I know I have to work harder than them."

After several more students shared their own thoughts, I asked, "How does being successful make you feel?" Melissa, an Asian American student, said "Being successful makes me feel awesome." Brad quietly added, "Relieved." Paul then said, "I'm happy a lot, but rarely content because I'm always looking at what comes next." There was a pause in the room, and then Angela, the third Asian American girl, said, "I don't know what happiness is anymore. I can tell before the quarter starts what grade I'm going to get because I know what I know and what I'm willing to go for. Getting an A doesn't make me happy because that's what I expect of myself. I feel like I'm sixty."

Sarah then looked around the room and said, "I'm getting a little depressed, listening to ourselves. Here we are, the best and the brightest of Wilton, and listen to us, we're stressed, we stay up all night working, and we don't know what happiness is. We have so much talent, it doesn't seem fair to me that we're the ones getting ground down. There are people who don't come to school, who don't have the gifts or anything to offer and they might as well just *die*, but it's the smart and talented people that get caught up in what society has created."

Sarah's last statement brings to mind the anthropologist Clifford Geertz's well-known description of the cultural predicament of human beings: as suspended in "webs of significance" that they themselves have "spun" (1973, 5). Certainly these AP students were very much caught up in the culture of personal advancement in Wilton. Their comments provide a succinct summary of many of the components of this cultural system presented in previous chapters—especially in their display of psychological capital and knowledge of instrumental approaches to learning and inflated assessments in the school.

Overall, this book has sought to present a finely grained description of a highly synthesized class cultural system oriented toward educational credentialism and individual advancement. It focused on several distinct components of this system: 1) a class culture and achievement ideology geared toward competitive success and the promotion of individual and community worth; 2) parental support, interventions in school, and manipulations of educational policies; 3) school policies and teaching practices that promote hypercredentialism; and 4) student identities and school strategies dedicated to control and success. The book's class cultural perspective illuminated how the educational philosophy in Wilton was based largely upon a keen local awareness of education and employment markets and a commitment to prepare students to successfully compete in them. It also showed how these components were bound together, in part, by several key linkages and feedback mechanisms that reinforced central meanings and practices, and underlay the system's robustness.

These linkages included a strong connection between individual and community worth and a resulting educational philosophy that authorized the community to extract private goods from its public schools; parental expectations and interventions that reinforced the school's emphasis on credentialing; the school's discourses of excellence and technologies of recognition that shaped students' perceptions of the purposes of education; the authority that achievement-oriented students attributed to themselves, which justified and reinforced their identities and practices; the articulation of the strategies of "point-hungry" students with the assessment practices of teachers who saw their primary work as credentialing; and finally, the academic climate and discourse of degradation which further alienated many average and low-achieving students from learning.

Overall, the book contributes an additional way of understanding the role of education in perpetuating class inequities in the United States: how middle-class children continue to pull further ahead of children from more disadvantaged backgrounds, and at the very least, remain in the middle class. This final chapter discusses the implications of study findings for our understandings of educational advantage, suggests directions for future research and makes recommendations for policy and practice in schools like Wilton Burnham. First, though, it seems appropriate to convey where the focal students went upon their graduation from Burnham.

Post-Graduation Paths of the Focal Students

Sharon Sosa received a full academic scholarship to Capital University in Columbus, Ohio. She had wanted to go to Ohio State, and had even explored some historically black colleges and universities, but Capital gave her a better scholarship offer, and her parents wanted her to be at a smaller school. Sharon came to terms with that, but did express her irritation with several teachers and students who assumed her scholarship was for athletics. In the long term, Sharon expressed an awareness that many other minority group members had not had the same opportunities as her. She said she wanted to "get back to community. . . . to do something. . . . that can give back to people."

After moving to Toledo in the middle of his junior year, *Nuako Konadu* continued to do well in school and became the starting running back for the football team. He had dreamed of going to USC, and was admitted, but received no scholarship money. It was, he said, "the biggest heartbreaker in the world." He earned a football scholarship to Wooster College in Ohio, but instead enrolled in the honors engineering program at the University of Toledo, where he received reduced tuition due to his father's administrative appointment. He explained that he was planning to stay with his "math and sciences work" and go into biomechanical engineering so that he would be "safe." He said he could just "get my major, get my job." By that, he explained that he had "little cash" and that making prostheses and prosthetics would be a marketable skill. He explained that he did not have to go through what his father did to land a respectable job. He said, "I feel like they've worked-up, so I have to . . . start-up, and then continue from there. . . . I should already be on that plane with them."

By the end of her senior year, *Julie Rice's* jaw had healed, though she still had occasional numbness in her chin. She wanted to go to a college close enough so that she could come home on weekends, but far enough away so that she felt like she was "away." She ended up matriculating at Baldwin Wallace outside of Cleveland. She thought its educational programs would prepare her for her desired work as a teacher and missionary. She also said, "I'm pretty sure it's a dry campus. They don't . . . party, which is something I was *really* looking for, because I *don't do that.*" She thought that in the future she might like to teach history in an inner-city high school. When I asked Julie if, in looking back, there was anything she would have done differently at Burnham, she said she would have "gotten better grades." She explained, "Because a 3.8 isn't too shabby, but I know that if I had applied myself, I could have been valedictorian."

David Sterling became class president his senior year and received a standing ovation from an auditorium full of students and parents when he sang a tenor solo with the all-male elite singing group. David had visited several schools, including some on the East Coast, but concluded that he did not want to be "too far from home." He said, "If something happens that I need to drive home, I want to be able to do it in a day." Much to his disappointment, however, David was not admitted to Notre Dame. He said in his final interview, "I did everything I could for . . . three and a half years, it wasn't good enough. You got to move on." He received a Valedictorian's

Scholarship at Miami University in Ohio, his parents' alma mater, where he matriculated in the fall. He said that he received "absolutely no help" from the Counseling Center in his college application process. He said his "life goals" included getting married, and that eventually he would probably like to go to law school and perhaps get into politics.

Sofia Rhoades said that she did not encounter a great deal of stress in high school until her college selection process. She said she relied on the support of her parents and played PlayStation to get through it. She ended up matriculating at Marietta College in southeastern Ohio. Like David, she said that the Counseling Center played virtually no role in her application process. During the spring of her senior year she did a senior project internship at a local radio station. This made such an impression on her that she said she was planning to major in broadcasting. Eventually, she hoped to work on ESPN's College "GameDay" program.

After leaving Burnham during her junior year, *Cindi Criswell* worked at several jobs, including a movie theater box office and a teen clothing store. After several months, the managers of the clothing store informed Cindi that they would like to consider her for management training, but that she would have to have a high school diploma or GED in order to qualify. Cindi began taking high school courses via correspondence. Though she said three years earlier that she didn't think school would get her "anywhere," during our last interview in July 2003, Cindi said she was "just really focused on getting my diploma, getting my management position." She said school would eventually "pay off."

Kevin Madsen became a starter on Burnham's boys soccer team, though in his senior year the team failed to win their conference championship for the first time in three years. Kevin said it was a big "letdown" for the seniors because they were "so used to winning," and "not winning was, like, real hard for us to take." Kevin ended up enrolling at the University of North Carolina at Charlotte so that he could be closer to his mother. He was not offered a soccer scholarship there but hoped to walk on to the team. His father planned to move the rest of the family to Charlotte after Kevin's younger brother finished high school. Kevin had fervently hoped to play soccer at the University of North Carolina at Chapel Hill, but was not admitted, he assumed, because of his low GPA. In the spring of his senior year he told us, "I mean, basically I screwed up my freshman year, I think you know that, but—that screwed me over for life, basically."

The systematic practices of personal advancement in Wilton have their basis in a long history of individual and community adaptations to the social class stratification inherent in American society. They are also sustained by a more recent and somewhat unconscious anxiety and insecurity regarding future class status. From an anthropological point of view, these practices are adaptations to an increasingly competitive yet sparsely regulated environment. When I have presented findings from the study to colleagues and educators over the last several years, many have expressed surprise and dismay that the school's morally questionable practices of institutional advantaging and parent's manipulations of special education policy went largely unchecked. Yet few such checks exist in the American system of public education, where, according to Varenne and McDermott, "gaining unfair advantage is what makes sense to do" (1998, 108). In this view, the way in which people in Wilton creatively leveraged their advantages certainly makes sense given the way in which they apprehended the world around them and the existing constraints on their actions.

A central argument of the book is that these morally questionable practices are a part of the overall culture of personal advancement that contribute to achievement "gaps" between students from different backgrounds. The fact that these practices are unregulated, and in fact were implicitly rewarded by a U.S. Department of Education "Blue Ribbon" designation, speaks to the profoundly balkanized nature of American public education. There is little oversight at the federal level, for example, to curb practices of hypercredentialing. Given the inequities between districts and schools to which these practices contribute, to refer to American public education as a "system" is a misnomer. It much more resembles an open field of power with districts and schools competing against each other with relatively few rules regulating their policies and practices. They have significant freedom to exercise their own sleight of hand to best position their own students to compete, and in turn, ensure the continuing worth of their own communities. More specific conclusions from the study are related below.

The achievement-oriented focal students for the most part benefitted from the support of their parents, and in some cases, their parents' interventions with teachers. In general, study data suggested that students seem to require a minimal amount of social support in order to compete academically. More specifically, the survey finding regarding the association between student SES and GPA suggests the presence of a critical set of class cultural competencies related to academic achievement that certainly bear further investigation.

It was particularly striking to notice some parents' seeming awareness of the ill-effects of their "pushing," but their inability to restrain themselves from continuing to urge their children to achieve. One vanity ad from the 2000 yearbook read:

> "Congratulations Tiffany! We are so proud of you. Keep all your energy and remember the sky's the limit, so go for the gold!"

Such an ad begs the question of how much "energy" Tiffany's parents knew she had already lost in her efforts to remain competitive. Julie Rice's mother wondered aloud to us about what Julie was giving up in high school: "But what's being sacrificed at the cost of loading a schedule, you know, are they being given a chance to be a kid?" These parents are seemingly in the same bind as those in Proweller's study of upper-middle-class girls in a private high school (1998): given the increasingly insecure class status of their families, they wanted an education for their daughters that would make them autonomous, confident, and economically independent.

More specifically, Wilton parents' appropriation of special education policy seems to be an instance of the "sleight of hand" that so character-izes middle-class parents' manipulations of educational systems (see, e.g., Ball 2003; Eckert 1989). They are also what George Lipsitz refers to as "social warrants" of consumer citizenship: practices that are authorized but not written down that encourage wealthy communities to "hoard their advantages" (2005). These practices raise serious questions about the al-location of public resources for private ends. They also contribute further to understandings of middle-class parents' "inter-institutional linkages" studied recently by Lareau (2003) and raise serious questions about the social profits realized by the investments of their social class resources. More research is needed in two distinct areas here. First, we need careful micro-ethnographic analyses of how linguistic categories, such as "disabil-ity," "average," and "on-task" get manipulated in processes of evaluation. It is through these networks, often made up of sympathetic class interests, that these cases get "built." Second, we need to better understand the class cultural competencies that underlie these parents' abilities to manipulate policy: how they are acquired, distributed across socioeconomic and eth-nic groups, and deployed. In this way we can get a sense of what kinds of parents do or do not have the dispositions or know-how to secure these sorts of advantages for their children.

The fact that Burnham's achievement-oriented students' very identities were oriented toward control and success suggests the deeply entrenched nature of the culture of personal advancement in the community. These student identities are another important feedback mechanism in the cul-tural system. The class cultural achievement ideology, home influences on academic achievement, and school emphasis on competitive success all represent a complex set of feedback loops that constantly shape and are shaped by youth. In this view, while these young peoples' selves are largely made by this cultural system, in turn, in their everyday encounters between their own subjective selves and their environments, they remake it anew. This last point is important, as it reflects newer insights concerning the mutually constitutive nature of cultural complexity (Hannerz 1997; Heath 1999). Buckingham succinctly summarizes this perspective by saying, "There is a kind of circularity here" (2000, 7). In addition, these findings concerning student identity show how Ortner's notion of psychological capital can be elaborated and usefully applied to educational achievement and aspirations. One interpretation of these student adaptations is that they are disciplining themselves to succeed in a social environment that is increasingly saturated with competition and risk (see Demerath, Lynch, and Davidson 2008). Most broadly, they are evidence of what the anthropologist Sharon Stephens referred to as, "the high price children must pay when their bodies and minds become the terrain for adult battles" (1995, vii).

Jim Greylock's AP students certainly demonstrated several components of the psychological capital that made up these identities, including a keen awareness of competition, internalized attachments to personal success, highly specific aspirations, and self-conscious attempts to habituate to stress and fatigue. After the meeting with his AP students, Greylock commented that many of them were so caught up in the system of academic competition that they simply couldn't "put on the brakes." This comment raises serious questions about the guidance these young people are receiving in preparing for the future. First of all, some sociologists estimate that given current trends related to neoliberal economic restructuring, in the near future people will have several careers in their lifetime. This possibility renders these students' dizzying need to control their lives by "colonizing their futures" with highly specific aspirations a seemingly somewhat wasteful expenditure of energy.

Second, chapter 6 recounted recent studies of the adolescent brain that illuminate how it may be very difficult for adolescent students to "put on the brakes" if left to their own devices (Giedd 2004; Thompson 2000). While more research is needed to adequately understand linkages between adolescent brain development and behavior, it is possible that attributing too much decision-making authority to young people at this age (as Burnham's policies of freedom and deferral certainly did) can result in poor decisions and elevated stress levels.

Jim Greylock's AP students also commented on their own somewhat instrumental approach to learning, as well as their teachers' tendencies to inflate assessments. These were at the core of the emphasis on the pursuit of "getting good grades" and the practice of hypercredentialing in the school which was described in chapters 3 and 5. Chapter 5 argued that the "point-hungry" students' pursuit of good grades and the inflated assessments provided by teachers who saw their primary function as credentialing made for another feedback mechanism in the cultural system. Most of the instrumental strategies that achievement-oriented students adopted to get the best grade with the "least amount of work" should come as no surprise to most educators. What is notable is the extent to which students saw cheating as "natural." This would surely be a part of the new "ethical calculus," which, according to David Callahan, is taking hold among people who aspire to become a part of what is now the "winning class" in the United States. The consequence, he argues, has been the rise of a new cheating culture (2004).

The study also uncovered important differences in the educational experiences of different kinds of students in Wilton. Female students seemed to be more immersed in the competitive culture and routines of the school and to experience more stress because of it. Study data revealed a pattern of achievement-oriented girls unable to let up in their academic and extracurricular efforts—even in the face of significant stress and fatigue. While it may be the case that the culture of success in the twenty-first century is gender neutral, many female students at Wilton still seemed to believe that they had to outperform boys in order to achieve the same educational and occupational success. The "warrior girl" mentality mentioned in chapter 6 is one descriptor of these young women's motivation. More specifically, it may be that they experience an early and intense sense of what Nikolas Rose refers to as "responsibilization" (1992, 149): internalized pressure to take responsibility for themselves and their imagined futures. Consequently, they suffer ill effects. Certainly, an important area of research and theorization will continue to be gender differences in the kinds of identities and adaptations students take on as they seek to meet the demands of an increasingly competitive education and employment marketplace.

The study also revealed ways in which African American students were marginalized within the school culture and were disadvantaged by the school's competitive routines. Qualitative data from the study suggest that most African American students did not develop particular components of psychological capital (such as confidence and predispositions to self-advocate) or adopt the instrumental strategies for success outlined above (such as cultivating the sorts of relationships with teachers that can contribute to positive academic gains). It also appears that many of them did not have the same social capital as their majority peers (networks of particular kinds of valuable relationships) that could serve them well regarding the ins and outs of the college admissions process.

The challenges faced by African American students in Wilton may stem both from different environments of socialization at home that may not equip them with some of the same class cultural dispositions as their peers, and normative assumptions made by school personnel regarding the class cultural knowledge that students bring to the college application process. I suggested in chapter 3 that racial differences regarding students' confidence, and relatedly, their abilities to self-advocate, are attributable in part to how the school handled diversity—specifically in the racial composition of its staff.

Such findings demonstrate that counter to the views of several contemporary writers (Steele 1990, 2006; Connerly 2000; McWhorter 2005; Thernstrom and Thernstrom 2003), explanations of black mobility must take into account institutional micro processes of racial exclusion (Akom 2006; Bonilla-Silva 2001). Study data show how these institutional practices influence student identities and possible futures. As such, this book seeks to contribute to efforts to ground interpretations of social mobility in the United States and elsewhere within a more "race and gender conscious framework" (Akom 2008, 1). The study, then, suggests that while the culture of success in the twenty-first century is not "raced," the means through which academic success is identified favor certain populations: those that have specific kinds of social, cultural, and psychological capital. Certainly this is another important direction for future inquiry and interpretation.

The study also raised questions about the extent to which the school was meeting the needs of a broader segment of average and lower-achieving students. I suggested in chapter 7 that the school's emphasis on credentialing and competitive academic achievement were stripping it of its mission to educate all students. It was inadvertently causing many students to become defeated, resulting in reduced academic effort and the adoption of attitudes of "passive noncompliance." In effect, many students became alienated from the central purpose of school: learning. Cindi's statement that she was "not a school person," suggests a disjunction between imperatives of learning and imperatives of schooling in Wilton. The anthropological theory of cultural transmission and acquisition tells us that we humans are wired to learn, and that we learn constantly in multiple modes and through multiple outlets (Spindler 1967; Wolcott 1994). The disengagement of students like Cindi and incivility of other average and under-achieving students during the study raises the question of whether they would be more motivated if the intrinsic value of learning, rather than competitive academic success, was emphasized more at the school.

Cindi's experience underscores the foundational importance of a high school education in the current "knowledge economy." She eventually learned of the essential value of a high school diploma from the workplace when her employer identified her as a potential management trainee. She realized that her own job security and potential social mobility would depend on her getting, at a minimum, a GED. Her experience also underscores the importance of making high schools places where no students fall through the cracks, and all can thrive and gain the knowledge they need for a variety of possible futures.

The way in which these students, the school, and the community all construed education as a high-stakes competitive enterprise meant that it was easy to fail, and that the costs of failure were grave. Kevin certainly was of this mindset, as he implied in his statement that his freshman year grades "screwed" him for life. Nuako was as well, in having his heart broken by not being able to go to USC. Even David, the highest achieving of the focal students and a school valedictorian, felt that after all he had done in high school he had still come up short, because he had failed to achieve his goal of going to Notre Dame. There were students in the WBHS Class of 2003 who were admitted to and attended some of the most selective colleges and universities in the United States, including Duke, the University of Pennsylvania, and Cal Tech. The highest achieving focal students did not apply to these sorts of schools (in part because they wanted to stay closer to home) yet were still thoroughly immersed in the culture of advancement at Burnham—a fact that attests to both its magnetic pull and somewhat deceptive promises. In the spring of his senior year in Toledo, Nuako reflected that he had probably "overachieved" while he was at Burnham. He said:

> If I knew in the long run I was going to UT, like I thought for sure I was going somewhere on a scholarship for academics, but I'm just going here, because my dad works there. . . . And so, had I known that then, I probably wouldn't have tried so hard. . . . had a lot more fun and a lot less—like, worries.

The extent to which students come up short of their aspirations suggests that school counselors need to be more proactive in helping students recast their future plans, given intensifying competition in the educational and employment landscape. In other words, while so many of these students are mobilizing themselves to ride the elevator to the penthouse, in reality, very few of them will actually do so. As the English teacher Lisa Riegel said during the study, "We need new definitions of success; otherwise we are setting students up for failure."

Making Anthropological Findings Public: Stimulating Reflection and Deliberation

From the outset, the book drew on several aspects of life, identity, and education in Manus in order to bring the cultural dimensions of particular beliefs and practices in Wilton into sharper relief. These included the communal basis for identity and the relatively small amount of time people spent alone; parents' more fatalistic attitudes toward education; the historically egalitarian social fabric and resulting ambivalence about personal success and being "somebody"; and finally, the ways in which those who did pursue such success could be ridiculed, ostracized, and pulled down.

The cultural basis of many of the assumptions and practices of parents, students, and teachers in Wilton means that they are open to discussion and deliberation. This is a foundational assumption of public anthropologists such as Margaret Mead, Peggy Sanday, and Michele Foster. For example, far from playing the detached observer, Margaret Mead applauded the Manus' strident efforts toward democracy and economic development. She synthesized her theoretical and empirical anthropological work with humane values and created novel roles for herself in showing the people of Manus their culture from a new perspective, discussing dilemmas with them, and actively assisting in their resolution. When my wife and I returned to Manus in 2001, the centennial of Mead's birth, we asked people what Mead had meant to them. Several said that her work had given them a way to "measure" (*scalim*) where they had been, how far they had come, and where they were going. In this sense, she provided a kind of reference point for how they located themselves in the modern world.

More recently, Peggy Sanday has advocated an activist anthropology that projects knowledge created from ethnography against the wider screens of history and power in order to identify "possibilities and strategies for change" (1998, 3). Michele Foster referred to her ethnographic work with teachers as a mirror, the surface of which could be altered in order to emphasize and reflect back to them different dimensions of their own beliefs and practices (1998). Sanday says that the ultimate aim of this kind of work is to help people imagine a "new way of being in the world" (2001).

Recommendations

While I embrace such lofty ideals, I am also well aware that the system of individualistic competition upon which American society is founded is unlikely to change in the near future. The key question that remains, however, is how public schools articulate with the competitive requirements of society. In this light, over forty-five years ago, Raymond Callahan wrote that American schools were "vulnerable" to the dictates of the "business society" within which they were situated. He observed that they tended to capitulate "to whatever demands were placed on them," and made many decisions not on educational grounds, and without a "steady guiding philosophy" (1962, 59). Jim Greylock's observation that the Burnham school culture *itself* is a "business culture" is troubling. The previous chapters demonstrated some of the negative effects of such a pronounced emphasis on individualistic competition and advancement. The point is that educators can control the extent to which competition is foregrounded in everyday school and classroom routines.

The most important recommendation from the study is that teachers and administrators engage in thoughtful conversations about how to go about that. For example, I encourage teachers to establish classroom cultures whereby assessments and discussions of them are always subordinate to what it is they are seeking their students to learn. In addition, I recommend that all forms of extra credit be eliminated. The study showed how extra credit promotes educational credentialism, and, through the incessant negotiations of "point-hungry" students for more of it, puts unnecessary additional pressure on teachers. Ted Sizer observed several years ago that a good school should be a place of "unanxious expectation" (1992a, 174). Wilton Burnham certainly has lofty expectations, but the way in which they are harnessed to competitive frameworks contributes greatly to student anxiety.

In addition, study data showed how the expenditure of effort students put forward during a typical school day and evening are out of balance. They typically spend much of their day in a state of "spectatorship" (this has changed little in many American high schools during the last several decades), yet spend a great deal of time at home doing highly concentrated schoolwork, resulting in fatigue, stress, and less time spent with family or engaging in community activities. Schools should explore ways to decrease student "spectatorship" and increase opportunities for students to engage in hands-on learning activities during the day, with an eye toward decreasing homework. An AP student told us, "Our lunch periods are so long and our time between classes is so much. We have huge chunks of the day where we do nothing." Though *The End of Homework* was published almost ten years ago, more teachers, administrators, and parents ought to participate in the "great homework debate" that it stimulated (Kralovec and Buell 2000). The central arguments of the book still ring remarkably true: homework is increasing, despite the facts that it advantages those children who have time in their homes to do it, has dubious educational value, and diminishes time for other activities and community involvements.

Finally, schools need to offer students more assistance in how to navigate the increasingly competitive fields of high school and the college admissions process. The danger here is that high-achieving students literally burn out in college or soon after, as in the case of Anna Norquist. Students, especially girls, appear to need assistance in learning how to sustain a high level of effort and concentration, and how to put on the brakes when necessary.[1]

I recently was asked by some family friends for some advice on how to achieve this balance. In the winter of 2008, my family sat down to dinner with two white friends from Ohio. Rachel, the mother, was an administrator at a selective liberal arts college, and Alyson, her daughter, was a sophomore at the local public high school. Our families had lived across the street from each other for eight years, and my wife and I had known Alyson from the time she was eight. Over time, she had played with our daughters, babysat them, and in general, became their all-time hero. She had also grown to five foot ten and developed into an accomplished basketball player, high jumper, saxophone player, and student. At the time, she was the number-one pupil in her class. Rachel knew about the book I was writing, and asked me if I thought they should sign Alyson up for the new international baccalaureate (IB) program in her school. She explained that it would mean little change in her schedule of classes, but that it would require that she attend a special IB class on theories of knowledge before the school day started, which would mean arriving at school nearly an hour earlier. I asked Alyson how often she was tired during the school year. She looked down, half smiled, and said "a lot." I told them that I thought she would probably be just fine not being in the IB program. She was thriving in high school as it was, and the important thing was to find ways for her to sustain her curiosity and effort into the future.

A starting point for a school like Wilton Burnham is to curtail the amount of freedom and choice it offers students—particularly in the area of schedule changes. This would free up guidance counselors to reassume responsibility for the most important task before them. Schools would also do well to explore proposals to move the school day back—to give students more time to sleep at night.

The book has argued that the tight, almost seamless linkages between class ideology, parental practices, accepted school policies, and ideal notions of personhood make this a cultural system. The result is an integrated network of meanings and practices geared toward positioning individuals to successfully compete in school, leveraging community resources to support the schools, building up the confidence of individual students, and recognizing their efforts as successes. In the end, it is this cultural system itself that is these students' primary advantage. By demonstrating another way in which class formation is mediated within a high school, the study shows how this integrated system of individual advancement is an important mechanism in the production of inequality in the contemporary United States. During the spring of their senior year, we asked each focal student about the purpose of high school—what they thought school was for. Sharon reflected for a moment and then said: "School is meant to separate social classes. How about that? That's what I think!"

I. Background & Home

Grade:

Sex: *Male / Female*

Ethnicity: *African American / Asian American / European American / Hispanic / Other* (please specify):

Whom do you live with at home?
___ One parent
___ Both parents
___ Guardian
___ Other (please specify)

Mother/Female Guardian's occupation:

Mother/Female Guardian's educational history (circle most recently completed):
High School / College (BA, BS) / Masters or Professional (MA, MS, MBA, JD) Doctorate (PhD/MD) / Don't know

Father/Male Guardian's occupation:

Father/Male Guardian's educational history (circle most recently completed):
High School / College (BA, BS) / Masters or Professional (MA, MS, MBA, JD) Doctorate (PhD/MD) / Don't know

On average, how many times per week do you have dinner together with your family? ___

How many hours on average do you spend by yourself at home during a typical school day? ___ During a typical weekend day? ___

Do you like to have some sort of music or background noise on when you read? *Yes / No*

Do you have your own bedroom at home? *Yes / No*

Do you have any of the following in your bedroom? (Please check all that apply)
___ CD player
___ TV ___ w/ cable? ___ w/ VCR?
___ DVD player
___ Computer ___ w/ internet hookup?
___ Playstation/Nintendo

How many hours do you spend watching TV on an average school day/night? ___

How many hours do you spend on the internet on an average school day/night? ___

Do you have a job? *Yes / No* If so, how many hours per week do you work? ___

Do you receive an allowance from your parents or guardian? *Yes / No*
If so, how much is it? (please specify per week or per month) ___

How much do you trust that your parents or guardian know what is best for you?
___ Very much ___ Somewhat ___ Not very much ___ No opinion

Do you think your parents or guardian could be more strict with you? *Yes / No*

Are you familiar with the term "The Wilton Way?" *Yes / No* If so, what does it mean to you?

II. School
How much do you see yourself as being in competition with other students at, as well as outside of Burnham?
___ Very much ___ Somewhat ___ Not really ___ No opinion

Estimated GPA:

What kinds of competition are there at Burnham?

What, in your view, is a "successful" person?

Are you an "involved" student? *Yes / No*

Do you think your teachers give you enough opportunities to earn extra credit? *Yes / No*

Is extra credit important to you? *Yes / No* If yes, why?

Do the grades you receive influence how much you like your classes? *Yes / No*

Do you think Burnham has enough ways of recognizing students? *Yes / No*

How much freedom does Burnham give you?
___ Not enough ___ Just enough ___ Too much ___ No opinion

Would you consider yourself a confident student? *Yes / No*
If yes, where does this confidence come from? If no, how have you come to be not very confident?

How much time do you spend on homework on an average school night? ___
Over the weekend? ___

How often do you feel stressed out?
___ All the time ___ Frequently ___ Infrequently ___ No opinion

If you answered either "All the time" or "Frequently" to the above question, which of the following stress you out the most? (Please rank order: 1 = most stressful; 6 = least stressful)

___ Schoolwork
___ Social life / Relationships with people in school
___ Things at home / family
___ Extracurriculars
___ The future / reaching aspirations
___ Other (please specify):

If you do often feel stressed out, how do you cope with it?

Do you sometimes think that you know better than your teachers what or how you ought to learn? *Yes / No* Can you explain or give an example?

How much do you trust that your teachers know what is best for you?
___ Very much ___ Somewhat ___ Not very much ___ No opinion

Can you think of a time when you thought you were treated unfairly by one of your teachers? What happened?

How serious a problem do you think cheating currently is at Burnham?
___ Very serious ___ Somewhat serious ___ Not very serious ___ No opinion

What kind of plans do you have for your future life? Please be as specific as you can.

Are you planning to go to college? *Yes / No* How are you preparing yourself to gain admission to the college of your choice?

Outside of your classes, what have been the most helpful programs/activities at Burnham in terms of your:

A) Overall well-being:

B) Academic success:

For what purposes do you mainly use the Guidance Office?

Is Burnham a multicultural community? *Yes / No* Why or why not? If not, what could be done to make it one?

III. Life Space

Do you think you could use more adult presence in your life? *Yes / No*
Why or why not?

Please rank in importance the following influences in determining a person's future (1 = most important; 4 = least important):
___ Individual effort
___ Parent's background
___ Social support
___ Quality of education

Has your life changed since the Columbine High School shootings in April 1999? *Yes / No* If so, how?

Has your life changed since the events of September 11, 2001? *Yes / No*
If so, how?

If you have a serious problem, whom would you most likely want to talk with about it? (Please rank the following options: 1 = most likely to turn to; 7 = least likely to turn to)

___ Friend

___ Parent/Guardian

___ Sibling

___ Burnham teacher

___ Burnham counselor

___ Burnham administrator

___ Other (please specify):

Thanks very much for sharing these thoughts. Once you are finished, please seal your survey in the envelope provided.

Notes

1. "Wilton" is a pseudonym, as are the names given to local institutions and all students, parents, teachers, and administrators.

2. In her middle and later years, Mead became a true public intellectual, using her comparative knowledge of different human societies to critically discuss various aspects of American culture, such as our child-rearing practices. She had a regular column in *Redbook* magazine and appeared on television programs such as *The Mike Douglas Show*. To commemorate the hundredth anniversary of Mead's birth, in 2001, the Library of Congress opened an exhibit of ten thousand of her documents—the largest exhibit ever dedicated to the work of a single individual. In 2006, *Atlantic Monthly* identified her as on of the "most influential figures in American history," stating that she made anthropology "relevant—and controversial."

3. See also Foley and Moss 2001.

4. The survey consisted of forty-four forced-choice and sixteen open-ended items and aimed to: 1) assess the extent to which the findings from the study of focal students were representative of the experiences and concerns of the larger student body, and 2) examine the relative impact of factors such as gender, ethnicity, SES, grade level, and family structure as they related to various aspects of student experience. Cumulative GPA (used as the main outcome measure of student achievement) was compared between males and females using an unpaired t-test. Differences in GPA on the basis of caregiving arrangements, mother's educational attainment, and SES were compared using the χ^2 statistic. Differences in student responses to specific survey responses (such as "How frequently do you eat dinner with your family during the school week?" and "How frequently do you feel 'stressed out' in school?") were compared across sex, SES, GPA, grade, and residing caregiver groups in bivariate models also using the χ^2 statistic. These models were expanded to include multiple student attributes (sex, SES, age, residing caregiver, etc.) using multinomial logistical regression with key response contrasts (such as "stressed out" "frequently" or "all the time" vs. "infrequently") as the dependent variables.

1. Here and elsewhere extensive quotations are identified as having been recorded in field notes or in formal interviews that were tape-recorded. Brackets ([]) mark text that has been inserted for clarification—either explanation or nonverbal communication. Three ellipses (. . .) indicate a pause in the dialogue. Four ellipses (. . . .) indicate that a segment of protocol has been omitted. Italics indicate an emphasis of the speaker.

2. Throughout the book, unless otherwise noted, all punctuation, spelling, and grammar are the respondents' own.

3. The Federal No Child Left Behind Act (NCLB) was instituted in Ohio on January 8, 2002. For the 2002–2003 academic year, the state proficiency test data reported above by the superintendent was supplemented with various requirements of NCLB, such as Adequate Yearly Progress (AYP). For the 2002–2003 academic year the school met all twelve state indicators, met its AYP requirement, and was given a rating of "excellent" (Ohio Department of Education, 2003).

4. Nearly ten years earlier, the cultural psychologist William Damon (1995) referred to such parenting styles as "overindulgent."

CHAPTER TWO

1. $\chi^2 = 39.5481; p = .0001$
2. $\chi^2 = 33.5284; p = .0417$
3. $\chi^2 = 69.5028; p = .0005$

CHAPTER FOUR

1. Three terms are used throughout the study to refer to students' relative levels of academic achievement. "High-achieving" and "under-achieving" are terms given to the eight focal students who were selected through consultation with teachers and review of GPA. "Achievement-oriented" refers to a larger group of students at the school with various GPAs and in various classes who exhibited characteristics of striving for academic success.

2. Throughout the book I follow Bonilla-Silva's distinction between ethnicity and race: while ethnicity connotes a primarily sociocultural orientation with significant malleability in terms of membership, racial "ascriptions" are largely imposed externally and often used to preserve status differences (2001, 55).

3. This notion grew out of Ortner's concern that Bourdieu's theory of capital (1986) lacked "a complex theory of subjects as persons" (Ortner 2002, 12).

CHAPTER FIVE

1. t statistic, 2.8183; $p = .0025$
2. $\chi^2 = 50.3363; p = .0001$
3. $\chi^2 = 29.4869; p = .0009$
4. See Pace and Hemmings's comprehensive discussion of the changing bases of authority between teachers and students in schools (2005).

CHAPTER SIX

1. This exchange involved both Melanesian Tok Pisin and Titan, the latter of which is an one of the indigenous languages of Manus.

2. OR = 0.2784; 95% CI, 0.1157, 0.6702; p = .004

3. χ^2 = 82.8074; p = .027

4. χ^2 = 42.09; p = .0001

5. χ^2 = 16.9407; p = .0497

6. χ^2 = 16.9407; p = .0497

7. χ^2 = 13.8459; p = .0314

8. χ^2 = 17.6118; p = .04

9. OR = 1.991; 95% CI, 1.10, 3.61; p = .023

10. χ^2 = 44.56; p = .0001

CHAPTER SEVEN

1. 55%; χ^2 = 61.054; $p <$ .0001

CHAPTER EIGHT

1. Parents and teachers would do well to learn about grassroots initiatives, such as Balance 4 Success, which seeks to "replace busyness with balance to ensure kids' success" (http://balance4success.net/).

References

Akom, A. A. 2006. The racial dimensions of social capital: Toward a new understanding of youth empowerment and community organizing in America's urban core. In *Beyond resistance: Youth activism and community change,* ed. G. Ginwright, P. Noguera, and J. Cammarota, 81–92. New York: Routledge.

———. 2008. Racializing reproduction theory: Reexamining the declining significance of race in 21st century America (unpublished manuscript). Cesar Chavez Institute, San Francisco State University, San Francisco.

Anyon, J. 2005. *Radical possibilities: Public policy, urban education, and a new social movement.* New York: Routledge.

Apple, M. 1996. *Cultural politics and education.* New York: Teachers College Press.

———. 1997. Consuming the other: Whiteness, education, and cheap french fries. In *Off white: Readings on society, race, and culture,* ed. L. P. M. Fine, L. Weiss, and L. Mun Wong, 121–28. New York: Routledge.

———. 2001. Comparing neo-liberal projects and inequality in education. *Comparative Education* 37:409–23.

Atlantic Monthly. 2006. The top 100: The most influential Americans in history. December. http://www.theatlantic.com/doc/200612/influentials.

Ball, S. J. 2003. *Class strategies and the education market: The middle classes and social advantage.* New York: RoutledgeFalmer.

Bartlett, L., M. Fredrick, T. Gulbrandsen, and E. Murillo. 2002. The marketization of education: Public schools for private ends. *Anthropology & Education Quarterly* 33 (1): 5–29.

Bateson, M. C. 2001. Invited address given at the Presidential Mead Centennial Session. American Anthropological Association annual meeting, Washington DC, November.

Beck, U. 2000. Risk society revisited: Theory, politics and research programmes. In *The risk society and beyond,* ed. B. Adam, U. Bech, and J. Van Loon. London: Sage.

Bonilla-Silva, E. 2001. *White supremacy and racism in the post-civil rights era.* London: Lyne Rienner Publishers.

Bourdieu, P. 1984. *Distinction: A social critique of the judgment of taste.* Cambridge, MA: Harvard University Press.

———. 1986. The forms of capital. In *Handbook of theory and research for the sociology of education,* ed. J. G. Richardson. New York: Greenwood Press.

———. 1998. *Practical reason: On the theory of action.* Palo Alto, CA: Stanford University Press.

Bourdieu, P., and J.-C. Passeron. 1977. *Reproduction: in education, society, and culture.* Beverly Hills, CA: Sage.

Brantlinger, E. 2003. *Dividing classes: How the middle class negotiates and rationalizes school advantage.* New York: RoutledgeFalmer.

Brooks, D. 2001. The organization kid. *Atlantic Monthly,* April, 40–54.

———. 2002. Making it: Love and success at America's finest universities. Review of Reviewed Item. *Weekly Standard,* December 23. http://www.weeklystandard.com/Content/Public/Articles/000/000/002/017ickdp.asp.

Brown, D. K. 2001. The social sources of educational credentialism: Status cultures, labor markets, and organizations. *Sociology of Education* (Extra Issue):19–34.

Brown, L. 1998. *Raising their voices: The politics of girls' anger.* Cambridge, MA: Harvard University Press.

Buckingham, D. 2000. *After the death of childhood: Growing up in the age of electronic media.* Cambridge: Polity.

Callahan, D. 2004. *The cheating culture: Why more Americans are doing wrong to get ahead.* New York: Harcourt.

Callahan, R. E. 1962. *Education and the cult of efficiency.* Chicago: University of Chicago Press.

Carrier, J. G., and A. H. Carrier. 1989. *Wage, trade, and exchange in Melanesia: A Manus society in the modern state.* Berkeley: University of California Press.

Clark, C. 2004. *Hurt: Inside the world of today's teenagers.* Grand Rapids, MI: Baker Academic.

Connell, R. W., D. J. Ashenden, S. Kessler, and G. W. Dorsett. 1982. *Making the difference: Schools, families and social division.* Sydney: George Allen & Unwin.

Connerly, W. 2000. *Creating equal: My fight against racial preferences.* San Francisco: Encounter Books.

Cookson, P. 1985. *Preparing for power: America's elite boarding schools.* New York: Basic Books.

Cowan, A. L. 2005. In an affluent town, parents and schools clash over special education. *New York Times,* April 24.

Csikszentmihalyi, M., and B. Schneider. 2000. *Becoming adult: How teenagers prepare for the world of work.* New York: Basic Books.

Currie, E. 2004. *The road to whatever: Middle class culture and the crisis of adolescence.* New York: Henry Holt and Company.

Damon, W. 1995. *Greater expectations: Overcoming the culture of indulgence in our homes and schools.* New York: Free Press.

Delpit, L. 1995. *Other peoples' children.* New York: The Free Press.

Demerath, P. 1999. The cultural production of educational utility in Pere village, Papua New Guinea. *Comparative Education Review* 43 (2):162–92.

———. 2007. Are student-determined goods good for students? Unseen effects of student identity, policy, and pedagogy in a U.S. suburban high school. Working paper, The Ohio State University.

Demerath, P., J. Lynch, and M. Davidson. 2008. Dimensions of psychological capital in a U.S. suburb: Identities for neoliberal times. *Anthropology & Education Quarterly* 39 (3): 270–92.

Donmoyer, R. 2001. Paradigm talk reconsidered. In *Handbook of research on teaching,* ed. V. Richardson, 174–97. 4th ed. Washington DC: American Educational Research Association.

Dorst, J. D. 1989. *The written suburb: An American site, An ethnographic dilemma.* Philadelphia: University of Pennsylvania Press.

Eckert, P. 1989. *Jocks and burnouts: Social categories and identity in the high school.* New York: Teachers College Press.

Eder, D. 1997. *School talk: Gender and adolescent culture.* New Brunswick, NJ: Rutgers University Press.

Education Council and Drug-Free Schools Consortium. 2003. Primary prevention awareness, attitude, and use survey: Student perspectives on the use of alcohol, tobacco, other drugs, and violence, [Wilton] City Schools. Wilton, OH.

Education Trust. 2001. *The funding gap: Low-income and minority students receive fewer dollars.* Washington DC : Education Trust.

Ehrenreich, B. 1989. *Fear of falling: The inner life of the middle class.* New York: Pantheon.

Elkind, D. 2001. *The hurried child: Growing up too fast too soon.* New York: Da Capo.

Erickson, F. 1986. Qualitative methods in research on teaching. In *Handbook of research on teaching,* ed. M. C. Wittrock, 119–61. 3rd ed. New York: Macmillan.

Finders, M. 1997. *Just girls: Hidden literacies and life in junior high.* New York: Teachers College Press.

Fine, M. 1991. *Framing dropouts.* Albany: State University of New York Press.

Foley, D. E. 1990. *Learning capitalist culture.* Philadelphia: University of Pennsylvania Press.

Foley, D. E., and K. Moss. 2001. Studying American cultural diversity: Some non-essentializing perspectives. In *Studying cultural diversity in the United States,* ed. I. Susser and T. Patterson, 343–64. Oxford: Blackwell.

Fordham, S. 1996. *Blacked out: Dilemmas of race, identity, and success at Capital High.* Chicago: University of Chicago Press.

Fordham, S., and J. U. Ogbu. 1986. Black students' school success: Coping with the "burden of 'acting White.'" *Urban Review* 18:176–206.

Foster, M. 1998. Critical race theory and the "translation" of ethnographic knowledge for empowerment. Paper presented at the annual meeting of the American Anthropological Association, Philadelphia.

Foucault, M. 1972. *The archaeology of knowledge and the discourse on language.* Trans. A. M. S. Smith. New York: Pantheon.

———. 1983. The subject and power. In *Michel Foucault: Beyond structuralism and hermeneutics,* ed. H. L. Dreyfus and P. Rabinow, 208–26. Chicago: University of Chicago Press.

———. 1988. The ethic of care for the self as a practice of freedom. In *The final Foucault,* ed. J. Bernauer and D. Rasmussen, 1–20. Cambridge, MA: MIT Press.

Friedman, T. 2005. *The world is flat: A brief history of the twenty-first century.* New York: Farrar, Straus, and Giroux.

Gallegos, B. P. 2005. Performing school in the shadow of imperialism. In *Performance theories in education: Power, pedagogy and the politics of identity,* ed. B. K. Alexander, G. L. Anderson, and B. P. Gallegos, 103–22. Mahwah, NJ: Lawrence Erlbaum.

Geertz, C. 1973. *The interpretation of cultures.* New York: Basic Books.

Gergen, K. J. 1991. *The saturated self: Dilemmas of identity in contemporary life.* New York: Basic Books.

Giddens, A. 1991. *Modernity and self-identity: Self and society in the late modern age.* Palo Alto, CA: Stanford University Press.

Giedd, J. N. 2004. Structural magnetic resonance imaging of the adolescent brain. *Annals of the New York Academy of Science* 1021:77–85.

Gnezda, N. M. 2005. *Teaching difficult students: Blue Jays in the classroom.* Lanham, MD: Rowman & Littlefield Education.

Graue, M. E. 1993. Social networks and home-school relations. *Educational Policy* 7 (4): 466–90.

Hannerz, U. 1997. Borders. *International Social Science Journal* 49 (154): 537–48.

Harris, J. R. 1995. Where Is the child's environment? A group socialization theory of development. *Psychological Review* 102 (3): 458–89.

Heath, S. B. 1999. Discipline and disciplines in education research. In *Issues in educational research: Problems and possibilities,* ed. E. Condliffe Lagemann and L. S. Shulman, 203–23. San Francisco: Jossey-Bass.

Henry, J. 1963. *Culture against man.* New York: Vintage.

Hersch, P. 1998. *A tribe apart.* New York: Ballantine.

Hewlett, S. A. 1992. *When the bough breaks: The cost of neglecting our children.* New York: Perennial.

Hilliard, A. 2002. Beneficial research in education: Paradigm, priority, and valid practice. Paper presented at the American Educational Research Association annual meeting, New Orleans.

Hollingshead, A. B. 1949. *Elmtown's youth.* New York: Wiley & Sons.

Holme, J. J. 2002. Buying homes, buying schools: School choice and the social construction of school quality. *Harvard Educational Review* 72 (2): 177–205.

Howard, A. 2008. *Learning privilege: Lessons of power and identity in affluent schooling.* New York: Routledge.

Josephson Institute of Ethics. 2002. Report card 2002: The ethics of American youth. Los Angeles: Josephson Institute of Ethics.

Knauft, B. M. 2002. *Critically modern: Alternatives, alterities, anthropologies.* Bloomington: Indiana University Press.

Kohn, A. 1986. *No contest: The case against competition.* Boston: Houghton Mifflin.

———. 1993. *Punished by rewards: The trouble with gold stars, incentive plans, A's, praise, and other bribes.* Boston: Houghton Mifflin.

———. 1999. The costs of overemphasizing achievement. *School Administrator* 56:40–46.

Kozol, J. 2006. *The shame of a nation: The restoration of apartheid schooling in America.* New York: Three Rivers Press.

Kralovec, E., and J. Buell. 2000. *The end of homework: How homework disrupts families, overburdens children, and limits learning.* Boston: Beacon Press.

Labaree, D. F. 1997. *How to succeed in school without really learning: The credentials race in American education.* New Haven, CT: Yale University Press.

Ladson-Billings, G. 2006. From the achievement gap to the education debt: Understanding achievement in U.S. schools. *Educational Researcher* 35 (7): 3–12.

Ladwig, J. 1996. *Academic distinctions: Theory and methodology in the sociology of school knowledge.* New York: Routledge.

Lareau, A.. 2000. *Home advantage.* Lanham: Rowman & Littlefield.

———. 2003. *Unequal childhoods: Class, race, and family life.* Berkeley: University of California Press.

Lasch, C. 1991. *The culture of narcissism: American life in an age of diminishing expectations.* New York: W. W. Norton & Company.

Leadership Wilton. 2001. People make the difference (brochure). Wilton, OH.

Levinson, B. A., D. E. Foley, and D. C. Holland, eds. 1996. *The cultural production of the educated person.* Albany: State University of New York Press.

Lightfoot, S. L. 1983. *The good high school: Portraits of character and culture.* New York: Basic Books.

Lipsitz, G. 2005. Rethinking American culture with George Lipsitz. Paper read at American Anthropological Association 104th annual meeting, Washington, D.C.

Lynd, R., and H. Lynd. 1929. *Middletown: A study in contemporary American culture.* New York: Harcourt, Brace and Company.

Martin, E. 2000. Flexible bodies: Science and a new culture of health in the U.S. In *Health, medicine, and society,* ed. S. Williams, J. Gabe, and M. Calnan, 123–45. London: Routledge.

McCarthy, C. 1998. *The uses of culture: Education and the limits of ethnic affiliation.* New York: Routledge.

McWhorter, J. 2005. *Winning the race: Beyond the crisis in Black America.* New York: Gotham Books.

Mead, M. 1942/1965. *And keep your powder dry: An anthropologist looks at America.* New York: William Morrow and Company.

———. 1964. *Anthropology: A human science.* Princeton, NJ: Van Nostrand.

Miller, D. 1998. *A theory of shopping.* Ithaca, NY: Cornell University Press.

Milner, M. 2004. *Freaks, geeks, and cool kids: American teenagers, schools, and the culture of consumption.* New York: Routledge.

Nack, W., and L. Munson. 2000, Special report: Out of control. *Sports Illustrated,* July 24, 86–95.

Nader, L. 1969. Up the anthropologist—Perspectives gained from studying up. In *Reinventing anthropology,* ed. D. Hymes, 285–311. New York: Pantheon.

———. 2001. Anthropology! Distinguished lecture—2000. *American Anthropologist,* 103 (3): 609–20.

National Center for Education Statistics. 2003. *The condition of education: An annual snapshot, 2003.* Washington DC: U.S. Department of Education.

———. 2005. *Digest of educational statistics, tables, and figures.* Washington DC : U.S. Department of Education.

Newman, K. 1993. *Declining fortunes: The withering of the American Dream.* New York: Basic Books.

Nichols, S., and T. Good. 2004. *America's teenagers—myths and realities: Media images, schooling, and the social costs of careless indifference.* Mahwah, NJ: Lawrence Erlbaum.

Noah, H., and M. Eckstein. 2001. *Fraud and education: The worm in the apple.* Lanham, MD: Rowman & Littlefield.

Oakes, J. 2005. *Keeping track: How schools structure inequality.* New Haven, CT: Yale University Press.

Ogbu, J. 1978. *Minority education and caste: The American system in cross-cultural perspective.* New York: Academic Press.

Ohio Department of Education. 1995. Operating standards for Ohio's schools serving children with disabilities. Columbus: Ohio Department of Education.

———. 2003. 2002–2003 School year report card. Columbus: Ohio Department of Education.

Ortner, S. B. 1993. Ethnography among the Newark: The Class of '58 of Weequahic High School. *Michigan Quarterly Review* 32:411–29.

———. 2002. Subjects and capital: A fragment of a documentary ethnography. *Ethnos* 67 (1): 9–32.

Pace, J., and A. Hemmings, eds. 2005. *Classroom authority: Theory, research, and practice.* Mahwah, NJ: Lawrence Erlbaum.

Page, R. N. 1991. *Lower track classrooms: A curricular and cultural perspective.* New York: Teachers College Press.

Partners for Citizenship and Character. 2001. Informational flyer. Wilton, OH.

Peshkin, A. 2000. *Permissible advantage? The moral consequences of elite schooling.* Mahwah, NJ: Lawrence Erlbaum.

Pope, D. C. 2001. *"Doing school": How we are creating a generation of stressed out, materialistic, and miseducated students.* New Haven, CT: Yale University Press.

Power, S., T. Edwards, G. Witty, and V. Wigfall. 2003. *Education and the middle class.* Buckingham: Open University Press.

Proweller, A. 1998. *Constructing female identity: Meaning making in an upper middle class youth culture.* Albany: State University of New York Press.

Putnam, R. D. 2001. *Bowling alone: The collapse and revival of American community.* New York Simon & Schuster.

Reay, D. 2004. Exclusivity, exclusion, and social class in urban education markets in the United Kingdom. *Urban Education* 39 (5): 537–60.

Reich, R. B. 1994. The revolt of the anxious class. Speech given at the Democratic Leadership Council, Washington, DC. http://www.dol.gov/oasam/programs/history/reich/speeches/sp941122.htm.

Resnick, M. D. 2000. Protective factors, resiliency and healthy youth development. *Adolescent Medicine* 11 (1): 157–64.

Richardson, J. L., K. Dwyer, K. McGuigan, W. B. Hansen, C. Dent, C. A. Johnson, S. Y. Sussman, B. Brannon, and B. Flay. 1989. Substance use among eighth grade students who take care of themselves after school. *Pediatrics* 84 (3): 556–66.

Riesman, D. 1950. *The lonely crowd.* New Haven, CT: Yale University Press.

Robbins, A. 2006. *The overachievers: The secret lives of driven kids.* New York: Hyperion.

Rose, N. 1992. Governing the enterprising self. In *The values of the enterprise culture: The moral debate,* ed. P. Heelas and P. Morris, 141–64. New York: Routledge.

Rosenfeld, A., and N. Wise. 2000. *The over-scheduled child: Avoiding the hyper-parenting trap.* New York: St. Martin's Griffin.

Rusk, D. 1999. *Inside game/outside game: Winning strategies for saving urban America.* Washington DC: Brookings Institution.

Sanday, P. 1998. Defining a public interest anthropology. Paper presented at the annual meeting of the American Anthropological Association, Philadelphia.

———. 2001. Prepared remarks. Paper presented at the Spender Foundation Advanced Institute on the Interrelationship between Anthropology and Education, September 27–30, Chapel Hill, NC.

Schneider, B. 2003. Pathways linking education to health: New directions and opportunities for research. Paper presented at the American Educational Research Association annual meeting, Montreal.

Schneider, B., and D. Stevenson. 1999. *The ambitious generation: America's teenagers, motivated but directionless.* New Haven, CT: Yale University Press.

Simmel, G. 1964. *Conflict and the web of group affiliations.* New York: Free Press.

Sizer, T. R. 1992a. *Horace's compromise: The dilemma of the American high school.* Boston: Houghton Mifflin.

———. 1992b. *Horace's school: Redesigning the American high school.* Boston: Houghton Mifflin.

Smith, D. 2000. The underside of schooling: Restructuring, privatization and women's unpaid work. In *Sociology of education: Major themes,* ed. S. J. Ball, 698–715. London: RoutledgeFalmer.

Sokolove, M. 2008. The uneven playing field. *New York Times Magazine,* May 11, 54–61, 76, 81. http://www.nytimes.com/2008/05/11/magazine/11girls-t.html.

Solomon, D. 2005. School monitor: Questions for Jonathan Kozol. *New York Times Magazine,* September 4, 14.

Sontag, D. 2002. Who was responsible for Elizabeth Shin? *New York Times Magazine,* April 28, 56–61, 94, 139, 140.

Spindler, G. D. 1967/1987. The transmission of culture. In *Education and cultural process,* ed. G. Spindler, 303–34. 2nd ed. Prospect Heights, IL: Waveland Press.

Spindler, G., and L. Spindler. 1998. Cultural politics of the white ethniclass in the midnineties. In *Ethnic identity and power: Cultural contexts of political action in school and society,* ed. E. T. Trueba and Y. Zou, 27–41. Albany: State University of New York Press.

Stambach, A. 2007. Discussant comments at Comparative and International Education annual conference. Baltimore.

Steele, S. 1990. *The content of our character.* New York: HarperCollins.

———. 2006. *White guilt.* New York: HarperCollins.

Steinberg, L. 2005. Cognitive and affective development in adolescence. *Trends in Cognitive Science* 9 (2): 69–75.

Stephens, S. 1995. Children and the politics of culture in "late capitalism." In *Children and the politics of culture,* ed. S. Stephens, 3–48. Princeton, NJ: Princeton University Press.

Strathern, M. 1991. Partners and consumers: Making relations visible. *New Literary History* 22 (3): 581–601.

Stout, M. 2000. *The feel-good curriculum: The dumbing down of America's kids in the name of self-esteem.* Cambridge, MA: Da Capo.

Thernstrom, S., and A. Thernstrom. 2003. *No excuses: Closing the racial gap in learning.* New York: Simon & Schuster.

Thompson, P. M. 2000. Growth patterns in the developing brain detected by using continuum mechanical tensor maps. *Nature* 404:190–93.

Tocqueville, de, A.. 1838. *Democracy in America.* Repr., London: Penguin, 2003.

U.S. Census Bureau. 2000. American FactFinder. http://factfinder.census.gov/ servlet/SAFFFacts?_event=Search&geo_id=&_geoContext=&_street= &_county=[Wilton]&_cityTown=[Wilton]&_state=04000US39&_zip= &_lang=en&_sse=on&pctxt=fph&pgsl=010&show_2003_tab=&redirect=Y.

Varenne, H. 1977. *Americans together: Structured diversity in a Midwestern town.* New York: Teachers College Press.

Varenne, H., and R. McDermott. 1998. *Successful failure: The school America builds.* Boulder, CO: Westview.

Weiss, B. 2004. *Producing African futures: Ritual and reproduction in a neoliberal age.* Leiden: Brill.

Wexler, P. 1983. *Critical social psychology.* Boston: Routledge.

———. 1992. *Becoming somebody: Toward a social psychology of school.* London: Falmer.

Whittier, N. 2000. To the Class of 2000. *In the Space* [WBHS student newspaper]. June.

Wilgoren, J., and J. Steinberg. 2000. Under pressure: A special report; Even for 6th graders, college looms. *New York Times,* July 3.

Willis, P. 2003. [Southern] resigns as [Colonial Hills] principal. *Wilton News,* July 2.

Willis, P. E. 1977. *Learning to labour.* Westmead: Saxon House.

———. 1982. Cultural production is different from social reproduction is different from reproduction. *Interchange* 12 (2): 48–67.

———. 2003. Footsoldiers of modernity. *Harvard Educational Review* 73 (3): 390–415.

Wilton Burnham High School. 1990. Untitled planning document. Wilton, OH.

———. 1999. Student/staff/parent handbook. Wilton, OH: Wilton Burnham High School.

Wilton Educational Foundation. 2001. Building a foundation today for the leaders of tomorrow (brochure). Wilton, OH.

Wilton Historical Society. 2003. Wilton 1803–2003: Building the future with pioneering spirit. Wilton, OH: Wilton Historical Society.

Wilton School District. 2002a. District Profile. Wilton OH: Wilton School District.

———. 2002b. State of the Schools Presentation. Wilton, OH: Wilton School District.

———. 2003. Wilton School District Budget Reduction Backgrounder. Wilton, OH: Wilton School District.

Wolcott, H. 1994. Education as cultural transmission and acquisition. In Vol. 3, *International Encyclopedia of Education,* ed. T. Husen and T. N. Postlewaite, 1724–29. 2nd ed. Tarrytown, NY: Elsevier.

———. 2008. *Ethnography: A way of seeing.* 2nd ed. Lanham, MD: Alta Mira Press.

Index

Buell, J., 183
bullying. *See* incivility

Callahan, D., 119, 124, 178
Callahan, R., 182
capital, 11, 47, 192n3; cultural, 6, 73, 97, 112, 179; institutional, 73–78, 121–22; psychological, 85, 88–102, 130, 133, 167, 171, 177–79
Carrier, A. H., 61
Carrier, J. G., 61
charitable activities. *See* community service
cheating, 3, 105, 118–22, 134, 169, 178
citizenship, 4
Clark, C., 126, 129
class: culture, 5, 10–13, 20f, 171–72, 176, 179; ideology, *see* Wilton Way; stratification, 4, 6, 46, 167, 172, 174–75, 184 (*see also* inequality)
cocurriculum. *See* extracurriculum
college: application process, 1, 3, 96, 107–8, 179; planning, 89–90, 92, 103, 107, 113, 118, 125, 153, 163–64, 174
commodification of education, 104–5, 115, 125
competition: in American society, 3, 4, 12, 101, 182–84; awareness of, 27, 41, 60, 88–90, 106, 124–25, 133–34, 170–71, 177; in the cocurriculum, 67–68; as a mechanism within neoliberalism, 87, 175; as a natural social process, 33, 37, 46; as an organizing principle in school, 149–50, 152–53, 155–56, 172, 179–80, 182–84; role of positive self-regard in, 37, 43–44
confidence, 93–95, 167, 178, 184
consumerism, 5, 31, 130
credentialism, educational, 3, 62, 104–5, 115, 122–23, 125, 172, 178–79, 182
Criswell, C. (focal student): background and description, 14–15, 17–18; post-high school path, 179–80; school experiences and perceptions, 132, 153–55, 158, 166, 174

cross-cultural perspective, 6–9, 149, 181
community service 29, 67, 115, 160, 172–73
Connell, R., 11
Connerly, W., 179
Cookson, P., 11
cortisol, 149–50
Cowan, A., 57
Csikszentmihalyi, M., 132
counseling center, 94–97, 108, 155–56, 167–68, 174, 72–73, 163–64, 180, 183–84
culture, 9–10 (*see also* anthropology); American, 5, 7, 86, 174–75, 181–82; appropriation of, 164; popular (electronic and commodity), 87
cultural production, 4, 12
curriculum, 64–66
Currie, E., 166

Damon, W., 192n4
Delpit, L., 9, 168
depression, 148–49
diversity, 64, 167, 179. *See also* multiculturalism
Donmoyer, R., 14
Dorst, J., 31
drug use: caffeine pills, 170; growth hormones, 4; illegal, 148; prescription, 4, 146, 148

Eckert, P., 12, 96, 176
Eckstein, M., 125
Eder, D., 166
education "debt," 4
educational philosophy, 27, 47, 48, 172
Ehrenrich, B., 3
Elkind, D., 3, 129
entitlement, 49, 87, 101
Erickson, F., 7
extra credit, 105, 110–11, 115–18, 125, 134, 182
extracurriculum (cocurriculum), 64, 67–68, 108, 151

fatigue, 1, 85, 102, 129–31, 137–38, 149–50, 154, 169–71, 177, 182

feedback mechanisms. *See* key linkages
Finders, M., 166
Fine, M., 167
Foley, D., 9, 10–11, 70, 98, 167, 191n3
Fordham, S., 167
Foster, M., 181
Foucault, M., 86
Friedman, T., 3

Gallegos, B., 167
gangs, 154
Geertz, C., 171
gender: equity, 166; and GPA (grade
    point average), 105, 135; and harass-
    ment and vandalism, 160–62; identity,
    178; and immersion in culture of
    competition, 135–36, 176, 178; and
    importance of extra credit, 116; paren-
    tal interventions in school, 55; and
    school experience, 1–2, 85, 92, 101–2,
    105, 158, 191n4; and stress, 130, 149–50,
    178
Gergen, K., 102
Giddens, A., 85, 97, 102
Giedd, J., 150, 177
gifted education, 38, 42
Gnezda, N., 156
Good, T., 132
grade inflation, 114–18, 125, 169–71, 178
Graue, M., 55

Hannerz, U., 177
Harris, J., 160
Heath, S. B., 177
Hemmings, A., 192n4
Henry, J., 152
Hersch, P., 132
Hewlett, S., 132
Hilliard, A., 6
Holland, D., 167
Hollingshead, A., 5
Holme, J., 30
homework, recommendations concern-
    ing, 182–83
Howard, A., 12, 85

hypercredentialing, 19, 81–82, 103–26,
    172, 178

identity, student 4, 6, 21, 49, 85–102, 105,
    125, 167, 172, 176–77, 179, 181, 184
impression management, 10, 70, 85,
    97–99
incivility, 152–53, 165–67, 180; discourse
    of degradation, 159–60, 166–67, 172;
    harassment and bullying, 18, 22,
    160–62, 166–67; vandalism and theft,
    22, 161–62, 166–67
inequality, 2, 4, 6, 22, 47, 167, 175, 184. *See
    also* race, gender
institutional advantaging, 19, 63–82, 125,
    175

Japanese students, 109–10
jobs, student, 88, 105, 130, 134, 137–38, 154
Josephson Institute of Ethics, 125–26
judgments: of classes by students, 105; of
    students, 134; of teachers by students,
    112

key linkages, 19, 27, 47, 48, 62, 81–82, 87,
    125, 166, 172, 176–77, 178
Knauft, B., 85
Kohn, A., 82, 126
Konadu, N. (focal student); back-
    ground and description, 14–17; post-
    graduation path, 173; school experi-
    ences and perceptions, 88, 90, 91,
    103–4, 106–8, 111, 130–33, 137, 180
Kozol, J., 4
Kralovec, E., 183

Labaree, D., 3, 104–5
Ladson-Billings, G., 9
Ladwig, J., 11
Lareau, A., 3, 11–12, 38, 43, 48–49, 87, 101,
    129, 176
Lasch, C., 4
Levinson, B., 167
Lightfoot, S., 104
Lipsitz, G., 176

Lynch, J., 13, 85, 99, 103–4
Lynd, H., 5
Lynd, R., 5

Madsen, K. (focal student): background and description, 15, 18; post-graduation path, 174; school experiences and perceptions, 106, 153, 158–62, 180
Manus, Papua New Guinea, 6–7, 9, 13, 18, 85, 132, 167, 181, 193n1; parents, 61–62, 181
Martin, E., 150
McCabe, D., 126
McCarthy, C., 4
McDermott, R., 151–52, 175
McWhorter, J., 179
Mead, M., 5, 9–10, 181, 191n2
middle class, 3, 4–5, 11–13, 27, 28, 46, 48, 81–82, 101, 129, 172, 176
Miller, D., 125
Milner, M., 166–67
Milner, R., 13, 18, 94, 98, 103–4, 164
mobility. *See* social mobility
modernity as a risk culture, 85–86, 101–2, 177
Moss, K., 10, 191n3
motivation, student, 122, 156, 180
multiculturalism, 79–80. *See also* diversity
Munson, L., 4
music program, 68

Nack, W., 4
Nader, L., 6, 10
Native American students, 28
NCLB, 192n3
neoliberalism, 3, 5, 85–87, 101, 150, 177–78
Newman, K., 3
Nichols, S., 132
Noah, H., 125
No Child Left Behind Act. *See* NCLB

Oakes, J., 4
Ogbu, J., 162
Ortner, S., 6, 9, 101, 177, 192n3

Pace, J., 192n4
Page, R., 4
parents, 14–18, 19, 184, 192n4, 193n1; anxiety related to children's school success, 33–35, 54; appropriation of special education policy and resources, 48, 55–62, 172, 175–76; concerted cultivation, 38, 48–49, 95, 101; hiring of consultants, 3; interventions in school, 39, 42, 48–49, 53–55, 62, 171–72, 175; "pushing," 48, 51–52, 57, 61–62, 175–76; support, 48, 50–52, 171, 175
Passeron, J.-C., 47
passive noncompliance, 156–58, 166, 179
Papua New Guinea, 6–7, 18. *See also* Manus
Parker, J., 161
Pere village, Papua New Guinea, 9. *See also* Manus
Peshkin, A., 7, 12, 85
Peters, A., 13, 155
placement of students (into gifted and talented, enriched, and AP classes), 35, 53
plagiarism. *See* cheating
policy: drug and alcohol, 119–20; hiring (and racial exclusion), 79–82; local control of U.S. schools, 23, 175; logic of freedom and deferral, 72–73; of the school, 44, 48, 64, 81–82, 181–84
political correctness, 97–99, 101. *See also* impression management
Pope, D., 105, 123, 129, 155
Power, S., 11
privilege, 12, 28
Proweller, A., 3, 176
Putnam, R., 4

race: discrimination, 79, 165; and ethnicity, 192n2; and school experience, 85, 96, 102, 162–65, 167–68, 191n4
Reay, D., 12
recognition (forms of), 38, 43–47, 75–78, 81–82, 124, 134, 172, 184

Wilton School District, 29–31, 39–42 (*see also* educational philosophy); funding, 41–42
Wilton (town), 27–31
Wilton Way (class cultural ideology), 2, 6, 19, 27–48, 53, 60–62, 121–22, 171–72, 176–77, 184. *See also* middle class
Wise, N., 3, 130
Wolcott, H., 9–10, 179
work ethic, 85, 99–101, 108